THE
VARIED
KITCHENS OF
INDIA

THE VARIED KITCHENS OF INDIA

CUISINES OF THE
ANGLO-INDIANS OF CALCUTTA,
BENGALIS, JEWS OF CALCUTTA,
KASHMIRIS, PARSIS, AND
TIBETANS OF DARJEELING

COPELAND MARKS

M. EVANS
Lanham • New York • Boulder • Toronto • Plymouth, UK

LIBRARY OF CONGRESS CATALOGING-IN-PUBLICATION DATA

Marks, Copeland.
 The varied kitchens of India

 Bibliography: p.
 Includes index.
 1. Cookery, Indic. I. Title.
TX724.5.I4M343   1986   641-5954   86-2028

ISBN 978-0-87131-672-1

Distributed by NATIONAL BOOK NETWORK

M Evans
An imprint of Rowman & Littlefield
4501 Forbes Boulevard, Suite 200
Lanham, Maryland 20706
www.rowman.com

Design by Lauren Dong

Manufactured in the United States of America

Contents

Preface

*I*t all started in Calcutta where I had been working for some years and where I return regularly to continue my survey of the unusual regional kitchens. I kept finding personal and family recipes that had not, to my knowledge, been integrated into the menus of restaurants where they would become familiar to the dining public. They are, therefore, relatively unknown, and are outside of the recorded cooking of the great Indian subcontinent from which they emerged.

Calcutta has always been my working headquarters in India, and the Calcutta Jewish kitchen was the first to attract my interest. It was one that I was determined to record—with the help of a large number of cooperative people from that community.

At first it seemed that the broad range of their cuisine would merit a complete volume. I proceeded to cook and collect recipes and historic information on that basis, but there were far too many other culinary inducements for me to resist. There were, for example, three other unique communities in or near Calcutta—the Parsis, the Anglo-Indian and Bengali. Then my attention was caught by the Tibetans of Darjeeling, and finally Kashmir, distant but with a distinctly important style of cooking, became my last choice.

All the religions are represented in my book, not because I made a conscious effort to include them but simply because religious beliefs frequently influence the diet. The Jews of Calcutta, the Muslims and Hindus of Kashmir, the Tibetan Buddhists of Darjeeling, the Parsis who are Zoroastrians, the Anglo-Indian Christians, and the Hindus of Bengal have been profoundly influenced by the dietary regulations (or lack of them) of their religions. Buddhists will not kill except for food, yet many are meat eaters who turn over their slaughtering requirements to non-Buddhists. The Christians will eat pork, which is abhorred by the Jews and Muslims. The Parsis decided centuries ago to respect the wishes of their Hindu benefactors by not eating beef. Vegetarians have their own special beliefs so that they may even dispense with strong flavorings such as chili, garlic and onion. Thus recipes developed within the same country along the lines established by religious antipathies.

However, my principal purpose was to catch and record the regional differences in home kitchens while the old ways were still respected, and preserve them for future generations. That has been my hope and my aim.

Acknowledgments

When I was collecting the recipes and the historical folklore of the unconventional cooking of India, I had already prepared myself for the variety of the people. Yet, in spite of racial and regional differences, they all had one thing in common, and that was an innate enthusiasm for their cuisine and a nostalgic attachment to the taste and texture. Nostalgia, after all, is what it is all about.

I am grateful to all those who allowed me to enter their culinary tradition and record their secrets.

The Bengali Kitchen
Nirupama Basu
Manju Gupta
Jaya Sen

The Jewish Kitchen
I am especially indebted to Diana Meyers, who gave unstintingly of her time over a period of several years to reveal the extent of the cuisine. Also, Bernard Jacob of Calcutta and London, whose insight into the origin of the names of the Jewish dishes, speculative or not, was of inestimable value.

Also,

Hilda Metook Abraham	Ann Curlendar Shellim Lawson
Ramah David	Sally Meyer Lewis
Cynthia Shellim Ebenau	Rachel Luddy Shellim
Flora Ezra Gubbay	Mercia Rassaby Rembaum
	Nahoum Nahoum

The Anglo-Indian Kitchen
Arlene Stokoe
Charles Wickins

The Parsi Kitchen

Hilla Ginwalla | Najoo Vakeel
Mrs. N. Batlivala | Mithoo Vatcha
Mrs. N. Contractor

The Hindu and Muslim Kitchens of Kashmir

Rochelal Bandari—the Hindu cook
Gulam Quadir Wani—the Muslim cook

The Tibetan Kitchen of Darjeeling

Cheojey Lama | Dorji Yudon Yuthok
Tashi Pemba (Majeela) | Tupchu Yuthok

My particular gratitude to Suresh and Sheila Kumar of Calcutta, whose hospitality and generosity provided the vital ingredient that allowed me to pursue my objectives.

Ingredients and Cooking Methods

AGAR-AGAR (*Porphyra umbilicalis*): A colorless derivative from a seaweed, dried and packaged in strings or pieces. Used as a substitute for gelatin to solidify desserts. Used in the Calcutta Jewish kitchens and available here in Asian food markets.

ASAFETIDA (*Ferula assafoetida*): A plant of the carrot family (Umbellife-rae) that grows 6 to 12 feet high. Known as *hing* in Bengal, it is used in very small quantities in curries. It is one of those strange seasonings that· to me has an unpleasant aroma and whose use must be considered optional.

BESAN: *Gram or chick-pea flour,* the powder or flour ground from dried chick-peas (*Cicer arietinum*) is a necessity for preparing batters in which vegetable slivers are dipped and deep-fried—*pakoras.* One of the commonest sights in Calcutta is a street vendor selling his *pakoras,* deep-fried to order. Whole dried chick-peas are used in vegetable curries after being soaked overnight in water and cooked until soft. The flour is available here in East Indian and Middle Eastern markets.

BETKI: This is the justly popular fish of Calcutta. It is a sea fish with a light pink cast through the flesh. The texture is similar to flounder, and flaky. It has soft flesh so that cooks scrape it off the skin with a knife rather than put it through a chopper. Flounder makes a good substitute.

BITTER MELON OR BITTER GOURD (*Momordica charantia*): Also known as balsam pear. An attractive, slightly bitter vegetable, beloved by the Bengalis. It is used in curries. The bitter taste can be lessened by soaking the vegetable in salt water for a while. It is available here in most Asian markets.

CARAWAY SEED (*Carum carvi*): Tibetans use the seeds in their cooking. Its distinctive flavor is best known to us from its use in the rye breads of Europe and the United States. Calcutta cooks use caraway as a flavoring in the Kaka, a doughnutlike biscuit (see recipe).

CARDAMOM (*Elettaria cardamomum*): An aromatic spice used in much of the regional cooking. The Kashmiris are especially fond of the taste, and it is used both ground as well as whole. The one available here has black seeds in green pods. The cardamom pods are often chewed as an after-meal digestive and breath sweetener. There is also a black cardamom pod from Bhutan resembling its green cousin in flavor. The black pod is about 1 inch long and 1/2 inch wide with a rather hairy thick skin.

CHULA: The *chula* is the simple kitchen stove used all over Calcutta by those who do not have modern stoves or where modern equipment does not exist. It is essentially an iron pail with a clay necklace 2 to 3 inches wide around the neck. It has an opening from 6 to 8 inches in diameter. A square hole has been cut out of the bottom of the pail to provide a draft and so that one can remove the ashes that accumulate.

Charcoal is added through the neck up to the top. It provides a steady, hot temperature for frying and stewing as well as an open flame for kabobs. The *chula* is probably the most useful (if not indispensable) piece of equipment in the lower income homes (or hovels) of Calcutta.

During the winter months, when the chill sets in in the late afternoon, the *chulas* all over Calcutta are providing a little heat while they are in operation. Millions of *chulas* burning charcoal have made Calcutta a nightmare of pollution since there is no other common method of cooking.

CINNAMON (*Cinnamomum zeylanicum*): A much-used spice in Indian cooking. The bark, in the form of cinnamon sticks, is used as well as the ground cinnamon.

CLOVES (*Eugenia caryophyllata*): This is also a very common spice in all Indian cooking.

COCONUT: Coconut milk is an ingredient required for many Indian recipes.

Rich Coconut Milk

1. Bake 1 large ripe coconut with hard brown shell in a 375°F. oven for 20 minutes. The outer shell may crack during this time and the heat will loosen the coconut meat.

2. Remove coconut from the oven. Over the sink give it several strong cracks with a hammer. The coconut water will run out and can be discarded or used for another purpose. Pry the coconut from the shell with a dull blade.

3. Cut all the coconut into thin 1/2-inch pieces. There should be about 4 cups. Put half in the container of a blender and add 3 1/4 cups hot water. Run the motor for 1 minute. Pour the mixture through a metal sieve and

squeeze to get all the liquid from the coconut. Repeat the process with the rest of the coconut and another 3¹/₄ cups hot water. Discard the pulp.

4. Let the coconut milk stand for 10 minutes, then carefully pour it off into another container. The sediment which has settled to the bottom should be discarded.

Grated Coconut

When preparing grated coconut to be used in desserts, trim the brown skin from the coconut meat after cutting it into pieces. This will keep the coconut white. Grate all you need on a hand grater or in a food processor.

CORIANDER (*Coriandrum sativum*): The ground seeds are one of the basic seasonings in Indian food. The fresh leaves and stems of the coriander plant are used in fresh table chutneys and as garnishes, and are included in the cooking as an important flavoring.

CRISPY ONIONS: A popular garnish on rice and curries in Calcutta and the northern areas of India. Ubiquitous in the cuisines of Burma and Indonesia, which have been influenced by Indian techniques.

Crispy Onions

1. Take ¹/₂ pound or more of small onions, about 4 or 5, peel them, and halve them from the stem to the root end, not across. Cut the halves into thin slices. This will make about 2 cups of sliced onions.

2. Sprinkle onions with ¹/₂ teaspoon salt and toss several times to separate each slice. Let stand for 10 minutes.

3. Put the onions in a thin kitchen towel and gently squeeze out as much liquid as you can.

4. Heat about ²/₃ cup corn or peanut oil, preferably in a wok although a skillet will do. Put the onions in the oil and fry them over moderate heat for 5 to 6 minutes, or until the onions begin to turn light brown. Stir them continuously with a slotted spoon to prevent burning, which they have a tendency to do. Turn off the heat, stir rapidly for a moment, and remove the onions, scattering them over paper towels. Draining the oil in this way makes them crispy.

5. Cool and drain onions for 10 minutes. Store in an airtight glass or plastic container. They may be refrigerated or frozen and used when needed. Warm them briefly in an oven before using as a garnish.

As an added bonus, the aromatic oil can be reserved and used later in any type of Indian food preparation. I prefer to refrigerate it in a glass jar, tightly covered.

CUMINSEED (*Cuminum cyminum*): One of the common spices in Indian cooking, used either as whole seeds or ground.

DAL: There are various kinds of *dal* used in this book: the red lentils used in the Jewish fritters of Calcutta; the *moong dal* with its black skin; the pink *masoor dal*; and the *chana ka dal*—yellow split lentils. Lentils provide a good deal of the protein used throughout India, especially when made into a soup and poured over rice. They are available here in Indian food shops. Although I have been known to use yellow split peas (for the *chana ka dal*) successfully, it is only in desperation since I prefer the authentic ingredients.

FENNEL (*Foeniculum vulgare*): The anise-flavored whole seeds and ground spice are frequently used in Kashmiri food.

FENUGREEK (*Trigonella foenumgraecum*): Quite definitely a peculiar spice with a slightly bitter medicinal taste. The ground spice becomes thick and viscous when mixed with water. Its principal use in these pages is for Halba, a table chutney (see recipe). Also called *methi*.

FIVE-SPICE MIX: A mélange of Chinese origin used in many Tibetan dishes to enhance the flavor. It may consist of star anise, cinnamon, fennel seed, cloves and black pepper or Szechuan pepper all ground together. It is available packaged in Chinese food shops.

GARAM MASALA: A combination of spices, freely translated in Hindi as "hot spice." Contains pepper, clove, cardamom, cuminseed, coriander and turmeric in combinations according to personal preference and regional taste. The mixture in my collection in addition to the above list includes ginger, bay leaves and nutmeg all ground together. I bought it already ground and packaged.

GINGER (*Zingiber officinale*): The fresh gingerroot, now easily available in most Asian food shops and public supermarkets, has acquired a high reputation in our kitchens. It achieved this status centuries ago in India and other Asian countries before reaching our shores. The pungent flavor of fresh ginger is an indispensable ingredient in most Indian regional cooking.

GRINDING STONE: This is a tool similar to the Central American *metate* or *piedra* (stone) of Guatemala. The one used in Calcutta, where I cooked for several years, was 20 inches long, 10 inches wide and 3 inches or so thick, with a V-shaped forward section. The surface of this gray stone had low fishbone ridges to provide a rubbing surface. The stone pestle was 10 inches long and 2 inches thick, with a smooth surface and round end. The Muslim cook, Alam, reduced scallions (among other things) to a smooth green paste on the stone by a constant back and forth motion. The green paste was so smooth it did not require sieving to remove any rough pieces.

HAMISS: This famous word crops up all the time when cooking Jewish food. It is simply rubbing back and forth with a wooden cooking spoon when frying onions, garlic, gingerroot and perhaps tomatoes so that the sauces can be reduced to a smooth texture.

LOOBIA (*Vigna unquiculata*): Known as Chinese long bean, asparagus bean or yard-long bean and *loobia* in Calcutta. They are used in the same manner as the supermarket green bean but are more tender and flavorful. I have eaten them in India, Burma and Indonesia and associate *loobia* with the Asian tropics. They are sometimes available here wrapped in bundles of 12 to 14, and are well worth searching for.

LOTUS (*Nelumbium nuciferum*): The Kashmiri lotus is a whitish tube about 25 to 30 inches long, found in the lakes of Srinagar. The interior of the lotus tube is perforated in a series of walls and openings that resemble bamboo. They must be thoroughly rinsed in cold water to remove mud from the interior. The crunchy tube is fried crisp in a batter or cooked in a yogurt sauce. Kashmir was my first encounter with the edible lotus and my seduction has been complete. I have found it in New York's Chinatown and in other cities with Southeast Asian neighborhoods.

METHI: *see* Fenugreek.

MINT: One of the species and varieties of *Mentha*. This universally available herb is used fresh.

MUSHROOMS, DRIED (*Lentinus edodes*): Dried Chinese mushrooms are often used by the Tibetans. Kashmiri cooking also includes dried mushrooms of a different type that have been gathered in their own hills.

MUSTARD SEED, BLACK (*Brassica nigra*) AND WHITE (*Brassica hirta*): Both are used in Bengali cooking to a great degree and impart a characteristic mustard taste to food. Mustard oil derived from the seeds is an important cooking medium in Bengal. Available only in Indian shops.

NUTMEG *(Myristica fragrans)*: Nutmeg is not used too frequently in Indian cooking but is more a favorite spice of the Indonesians. Several Parsi recipes in this volume do use it, especially Nankhatai, Classic Cookie (see recipe).

OKRA *(Hibiscus esculentus)*: Okra belongs to the same botanical family as cotton. The Indians prepare okra in various ways, especially in vegetarian curries. It is also known as "lady's-fingers." My cook in Calcutta had never heard of the word okra. The Jewish dish, Sweet-and-Sour Chicken and Okra, is one of its finest preparations (see recipe).

PEPPER *(Piper nigrum)*: A standard spice used in ground form as well as the whole peppercorns. India is one of the world's largest producers. Before the arrival of the hot chili from Central America in the sixteenth century, it was pepper that gave food its sting. It is the most important spice in world commerce.

PHING: This is the name used by Tibetans for bean threads, also called bean-thread noodles, cellophane noodles and transparent noodles. These are made from mung bean flour. They are used in soups and stir-fry dishes. The dry threads are made in several thicknesses from hair-thin to the standard spaghetti size. They are available in Asian groceries packed in plastic bags. Soaking in warm water for 10 minutes softens the noodles so they can be handled.

POPPY SEED *(genus Papaver,* probably *P. Somniferum)*: One of the esóteric ingredients in Indian curries that give them depth and individuality. Seeds may be used ground or whole.

RADISH, WHITE *(Raphanus sativus)*: The large white Chinese radish (in a Korean shop it was called Japanese radish) is cultivated all over Asia. It is used fresh or cooked. The Tibetans include it in a soup, Faktu(see recipe). Some of the radishes reach weights of 4 pounds or more. We find it here in Chinatowns and Korean markets.

RED SPINACH *(Amaranthus tricolor)*: A leafy green with red blotches through the center, very evident in the vegetable markets and with street vendors of Calcutta. It has an appealing beet-green taste and does not require a lot of seasoning when simply stir-fried.

SEMOLINA: This cereal, known throughout India as *soojee*, is a wheat product. It is used in several desserts, especially in Kashmiri and Parsi cooking. Cream of Wheat, the American cereal, is like *soojee* and can be used in all recipes that call for it.

SYED KA ROTI: Flat, unleavened bread, the large round flat bread baked by the Jewish women in Bow Bazaar, Calcutta, for daily use and as matzoh for Passover. The loaf or sheet is about 18 inches in diameter and 1/4 inch thick, crispy and dry. The nearest we can get to this is the lavash or Armenian flat bread, which is occasionally sold in Mideastern grocery stores. The bread is prepared with flour and water, kneaded into a dough, and baked in a *tandoor*, a clay oven.

TAMARIND (*Tamarindus indica*): Many cultures in Asia and Central America rely on the acid flavor of the tamarind pulp for its unique taste. The pulp is removed from the ripe, brown beanlike casing, which contains large seeds and fiber. Asian shops carry tamarind, of a fine quality, imported from Thailand, although Central American shops sell both the clean pulp and the pods. Soaking the pulp in warm water for about 30 minutes and straining the liquid through a metal sieve prepares this popular flavoring for cooking.

TREE EARS (*Auricularia polytricha*): We are familiar with these from Chinese cooking. They are available in dried form in Asian food shops. Tibetans call for them in their family-style Gyako (see recipe). Cloud ears are bigger and thicker.

TURMERIC (*Curcuma longa*): This provides the yellow color in standard curry powders. The French refer to it as "Indian saffron" since it provides a yellow hue to foods and has a faint curry odor. It is in the same botanical family as ginger and like ginger, the ground spice is made from the dried rhizome.

WHITE PUMPKIN (*Benincasa hispida*): Also called winter melon, wax gourd or ash pumpkin by the Chinese since it is covered by a white dust at maturity. The crisp, white pulp is covered by a hard, green skin; the pumpkin sometimes grows to 25 pounds. It is used in soups, desserts, chutney and curry. In New York's Chinatown, the pumpkin is sold by the pound, cut into pieces.

Note on Sources of Ingredients

A new era in food emporiums has arrived that promises well for the American kitchen. No longer is the adventurous cook discouraged by the difficulty of obtaining ingredients' that are vital for the preparation of dishes from Asia. Fresh gingerroot, turmeric, the family of lentils, ground spices such as cumin, coriander and nutmeg, and the hot chili in all its manifestations are available in markets and shops or by mail order.

Twenty years ago, in the early days of my investigations into the cuisines of Indonesia and India, Americans had not yet been introduced to foods that are now commonplace. Asian tropical vegetables such as loobia (the long Chinese green bean), the bok choy family, and even snow peas were mysteries that had to be unravelled before they could be integrated into the American repertoire.

How did these changes and the new enthusiasm for Asian food come about? To begin with, there were the well-established Chinese communities around the United States, which were already using their own traditional foods. In the past ten years, there has been an enormous influx of people from Southeast Asia, including Vietnamese, East Indians, Cambodians, Burmese, and Tibetans. All of these people yearned for their ginger, garlic, turmeric, cardamom, lemon grass, and Asian tropical vegetables. Where there is a demand, a supply soon follows in the freewheeling American economy. Restaurants and shops have sprung up. Finally, the traveling Americans of the seventies and eighties who were seeing and tasting the outer reaches of Asian cooking responded enthusiastically and sought out restaurants and foods at home.

The American kitchen is the benefactor of the newly arrived foods. Nothing in the present book is so unusual that it cannot be found easily in metropolitan areas and even in moderate-sized cities. My own favorite and most effective shopping stops are the Chinese, East Indian and Latin American food shops that have proliferated across the country. There is an overlapping in the culinary list of ingredients, so that it is possible to find fresh coriander, ground cumin and coriander, and hot chilies in the Latin American shops. East Indians have their chick-pea flour, lentils, and spices. Chinatown shops are eclectic, and a good shopping eye will observe the seasonings and vegetables that are required in Indian cooking.

You will also find that many supermarkets, health-food stores and gourmet shops carry an array of ingredients you will need.

The chapter on ingredients and cooking methods offers suggestions on where to find specific items. Following is a list of stores that sell necessary ingredients. These stores accept mail orders, and stores that offer a catalog are marked with an asterisk (*).

CALIFORNIA
*Bazaar of India
1810 University Avenue
Berkeley, California 94703
415-548-4110

Mr. K's Gourmet Foods and Coffees
Stall 430, Farmer's Market
Third and Fairfax
Los Angeles, California 90036
213-934-9117

FLORIDA
Indian Grocery Store
2342 Douglas Road
Miami Beach, Florida 33134
305-448-5869

ILLINOIS
*Conte di Savoia
555 West Roosevelt, #7
Chicago, Illinois 60607
312-666-3471

India Gifts and Foods
1031 West Belmont Avenue
Chicago, Illinois 60650
312-348-4392

NEW YORK
*House of Spices
76-17 Broadway
Jackson Heights, New York 11373
718-476-1577

*K. Kalustyan, Orient Export Trading Corporation
123 Lexington Avenue
New York, New York 10016
212-685-3416

TEXAS
Jay Store
6688 Southwest Freeway
Houston, Texas 77004
713-783-0032

WASHINGTON
*Specialty Spice House
Pike Place Market
Seattle, Washington 98105
206-622-6340

The
Bengali
Kitchen

Calcutta has always had a bad press ever since Job Charnock founded the city in 1690 on the mud flats of a tributary of the Ganges—the Hooghly River—for the British East India Company. It is now a city in the process of slowly sinking into the Hooghly whence it came. Rudyard Kipling penned these lines about Calcutta, which are as true today as they were in the nineteenth century.

> Where the cholera, the cyclone, and the crow,
> Come and go.

It was not helped by the 1756 Indian Mutiny and its Black Hole of Calcutta suffocation, now only remembered by a small plaque in the general post office in Central Calcutta's Dalhousie Square. Yet, another author in the twentieth century refers, "to Calcutta, much abused, much loved and always interesting." And that too is true, this ambivalent love-hate relationship that drives those old Calcutta hands who once lived there as I did to return now and then to renew acquaintance.

The Bengali nation, or Bengalis as they are called, really give Calcutta the character that it now has. They were the original inhabitants of the city but were followed very quickly (some say preceded) by the Armenians, another surprise. Nothing that happens in Calcutta is ordinary.

Rabindranath Tagore, the great poet, philosopher and artist, was a Bengali and Jamini Roy, the primitive artist, whom I knew and whose paintings adorn my apartment, was a celebrated Bengali. The most literary people in India are reputed to be the Bengalis.

The architecture of the city, constructed during the British Colonial period, gave Calcutta its marvelously grand look as private palaces, public monuments, imposing estates, vied with Hindu temples, Muslim mosques, the Armenian Church (the oldest Christian monument in Calcutta), the Synagogue and the famous Old Park Street Cemetery. The cemetery was new in 1769 and by 1790 was full—most of the graves being for the young who died in the pestilential, dank climate. The extravagant mausoleums, gravestones, epitaphs are now being restored as decay threatens to obliterate even the cemetery. But the rest of the city continues to deteriorate.

Yet, and there is always a "yet" in discussing Calcutta, in spite of the decay that surrounds one and all, extraordinary cuisines flourish in the city.

The Bengalis love fish and are perhaps the most dedicated fish eaters in India. It is logical in a province situated on the Bay of Bengal and threaded by the estuaries of the Ganges River. Prawns especially are treated royally and just about anything that swims is given special attention. Vegetables in profusion are eaten, such as eggplant, cauliflower, cabbage, potato and the tender leaves and shoots of the local greens grown in the tropical, bone-melting heat and monsoon rains.

Meat is the least interesting food and has only been eaten in recent years as a vogue rather than a way of life.

The spices and flavorings are the same as for the rest of India: turmeric, cuminseed, coriander, onion, gingerroot, garlic and hot chili as well as unusual spices such as fenugreek and asafetida. Mustard seeds and mustard oil are much used in Calcutta and influence the cooking profoundly, thus differentiating the food from other regional cuisines.

Coconut milk is the great lubricator; rice is the great filler and the staple of the Bengali diet.

The traditional Bengali style of dining has its ritual and courses are served in this order:

1. First course is bitter, like bitter melon dishes.
2. *Dal* and white rice.
3. A vegetable dish.
4. Fish in some form.
5. A meat dish, if desired.
6. A dried-fruit chutney (Aloo Bokhra—see Index for recipe) if included.
7. Dessert is the final course.

Bengalis have won distinction throughout India for the variety and ingenuity of their sweets, usually prepared with milk and its products. Sweetmeat shops abound in Calcutta. There is a great deal of dispute as to the quality of the milk and just how much water the milk vendor has added. The best sweets are prepared in the home and are richly sweet, lavished with coconut, pistachios, gold or silver leaf, fruits and spices.

Bengali food is unconventional even for India where the ordinary is unknown. The cuisine is, in fact, as different and interesting as Calcutta itself.

Kancha Kola
Fried Green Banana Chips

4 green bananas, peeled
3 cups water
1 teaspoon salt

1 teaspoon ground turmeric
1 cup corn or peanut oil

1. Cut the bananas into 1/4-inch-thick crosswise slices. Soak them in water with the salt and turmeric for 1 hour. Drain well and pat dry with paper towels.

2. Over moderate heat, deep-fry the slices, a few at a time, in the oil until crisp. Drain briefly on paper towels.

Serve at room temperature as a snack with drinks.

Note: The original recipe calls for mustard oil, which is aromatic if not strong. I suggest that if you wish to reproduce the mustard oil flavor without actually buying any, put 1/4 teaspoon dry mustard in the oil and mix well.

Murghir Jhol
Simple Chicken Curry

1/4 cup corn or peanut oil
1 pound potatoes (4 small), peeled and quartered
1 cup thin-sliced onions
1 chicken, 3 pounds, cut into 8 pieces, loose skin and fat removed
1/2 cup onion slices, ground to a paste
4 garlic cloves, ground to a paste
1 inch of fresh gingerroot, ground to a paste
1/2 cup plain yogurt
1 teaspoon dried hot red chili flakes
1 teaspoon cuminseeds
1/4 teaspoon ground cinnamon
1/8 teaspoon ground cloves
1 cardamom pod, cracked
1 teaspoon salt, or to taste
1 fresh green hot chili, whole
1 1/2 cups water
1/4 cup coarse-chopped fresh coriander

1. Heat the oil in a pan and brown the potatoes over moderate heat for 3 minutes. Remove them and set aside.

2. Brown the sliced onions in the same oil over moderate heat for 3 minutes. Add the chicken and stir-fry for 3 minutes. Add the onion paste, garlic and gingerroot and stir-fry for 2 minutes.

3. Add the yogurt, chili flakes, cuminseeds, cinnamon, cloves, cardamom pod, salt and fresh chili. Continue to stir-fry for 1 minute.

4. Add the water and the browned potatoes. Bring to a boil, cover the pan, and cook until the chicken is tender, about 40 minutes. Add the coriander and stir for a moment.

Serve warm with white rice.

Serves 6

Chingri Bamboo Jhol
Shrimp and Bamboo Shoot Curry

This was the first curry served to me upon my arrival in Calcutta one August 30 years ago. It was during the monsoon season when the bamboo shoots were available fresh in Calcutta's famous New Market. It won me over to the taste of curry, the hotter the better.

2 pounds medium shrimps, peeled and deveined
¹/₂ teaspoon ground turmeric
1 teaspoon salt, or to taste
1 tablespoon corn or peanut oil
1 cup onion slices
2 garlic cloves
1 inch of fresh gingerroot
1 teaspoon dried hot red chili flakes
2 cups Rich Coconut Milk (see Index)
¹/₂ teaspoon sugar
2 cups canned bamboo shoots, cut into julienne

1. Rub the shrimps with the turmeric and salt. Let stand for 15 minutes.

2. Heat the oil in a pan and stir-fry the shrimps over moderate heat for 2 minutes. Grind the onion slices, garlic, gingerroot and chili flakes together into a paste. Add to the shrimps and stir-fry for 3 minutes.

3. Add 1 cup coconut milk, the sugar and the bamboo shoots. Bring to a boil, stirring frequently, and cook for 5 minutes. Add the other cup of coconut milk and cook for 5 minutes more, stirring frequently so that the milk does not separate. Do not cover.

Serve warm with white rice, various chutneys and Indian breads.

Serves 6

Note: Coconut milk may be prepared fresh, or cans of a very good quality imported from Thailand may be purchased.

Chingri Macher Malai
Prawn Curry in Coconut Milk

This is a rich, eminently satisfactory curry with an especially intriguing flavor when mustard oil is used. The rice is a sponge for the textures and flavors of the curry. One should also remember that prawns or shrimps are purchased in Calcutta with the heads on and very often still alive. The freshness is an elusive quality hard to duplicate in seafood purchased in our local supermarkets.

1 pound prawns or large shrimps, legs and heads removed but unpeeled
1 teaspoon salt
1 teaspoon ground turmeric
3 tablespoons corn or peanut oil, or mustard oil
1/2 teaspoon dried hot red chili flakes

1 teaspoon ground fresh gingerroot
1/2 cup sliced onion, ground to paste
2 cups Rich Coconut Milk (see Index)
1 teaspoon sugar
1 teaspoon ground garam masala

1. Mix the prawns with salt and turmeric. Let stand for 15 minutes.

2. Heat the oil in a wok or skillet and fry the prawns over moderate heat until they turn pink, about 2 minutes. Add the chili flakes, gingerroot and onion paste and stir-fry for 2 minutes. Remove the prawns and set aside.

3. Add the coconut milk and sugar to the wok and bring to a boil. Return prawns to the wok and cook for 10 minutes, basting continuously. Add the *garam masala*, stir for 1 minute, and remove from the heat.

Serve warm with plain white rice.

Serves 4

Lau Chingri
Shrimps and White Pumpkin

3 tablespoons corn or peanut oil
1 pound small shrimps, peeled
and deveined
1/2 teaspoon mustard seeds
4 small hot green chilies, halved
lengthwise
2 bay leaves
2 pounds white pumpkin, cut into
slices 1/2 inch long and 1/8 inch
thick

1 teaspoon sugar
1 teaspoon salt, or to taste
1 teaspoon ground turmeric
1 teaspoon cuminseeds
1/4 cup water, if needed

1. Heat the oil in a pan and fry the shrimps over moderate heat for 3 minutes, or until lightly browned. Remove them from the oil.

2. Add the mustard seeds, chilies and bay leaves, and stir-fry for 1 minute. Add the pumpkin slices and stir-fry over moderate heat for 5 minutes or more, or until the liquid seeps out.

3. Return the shrimps and stir-fry for 5 minutes. Add the sugar, salt, turmeric and cuminseeds at this time. There should be a small amount of liquid. If not, add the water and stir-fry for 2 minutes to combine the flavorings.

Serve warm with white rice.

Serves 6

Tomato Mach
Tomato Fish

1 pound fish—sea bass, red snapper, scrod—cut into ¹/₂-inch-thick slices including the bone

¹/₄ teaspoon ground turmeric

1 teaspoon salt

¹/₄ cup corn or peanut oil

2 bay leaves

2 cardamom pods, cracked

1 inch of stick cinnamon, broken into halves

2 whole cloves, broken into halves

¹/₄ cup onion slices, ground to a paste

1 inch of fresh gingerroot, ground to a paste

¹/₄ teaspoon dried hot red chili flakes

1 garlic clove, ground to a paste

1 medium-size ripe tomato, peeled and chopped (¹/₂ cup)

1 cup water

1 teaspoon sugar

1 tablespoon cider vinegar

1. Rub the fish slices with turmeric and salt and let stand for 15 minutes.

2. Heat the oil in a pan and fry the fish over moderate heat for 1 minute on each side. Remove fish and set aside. Remove all the oil except 2 tablespoons.

3. Heat the 2 tablespoons of oil and stir-fry the bay leaves, cardamom pods, cinnamon and cloves over moderate heat for 1 minute. Add the onion paste, gingerroot and chili flakes and stir-fry for 2 minutes.

4. Add the garlic paste and tomato and stir-fry for 3 minutes to reduce the tomato and flavorings to a paste. Add the water and bring to a boil.

5. Add the fish, sugar and vinegar, and simmer, uncovered, over moderately low heat for 10 minutes more.

Serve warm with rice, dal, chutney.

Serves 4

Macher Jhol
Simple Fish Curry

Bengalis are addicted to fish curry and this easily assembled one fulfills all their requirements.

1 pound fish—kingfish, scrod, red
  snapper or similar fish—fillets or
  with bone, cut into 2-inch pieces
1 teaspoon turmeric
1 teaspoon salt
3 tablespoons corn or peanut oil
2 small potatoes, peeled and
  quartered (about 1 cup)

1 bay leaf
1/4 teaspoon cuminseeds
2 whole small green chilies
1/2 to 1 teaspoon dried hot red
  chili flakes, or to taste
1 1/2 cups water

1. Rub the fish pieces with 1/2 teaspoon turmeric and 1/2 teaspoon salt. Let stand for 30 minutes.

2. Heat the oil in a wok or skillet and fry the fish over moderate heat for 3 minutes on both sides. Remove fish from the oil and set aside. Brown the potatoes in the same oil over moderate heat for 5 minutes. Remove them and set aside.

3. Add the bay leaf, cuminseeds and whole chilies to the oil, and stir-fry over moderate heat for 1 minute. Add the chili flakes and remaining turmeric and salt. Stir-fry for 2 minutes.

4. Add the water, bring to a boil, then return the potatoes and fish. Cover the wok and cook over moderately low heat for 10 minutes or until the potatoes are soft.

Serve warm with white rice and other dishes.

Serves 4 to 6

Sukta

Bitter Vegetable Mix

The *sukta* is served as a starter in a Bengali meal. It is flavored with an unusual combination of ingredients, but it is essentially slightly bitter. The bitter gourd and radish are tempered by the potato, banana and eggplant, bland vegetables and fruit. The slightly bitter fenugreek, the sharpness of the mustard and chili, make this a dish for the brave. It is so interesting that a recipe must be included. Bengalis love it.

Mustard oil is not an easy ingredient to find although it is always available in East Indian food shops. I usually use corn or peanut oil and add to this ¼ teaspoon dry mustard for the flavor I require. The mustard seeds, which snap and pop when added to hot oil, also provide the flavor.

Badi are croutons prepared from *dal* that is soaked in water for several hours and crushed into a thick paste. Small ½-inch nuggets of the paste are put on a tray to dry in the sun. Afterward, they are fried in oil just enough to cook them, and included in the *sukta*.

1 tablespoon mustard oil	1 cup bitter gourd (melon) slices
⅓ cup badi, dal croutons (optional)	1 medium-size potato, peeled, cut into ½-inch cubes
1 teaspoon black mustard seeds	1 green banana, cut into ½-inch-wide slices
1 teaspoon methi, fenugreek seeds, or ½ teaspoon ground fenugreek	1 whole dried hot red chili
2 bay leaves	½ inch of fresh gingerroot, grated (1 teaspoon)
½ pound (2) small eggplants, cut into 1-inch cubes	½ teaspoon ground turmeric
1 cup ½-inch cubes of white radish	1 cup water
	1 teaspoon sugar
	1 teaspoon salt

1. Heat the oil in a wok (in India it is called a *kerai*) or large skillet and lightly brown the croutons over moderate heat for 1 minute. Remove them and set aside.

2. Add the mustard seeds, *methi* (fenugreek) and bay leaves, and stir over moderate heat for a moment. Add the eggplants, radish, bitter gourd, potato, green banana and chili, and stir-fry for 3 minutes. Add the gingerroot, turmeric, water, sugar and salt. Cover the wok and cook for 20 minutes.

3. Stir in the *dal* croutons if you wish to use them, and cook for another minute.

Serve warm with white rice as a first course.

Serves 6

Alu Daum
Spiced Potatoes

This style of *alu daum* does have some sauce. However, a continuous cooking for 10 minutes more will completely dry out the sauce and would be another method of presenting the *alu*.

As dried, brown, small whole potatoes, they are served at teas and cocktails as appetizers. They are also served with *luchi*, the Bengali puffed bread.

1 pound small potatoes, 5 or 6
1/2 cup corn or peanut oil
1 teaspoon ground cuminseed
4 bay leaves
1 small ripe tomato, peeled and chopped (about 1/4 cup)
1 teaspoon dried hot red chili flakes
1/2 teaspoon ground turmeric

1 teaspoon sugar
2 tablespoons plain yogurt
1 teaspoon ground fresh gingerroot
1/2 teaspoon garam masala
1/2 teaspoon salt, or to taste
1/8 teaspoon asafetida (hing) (optional)
1/2 cup water

1. Cook the whole potatoes in their skins in water until they are almost soft. Remove, cool and peel. Set aside.

2. Heat the oil in a pan and brown the potatoes over moderate heat for 3 minutes. Remove the potatoes and all but 1 tablespoon oil.

3. Heat the tablespoon of oil and stir-fry the cuminseed and bay leaves over moderate heat for 3 seconds. Add the tomato, chili flakes, turmeric and sugar, and stir-fry for 2 minutes. Add the yogurt, gingerroot, *garam masala*, salt, and asafetida if used. Stir for 1 minute.

4. Add the potatoes and water and simmer, covered, over low heat until the water evaporates and a thick sauce remains.

Serve warm with other dishes.

Serves 4

Channna Masala
Spiced Chick-Peas

The *channa masala*, being high in protein, makes a good basis for a complete vegetarian meal, with or without other vegetable dishes.

¹/₄ cup sliced onion
2 tablespoons corn or peanut oil
¹/₂ teaspoon ground turmeric
¹/₂ to 1 teaspoon dried hot red
  chili flakes, to taste
¹/₂ teaspoon freshly ground black
  pepper

4 cardamom pods
4 bay leaves
¹/₂ teaspoon salt
1 pound cooked chick-peas
¹/₂ cup water
¹/₄ cup thin-sliced scallions
fresh lime slices

1. Fry the onion in the oil over moderate heat until golden, about 3 minutes. Add the turmeric, chili flakes, black pepper, cardamom, bay leaves and salt, and stir-fry for 2 minutes.

2. Add the chick-peas and mix well, then add the water. Cook over moderately low heat until all the liquid has evaporated, about 10 minutes.

Serve warm garnished with the scallions and lime slices and accompany with any kind of Indian bread such as *puri, loochee, naan, parata*.

Serves 6

Sag Bhaja
Red Spinach Fry

Beet greens taste to me like the red spinach and would make a good substitute. Cut the stems into ¹/₂-inch pieces and coarse-chop the leaves.

Green spinach or Swiss chard are not substitutes but may be treated the same way as the red. Simply season and stir-fry until dry.

1 tablespoon corn or peanut oil
¹/₄ teaspoon mustard seeds
2 whole dried red chilies
1 pound red spinach, well rinsed
  and coarse-cut

¹/₄ teaspoon salt
¹/₂ teaspoon sugar

1. Heat the oil in a wok or large skillet. Add the mustard seeds and chilies and stir-fry over moderate heat for a few seconds. Add the spinach and stir-fry for a minute, adding the salt and sugar.

2. Continue to stir-fry for 5 minutes, or until the liquid that has accumulated has evaporated. This is a dry vegetable fry.

Serve warm with other dishes.

Serves 4

Tetor Dal
Bitter Lentils

This fine lentil dish has several textures and flavors. The gourd and *dal* provide a smooth texture on the tongue. The bitter melon, browned, has its own attractive, lightly bitter taste to contrast with the other ingredients.

$\frac{2}{3}$ *cup* moong dal, *rinsed and drained*
6 *cups water*
2 *cups 1-inch cubes of bottle or round gourd*
$\frac{1}{2}$ *teaspoon ground turmeric*
4 *whole small hot green chilies*
1 *teaspoon salt, or to taste*
1 *teaspoon sugar*

2 *tablespoons corn or peanut oil*
1 *small bitter melon, seeded and cut into $\frac{1}{4}$-inch-thick slices ($\frac{1}{2}$ cup)*
$\frac{1}{2}$ *teaspoon black mustard seeds*
$\frac{1}{2}$ *teaspoon fenugreek seeds, or $\frac{1}{4}$ teaspoon ground fenugreek*
2 *bay leaves*

1. Mix the *dal* and water; bring to a boil in a large pan over moderate heat. Remove the foam that accumulates. Add the gourd, turmeric and chilies, and cook for 5 minutes. Add the salt and sugar and cook for 10 minutes.

2. Heat the oil in a skillet and over moderate heat brown the bitter melon slices for 2 to 3 minutes. Add the mustard seeds, fenugreek and bay leaves and fry for 1 minute.

3. Add the entire mixture to the *dal* and continue to cook over moderately low heat for 10 minutes more.

Serve warm with rice and other dishes.

Serves 6

Anarash Chutney
Pineapple Chutney

Bengalis have a sweet tooth as shown by the popularity of this chutney. It contributes to the variety of flavors in a Bengali meal and is an especially attractive contrast to the fish curries.

5 dried apricots, halved, soaked in   *2 tablespoons sugar*
  water for 4 hours   *¹/₄ teaspoon salt*
1 cup grated fresh ripe pineapple   *1 tablespoon raisins*

1. Drain the apricots and mix all the ingredients together in a pan. Simmer over low heat for 15 minutes, stirring constantly, until all the liquid has evaporated and the chutney has thickened.

2. Turn out into a glass dish and refrigerate for 1 hour.

Serve with any type of Bengali fish or meat dish.

Makes 1 cup

Aloo Bokhra
Fruit Chutney

The Bengalis eat *aloo* between courses to clear the palate, but for Western taste it would serve well as a chutney with meat or fish dishes.

1 tablespoon corn or peanut oil   *6 ounces dates with pits, about 1*
1 whole dried hot red chili   *cup*
¹/₄ teaspoon mustard seeds   *1 tablespoon raisins*
4 or 5 medium-size prunes,   *¹/₄ cup sugar, or to taste*
  soaked in water for 1 hour, then   *¹/₄ teaspoon salt*
  drained   *1 cup water*

1. Heat the oil in a skillet and fry the chili over moderate heat for 5 seconds. Add the mustard seeds and stir-fry for another 5 seconds. Add all the fruits and stir-fry for 2 minutes.

2. Add the sugar, salt and water. Bring to a boil and cook for 5 minutes. Shake the skillet now and then. Do not mash the fruits and do not overcook.

Serve cool or at room temperature.

Serves 6

Panir Payes
Milk Custard with Cheese and Raisins

This fine, natural custard illustrates the Bengali attachment to milk and milk products. The custard is produced simply by cooking milk slowly to make the water evaporate, leaving the milk solids. No flour, cornstarch or other thickening agents are necessary, just a little heat and patience.

2 quarts whole milk
½ cup sugar
3 tablespoons raisins
⅔ cup Panir, Cheese (following recipe), cut into ½-inch cubes

1 drop of vanilla extract (optional)

1. Bring the milk to a boil in a pan over moderate heat. Continue to cook the milk over moderately low heat, stirring frequently, to reduce the milk by about one third. Add the sugar, mix well, and cook for 10 to 15 minutes more to thicken the mixture.

2. Add the raisins, *panir* (cheese), and vanilla, mix well, and cook for 5 minutes more. Turn out the mixture, which should be thick, into a bowl.

Serve well chilled.

Serves 6

Panir
Cheese

1 quart whole milk   1 tablespoon lemon juice

1. Bring the milk to a boil over moderate heat. Remove the pan from the heat and add the lemon juice; stir well. The milk will "crack"—the curd and whey will separate.

2. Pour everything into a cheesecloth and lightly squeeze out the liquid. Tie the cloth over a bowl and let the cheese drain for 1 hour. What is left is a relatively dry, white cheese, which may be used in various ways.

Refrigerate to be used when needed.

Makes 1 cup

Narkoler Nadu
Coconut Balls

1 cup white sugar   2 cardamom pods, cracked
1 cup freshly grated ripe coconut

1. Mix the sugar and coconut together in a wok or skillet. Cook over low heat, stirring constantly, for 10 minutes. The sugar will soften or even melt. Add the cardamom and stir for 5 minutes more.

2. Remove the mixture from the heat and process in a processor for a few seconds. Turn out, and shape firm balls, using 1 heaping teaspoon of the coconut mixture for each. The balls should be about 3/4 inch in diameter.

3. Allow to cool and dry on wax paper for about 1 hour. Store in a jar or metal can.

Makes about 30

Variation: One cup firmly packed light brown sugar may be used instead of the white for a slightly different flavor.

The Jewish Kitchen

*T*he punkahs (overhead fans) were whirling incessantly chasing the chick-chucks (the tiny mosquito-eating house lizards) from one side of the ceiling to the other. White-jacketed house servants glided barefoot across the marble dining-room floor, carrying bowls of cashews and almonds. Out on Camac Street, a main residential area, cows wandered aimlessly, chewing on street garbage in the bone-melting heat. Overhead, vampire bats flapped noiselessly through the night looking for victims.

No, dear reader, this is not Kipling's India but the setting for a Sabbath evening dinner at the home of a member of the vanishing Calcutta Jewish community. I was there to indulge myself in the wonderful food of a rare and little-known cuisine.

Twenty-five or more years ago I went to live and work in Calcutta, then and even now considered one of the world's strangest cities—with cyclones, plague and intense heat as well as other assorted phenomena of the Indian subcontinent. At that time I was introduced to the cooking of the ancient Sephardic community of the Calcutta Jews and became aware that here was an important and unknown style of cooking. It was a cuisine within cuisines and it celebrated the individuality of the transplanted Jewish community.

The community traces its antecedents to the immigrants from Baghdad (Iraq) and the Middle East, and through them 2,000 years back to the original Babylonian Jews. During the end of the sixteenth century there was some movement from Baghdad to Bombay and Calcutta, but by 1800 that trickle became a flood.

The immigrants brought their own culinary techniques and tastes with them but found in India new cooking styles and an unlimited variety of spices, vegetables, fruits, meat and poultry. Their neighbors were benevolent and the British Colonial rule was auspicious. It was a time when dissemination of foods from one part of the world to another was in full swing, as we see by the passage of tomatoes, hot chilies, squashes, potatoes and beans from Mexico and Guatemala to India. There was a general acceptance of new products and an experimenting with new food combinations everywhere.

For the Jews, the introduction to Indian spices was love at first sight.

Garlic they knew, but ginger and turmeric they enthusiastically embraced and appropriated for the Jewish cuisine. There was a culinary marriage between the cooking of Baghdad and that of Calcutta. The number of dishes proliferated with adaptions to suit the Jewish palate and outright inventions such as Sweet-and-Sour Beef and Beets (see recipes).

Beets, okra, tamarind, lemon and hot chilies were favorably integrated with cumin, coriander, cardamom and the gamut of vegetables both tropical and western. Coconut milk was occasionally used with fish and in the famous dessert, Dol Dol. Indian appetizers such as *pakora* were adapted to Jewish tastes. Beef dishes, perhaps in sympathy with the Hindu prohibition of the slaughter of cows, were few. And the kosher dietary laws were obeyed—pork and shellfish were never used.

And so, by the twentieth century, as a result of cultural habits and religious scruples, the adoption of local ingredients, the multiplication of all the personal preferences of the different families, through 100 years of development, there was brought forth a new hybrid but distinctive cuisine.

Servants and family retainers had a special authority in the Jewish kitchen. The family cook (in Calcutta men were the cooks) was highly skilled in reproducing Jewish cooking and frequently became the guardian of its tradition. The lady of the house kept track of what was going on, but the actual production in the kitchen was in the hands of the cook and his satellite assistants. The cook's son inherited his father's job when he retired. It was a good life for all.

Preparing a Calcutta dinner in the American kitchen will present no problem and should be pursued with confidence. I have cooked the food in Calcutta, London, Los Angeles, New York and Guatemala City to good account. No spices or ingredients are so esoteric that they cannot be easily found in supermarkets or Asian groceries. Since we are not blessed with an unlimited number of servants, a small formal dinner or large buffet can quite easily be presented with some judicious timing. Most of the dishes can be prepared the day before with the certain knowledge that the flavors will only be enhanced. Light reheating may be all that is necessary. Also, a menu that focuses on a great variety is more important than large quantities of a few dishes. What dazzles the eye can also excite the palate and offer expectation of a special event.

Store-bought hot and sweet mango chutneys and hot pickles of many imported varieties are available in Indian food emporiums. These too are commonly included in a Calcutta meal. Servants in the homes at one time prepared everything that appeared on the table, but in the twentieth century it became possible to purchase acceptable bottled products. Even today, in Calcutta, the famous Daw Sen Chutney brand, originated by the

Jewish Mordecai family, is bottled along with other marvelous creations and exported to many countries.

Jewish holy days are occasions for special efforts in the kitchen, when variety indeed becomes the spice of life. Not all of the repertoire of the cuisine is common daily fare. Simple poultry roasts of chicken or duck, spiced Calcutta-style, vegetable curries, the ubiquitous rice either plain or glorified in pilau, are timeless and neither ceremonial nor special.

In the autumn of 1982 and 1983, I returned to Calcutta and cooked daily and intensively with a marvelous cook from the rapidly dwindling community. It was an exhilarating experience. I believe now that my twenty-five-year quest to record the cuisine before its final disappearance has been accomplished.

Now the community with the large homes and gardens that reflected the tradition as it once was has disappeared. The community at the time of publication of this book is down to about fifty members. Most have gone freely to England, Australia and the United States. And my private mission has been accomplished.

Pilau Matabak
Old-Fashioned Rice

This is a *pukha* (real!) Jewish rice cooked by the Orthodox Jews of Calcutta on Simchat Torah. Any gala occasion would be a good time to prepare this pilau.

POTATOES

4 small potatoes, cut into
   1/4-inch-thick round slices
1 cup sliced onions
1/2 teaspoon ground turmeric

1/2 teaspoon salt
1 tablespoon oil
1/2 cup water

RICE

1 tablespoon corn or peanut oil
2 cups raw rice, rinsed and well
   drained
1/2 teaspoon ground turmeric

1/2 teaspoon salt
2 teaspoons garam masala
3 cups water

FISH

1/2 pound fillet of sole, flounder or
   similar fish, cut into 2-inch
   cubes

1/4 teaspoon salt
1/4 teaspoon ground turmeric
2 tablespoons corn or peanut oil

1. Mix the potatoes and onions with the turmeric and salt.

2. Put the tablespoon of oil in a large saucepan. Place the onion slices in the bottom of the pan and cover them with the potato slices. Fry the mixture slowly over low heat for 5 minutes. Do not stir to disturb the slices. Add the water, cover the pan, and continue to steam/fry for 15 minutes, or until the water has completely evaporated. Set aside.

3. Heat the oil for the rice in a saucepan. Over moderate heat lightly brown the rice for 3 minutes, adding the turmeric, salt and *garam masala* during the process. Add the water, stir the mixture, bring to a boil, cover the pan, and turn the heat to low. Cook for 10 minutes.

4. Rub the fish with the salt and turmeric. Heat the oil in a skillet and lightly fry the fish over moderate heat for 2 minutes. Remove fish cubes from the oil.

5. Spread the fish cubes over the potatoes in their original pan. Cover fish completely with the rice. Cover the pan and fry the pilau slowly over low heat for 15 minutes. This may also be done in a 350°F. oven for 15 minutes.

Serve warm.

Serves 6

Pilau

Spiced Rice with Green Peas

1 teaspoon cuminseeds
3 tablespoons corn or peanut oil
3 tablespoons chopped onion
2 cups raw Basmati rice, well
   rinsed and soaked for 30
   minutes
1/4 teaspoon ground turmeric

1/2 teaspoon salt, or to taste
1 cup green peas, fresh or frozen
1 cardamom pod
1 whole clove
1 cinnamon stick, 1 inch
3 1/4 cups water, or more as
   needed

1. Toast the cuminseeds in a dry skillet over low heat for 1 minute or until the aroma is released. Set aside.

2. Heat the oil in a pan and over moderate heat fry the onion for 2 minutes, or until it turns golden. Add the rice and stir well. Add the turmeric, salt and toasted cuminseeds and continue to fry the rice lightly for 2 minutes.

3. Add the peas, cardamom, clove and cinnamon. Stir and add the water. Bring to a boil and immediately turn the heat to low. Cover the pan and cook for 12 to 15 minutes. Stir once toward the end of that time. If the rice appears too firm, add another tablespoon or two of water. Cook for another minute, turn off the heat, and allow the rice to rest in the covered pan for 15 minutes before dining.

Serve warm. The rice may be lightly reheated just before dining.

Serves 6

Jungli Pilau
Country Rice

Jungli is a word that crops up now and then referring to a person who is a boor, a little uncouth or uncultured. The word implies a country hick just in town for the weekend. However, this is the only time I have encountered the word in reference to food. Here it refers to country vegetables used in a family-style vegetable dish.

1/2 cup 2-inch carrot sticks
1/2 cup 1/4-inch green bean slices
1/2 cup 1/2-inch potato cubes
1 cup 1-inch cauliflowerets
1 cup shredded cabbage
1/4 cup green peas, fresh or frozen
3 tablespoons corn or peanut oil
1/2 cup thin-sliced onion
1/2 teaspoon crushed fresh
  gingerroot
1/2 teaspoon crushed garlic
1/2 teaspoon ground turmeric
1 teaspoon salt, or to taste

2 cups raw rice, well rinsed and
  drained
3 1/2 cups water
1/2 cup chopped ripe tomato
3 whole cloves
1 cinnamon stick, 3 inches, broken
  into halves
4 cardamom pods, cracked
2 tablespoons raisins (optional)
12 almonds, blanched and halved
  (optional)
1/4 cup chopped fresh coriander

1. Cook the carrot sticks in boiling water for 2 minutes. Remove and set aside. Cook the green beans, potato, cauliflower and cabbage separately for the same length of time. The peas do not need this precooking. Drain each vegetable well.

2. Heat the oil in a pan and brown the onion until a light brown color develops, about 3 minutes. Add the gingerroot, garlic, turmeric and salt, and stir for 1 minute.

3. Add the rice and stir well to coat the grains with the flavorings, about 2 minutes. Add the cooked vegetables and peas, the water, tomato, cloves, cinnamon and cardamom. Bring to a boil; add the raisins and almonds if used. Turn the heat to low, cover the pan, and cook for about 15 minutes. The water should be completely absorbed and the rice dry.

4. At this stage, sprinkle with the coriander. Stir the rice to fluff it up. Cover the pan and let the mixture rest for 10 to 15 minutes more.

Serve warm.

Serves 6

Arook
Rice Balls

Arook means "veined" in both Hebrew and Arabic (from Baghdad) since the ground chicken appears as "veins" running through the rice.

½ cup raw rice
2 cups water
2 teaspoons salt, or to taste
½ pound boneless chicken, chopped fine
½ teaspoon ground turmeric
½ teaspoon crushed fresh gingerroot

½ teaspoon crushed garlic
¼ teaspoon garam masala
1 tablespoon chopped fresh mint, coriander or celery leaves
1 egg, beaten
2 tablespoons plus 2 teaspoons corn or peanut oil

1. Rinse the rice under cold water. Bring 2 cups water to a boil with 1 teaspoon salt, add the rice, and cook rapidly for 5 minutes. Drain the rice and set aside.

2. Mix the warm rice with the chicken, remaining salt, turmeric, gingerroot, garlic, *garam masala*, mint, egg and 2 teaspoons oil.

3. Moisten your hands with cold water. Scoop up 2 tablespoons of the rice mixture and shape into a ball 2 to 2½ inches in diameter. This can be done with practice by rolling the ball in a circular motion in the palm of your hand. Shape all the rice balls.

4. Place the rice balls in a baking pan well coated with 2 tablespoons oil. Bake in a 375°F. oven for 30 to 35 minutes. Do not turn the balls; let them bake to a light brown with a firm top.

Serve warm.

Makes 8 balls

Variation: A half-pound of boneless fish such as flounder, cod or haddock, chopped fine, can be used instead of the chicken. With the fish, use chopped mint or parsley. With the chicken, coriander or celery are preferable.

Note: The *arook* can be made a day or two in advance. These rice balls are an excellent buffet idea. They can be frozen but should be thawed out at room temperature for 1 hour and then warmed in a 375°F. oven for 10 minutes before serving.

Kooba

Stuffed Rice Dumplings

Kooba means "dome" in Arabic, and the name is a good description of these rounded or domed stuffed dumplings.

My Calcutta cook would grind the soaked rice with a stone mortar and pestle almost exactly the same size and shape as those I have seen used in Guatemala. The grinders are a gray stone, rectangular in shape, 12 inches wide and 24 inches long and about 3 inches thick. They are sturdy, hard and good for a lifetime of use. We, of course, use a processor.

DOUGH

1 cup raw rice
2 cups water

½ teaspoon salt

STUFFING

½ cup grated onion, squeezed dry in a towel
¼ teaspoon minced garlic
¼ teaspoon minced fresh gingerroot
½ teaspoon salt
¼ teaspoon ground turmeric

¼ teaspoon freshly ground black pepper
1 tablespoon chopped fresh coriander
¼ pound raw chicken or beef, ground

1. Soak the rice in the water overnight. Drain and process to a smooth dough with the salt. It will be firm.

2. Mix all the stuffing ingredients together and set aside.

3. Take 1 tablespoon rice dough and flatten it into a circle ¼ inch thick in the curved fingers and palm of your hand. Fill this with 1 heaping teaspoon of the stuffing. Fold the dough over this into a ball. Prepare all the dumplings in this way.

4. The dumplings are traditionally cooked in boiling Maraq, chicken soup (see Index) over moderate heat for 30 minutes and served warm as a side dish.

5. They may also be fried; in that case, after they have been made, flatten them out into round discs ½ inch thick. Using ½ cup corn or peanut oil, brown them in a wok or skillet for about 2 minutes. Drain on paper towels and serve warm as appetizers.

Makes about 12

Piaju
Two-Lentil Fritters

These fritters are served with drinks or at tea or coffee hour. Squeeze lemon juice, as much as wanted, over the *piaju* as you eat them.

I am told this is definitely Indian, not Jewish, but the difference is that in Burma it is prepared in a large football shape rather than as flat cakes. So one can toss *this* football back and forth to discover the origin of the recipe.

1 cup yellow lentils (chana ka dal)
1/2 cup red lentils (Egyptian)
1/2 teaspoon crushed fresh gingerroot
1 small garlic clove, crushed to a paste
1/2 teaspoon chopped fresh hot chili or to taste
1/2 teaspoon ground turmeric
1/2 teaspoon salt
2 medium-size onions, chopped (1 cup)
1 tablespoon minced fresh coriander
1 cup corn or peanut oil for deep-frying

1. Soak the yellow and red lentils separately in water for 4 hours. Drain. Crush them to a coarse paste in a processor.

2. Mix the lentils and the gingerroot, garlic, chili, turmeric, salt, onions and coriander together.

3. Heat the oil in a wok or skillet over moderate heat. Take 1 heaping tablespoon of the lentil mixture and shape a fritter 2 inches in diameter and about 3/8 inch thick. Continue to shape fritters with the rest of the mixture. Brown them in the oil for about 2 minutes on each side. Drain on paper towels.

Serve warm with lemon wedges.

Makes 14 to 15 fritters

Pantras
Beef-Stuffed Pancakes

I have been told that the recipe for *pantras* is not an exclusive dish of the Calcutta Jews. A Parsi lady told me that it originated in her community, whereas an Anglo-Indian acquaintance claims it for them. My Jewish cook says that without doubt it is Jewish. I believe all of the stories are correct but that the *pantras* are probably Jewish by adoption.

When I was being taught how to make this delicious dish, which can be served as an appetizer, the cook cut the top off the egg and emptied the shell of its contents. The empty shell was used to measure the batter and pour it into the frying pan. An effective method, resulting in all the crêpes being of the same size and thickness.

STUFFING

1 tablespoon corn or peanut oil
1 cup fine-chopped onions
1 pound ground beef
1/2 teaspoon crushed fresh
   gingerroot
1/2 teaspoon crushed garlic

1/4 teaspoon dried hot red chili
   flakes
1/2 teaspoon salt
1/2 teaspoon ground turmeric
1/2 cup chopped fresh coriander
1 teaspoon garam masala

PANCAKES

1 1/2 cups flour
2 cups cold water
1/4 teaspoon salt

1 egg, beaten
corn or peanut oil

FOR COOKING

1 egg, beaten
1 cup toasted fine bread crumbs

1/4 cup oil

1. To make the stuffing, heat the oil in a large skillet and over moderate heat fry the onions for 2 minutes. Add the beef and all other stuffing ingredients. Stir-fry for 5 minutes to evaporate all the liquid. The stuffing should be fairly dry. Cool it to room temperature.

2. For the pancakes, mix the flour, water and salt into a smooth batter. Add the egg and mix again. The batter will be thin.

3. Lightly oil a crêpe pan or other nonstick skillet. Pour in about 1/4 cup batter, tipping the pan so that the batter spreads evenly. Fry only one

side of the crêpe over moderate to low heat and turn out on a cloth towel. Prepare all the batter this way.

4. For each pancake, place 1 heaping tablespoon of the beef mixture on the end nearest you, roll it over once, fold the sides in towards the middle, and complete the roll. The *pantras* should be 4 inches long and 1 inch wide.

5. Dip the *pantras* into the beaten egg and roll them in the crumbs. Heat the oil in a skillet and brown them over moderate heat for about 3 minutes. Drain quickly on paper towels.

Makes 8 to 10

Variations: Several alternate stuffings may be prepared instead of the ground beef.

VEGETABLE STUFFING

1 cup julienne carrots	*1 cup ¹/₂-inch cubes of cauliflower*
1 cup ¹/₄-inch slices of green beans	*1 cup julienne beets*

1. Blanch the raw vegetables in boiling water for 5 minutes. Drain well and dry on a cloth towel. Cooked beets, either canned or fresh, need not be blanched; simply drain well.

2. Mix the vegetables together and prepare the *pantras* in the same manner as for those stuffed with beef.

CHEESE STUFFING

1¹/₂ cups farmer's cheese	*¹/₄ teaspoon sugar*
1 egg, beaten	*¹/₂ teaspoon salt (optional)*
¹/₂ teaspoon freshly ground black pepper	

1. Mash the cheese and mix it with the egg, black pepper, sugar, and salt if used.

2. Stuff the crêpes and continue as for the beef.

Sambusak
Beef and Lentil Turnover

STUFFING

3/4 cup yellow split lentils (chana ka dal)
3 cups water
3 tablespoons corn or peanut oil
1 medium-size onion, chopped (1/2 cup)
1/2 teaspoon ground turmeric
1 teaspoon salt
1/2 teaspoon crushed fresh gingerroot

1 small garlic clove, crushed to a paste
1/4 teaspoon dried hot red chili flakes
1/2 pound ground beef
2 tablespoons chopped fresh coriander
1 teaspoon garam masala

DOUGH

2 cups flour
1/2 teaspoon salt
1 tablespoon corn or peanut oil

about 4 tablespoons cold water, as needed

FOR COOKING

1 cup corn or peanut oil for deep-frying

1. Soak the lentils in the 3 cups water overnight. The next day cook the lentils in the same water for about 30 minutes, or until they are soft. Drain off the excess water, if any, and mash the lentils by hand, or in a processor if you wish.

2. Heat the oil in a wok or skillet and stir-fry the onion over moderate heat until it is golden, about 3 minutes. Add the turmeric, salt, gingerroot, garlic and chili flakes, and stir-fry for another minute. Add the beef and continue to stir until the color has changed.

3. Add the mashed lentils, the coriander and *garam masala*. Stir-fry the mixture together into a more or less coarse paste for 2 minutes more. Set aside and cool until ready to use. (*Note:* At this stage the beef/lentil mixture can be eaten as an appetizer with toast or Indian breads.)

4. Mix dough ingredients together, adding small amounts of water as needed to prepare a dough that can be easily handled. Let dough rest, covered, for 15 minutes.

5. Roll out the dough into a long sausage 1 inch in diameter. Cut or break off ³/₄-inch-wide pieces.

6. On a floured board roll out each piece of dough into a thin pancake 4 to 5 inches in diameter. Put 1 heaping tablespoon of the beef/lentil mixture on the lower half of the pancake, turn over the top to make a half-moon, and press the edges together firmly. Fold the edge over all the way around.

7. Heat the oil in a wok or skillet and lightly brown the turnovers on both sides over moderate heat. Drain on paper towels. Or bake on an oiled cookie sheet in a 375°F. oven for 30 minutes, or until lightly browned.

Serve warm as an appetizer.

Makes 20

Note: The *sambusak* freeze well and therefore a large number can be prepared for future use or storage. Cool them first, then store in plastic bags and freeze. To serve, let them defrost for 1 hour and warm briefly in a hot oven.

Egg Meetha

Hard-cooked eggs browned in hot oil are combined traditionally with *turai*, also called bitter gourd, bitter melon, or in Kipling's India, "gentlemen's fingers."

6 hard-cooked eggs, peeled	1/2 teaspoon ground turmeric
3 tablespoons corn or peanut oil	1/2 teaspoon salt, or to taste
1/2 pound bitter melon	2 bay leaves
1 teaspoon crushed fresh	2 cardamom pods
gingerroot	1/2 cup water
1 teaspoon crushed garlic	2 tablespoons lemon juice
1/2 cup sliced onion	2 teaspoons brown sugar

1. Brown the eggs in the oil over moderate heat for about 3 minutes. Remove and set aside.

2. Cut the bitter melon horizontally into halves. Scoop out and discard the seeds and loose pulp and cut half-moon slices 1/4 inch thick.

3. In the same oil used for the eggs, stir-fry the gingerroot, garlic and onion for 2 minutes. Add the bitter melon slices, the turmeric, salt, bay leaves, cardamom and water. Stir well, cover the pan, and cook over moderate heat for 5 minutes.

4. Add the eggs, lemon juice and brown sugar. Shake the pan several times and cook, uncovered, over low heat until the liquid has evaporated. Adjust the seasonings of lemon juice, sugar and salt to taste at this stage.

Serve warm as a side dish.

Serves 6

Maraq
Light Spicy Chicken Soup with Vegetables

This is a popular Jewish dish that is halfway between a soup and a stew. It is a complete meal. It may include as many vegetables as you wish. My own preference runs to any kind of squash or pumpkin, peas, carrots and potatoes. Since the type of vegetable influences the flavor of the *maraq*, personal preference is paramount. Potatoes, however, are always included.

½ cup chopped onion
¼ teaspoon crushed fresh
    gingerroot
¼ teaspoon crushed garlic
½ teaspoon ground turmeric
1 teaspoon salt, or to taste
3½ cups water
1 chicken, 3 pounds, cut into
    serving pieces, loose skin and fat
    discarded
½ cup coarse-chopped tomato,
    fresh or canned

1 cup cauliflowerets
¼ cup 1-inch slices of green
    beans
¼ cup green peas
½ cup cubed white turnip
½ cup thin-sliced carrot
½ cup cubed potato
1 tablespoon chopped fresh
    coriander

The traditional way of eating the *maraq* is to put 1 or 2 teaspoons of Halba (Hilbeh) (see Index) in the bowl first, then add 3 or 4 pieces of flat bread (*syed ka roti*) or matzoh, before pouring the soup over all. Even toasted pita could be used, if necessary.

1. Cook the onion, gingerroot, garlic, turmeric and salt in ½ cup water in a large covered saucepan over moderate heat for 5 minutes.

2. Add the chicken and the balance of the water and bring to a boil. Cook for 20 minutes.

3. Add the tomato, cauliflowerets, green beans, peas, turnip, carrot and potato and cook for 20 minutes more until the chicken and vegetables are tender and the liquid reduced a little. Sprinkle with the coriander and cook for 5 minutes more. Total cooking time is about 45 minutes.

Serve with white rice.

Serves 6

Hameen

Baked Chicken and Rice for the Sabbath

Hameen is a classic Sabbath food since it is prepared before sundown but cooked during the entire Friday evening since no cooking is allowed on Saturday. (Ashkenazis prepare the *chalunt* for Sabbath in the same fashion.) The style is to cook the chicken and rice very slowly so that the chicken melts away from the bones. All the flavors are locked into the cooking pot, which must be tightly sealed with the cover. The chicken fat combines with the rice to develop a brown rice crisp (*hakaka*) on the bottom of the pan after several hours of cooking. This is scraped out and served with the chicken as a garnish.

Sometimes hard-cooked eggs are wrapped in aluminum foil and cooked on top of the pan along with the chicken. They develop an unusual but delicious brown roasted flavor.

STUFFING

1/2 cup raw rice, well rinsed
1/4 cup chopped tomato
1/4 teaspoon crushed fresh gingerroot
1/4 teaspoon crushed garlic
1/4 teaspoon salt

1/4 teaspoon ground turmeric
1/4 teaspoon garam masala
1 chicken gizzard, heart and liver, chopped fine
1 chicken, 3 1/2 pounds

RICE

3 tablespoons corn or peanut oil
1/2 cup sliced onion
1/2 teaspoon crushed fresh gingerroot
1/2 teaspoon crushed garlic
1 teaspoon salt

1/2 teaspoon ground turmeric
1 cup cubed tomatoes
1 teaspoon garam masala
2 cups raw rice, well rinsed
5 cups water

1. Mix stuffing ingredients together. Stuff the chicken and sew up the opening. Set aside.

2. Heat the oil in a saucepan large enough to hold the chicken and rice. Brown the onion, gingerroot, garlic, salt, turmeric, tomato cubes and *garam masala*. Fry over moderate heat for 2 minutes.

3. Add the rice and fry for 2 minutes. Add the water and bring to a boil. Place the chicken, breast side up, into the rice. Cover the pot and cook the *hameen* very slowly over low heat for 2¹/₂ to 3 hours. Or, as done traditionally, bake in a 250°F. oven for 3 to 4 hours.

Serve warm. Serve the rice gruel as a side dish with the chicken and stuffing.

Serves 6

Hashua
Stuffed Chicken

¹/₂ cup raw rice, well rinsed
5 cups water
1 chicken gizzard, heart and liver
1 tablespoon chicken fat
1 teaspoon ground turmeric
1¹/₂ teaspoons salt
¹/₄ teaspoon crushed fresh
  gingerroot

¹/₄ teaspoon crushed garlic
¹/₄ teaspoon crushed fresh hot
  chili
1 chicken, 3 pounds, loose skin
  and fat removed
¹/₂ cup oil for deep-frying
  (optional)

1. Cook the rice in 2 cups of the water for 5 minutes. Drain and put aside.

2. Trim and chop fine the gizzard, heart and liver and mix in the chicken fat. There should be no more than 1 cup of the mixture. Mix with the cooked rice, ¹/₂ teaspoon of the turmeric, ¹/₂ teaspoon salt, the gingerroot, garlic and chili.

3. Stuff the chicken with this filling and sew up the opening with strong thread. Put the chicken in a saucepan slightly larger than itself.

4. Dissolve remaining 1 teaspoon salt and ¹/₂ teaspoon turmeric in remaining 3 cups water. Pour the water into the saucepan and bring to a boil. Cook, covered, over moderate heat for 30 to 35 minutes. Turn the chicken over once. At this stage, the chicken may be removed and served warm.

5. My own preference is to cool the chicken for 10 minutes and then fry it in the oil over moderate heat for about 10 minutes, or until it is crisp and brown on all sides.

Serve warm.

Serves 4 to 6

Harisi
Stuffed Chicken with Whole-Wheat Grains

This is one of the special holiday dishes that is cooked for Shavuot. Traditionally, the *harisi* was put in the oven the night before the holiday and baked very slowly all night. I believe the *harisi* must have originated in the Middle East because of its use of the wheat grains. It is the only recipe that I know of in the Calcutta Jewish cuisine that uses them.

1½ cups whole-wheat grains
5½ cups water
1 bay leaf
1 cardamom pod, cracked
1 whole clove
1 teaspoon salt
¼ teaspoon black pepper
¼ cup raw rice, cooked in 1 cup
  water for 5 minutes

½ teaspoon minced garlic
½ teaspoon minced gingerroot
¼ teaspoon ground turmeric
¼ teaspoon salt
1 chicken liver, chopped fine, and
  1 gizzard, trimmed and chopped
1 chicken, 3½ pounds

1. Soak the whole wheat in 2 cups water overnight.

2. Drain. Crack the grains slightly with a rolling pin or other instrument. Mix the grains with the bay leaf, cardamom, clove, salt and black pepper.

3. Prepare the stuffing by draining the cooked rice and mixing it with the garlic, gingerroot, turmeric, salt and chopped giblets. Stuff the chicken and sew up the opening.

4. Put the chicken in a large pot and surround it with the whole-wheat mixture. Cover with 3½ cups water and bring to a boil over moderate heat. Turn the heat to very low, cover the pot, and simmer on top of the stove for 30 minutes.

5. Place the chicken, tightly covered, in a 250°F. oven for 4 to 5 hours, the longer the better.

Serve warm.

Serves 4 to 6

Variation: Often included are 4 to 6 hard-cooked eggs in their shells, placed in the whole wheat and baked with the chicken.

Another style is to put 6 small Central American sugar bananas, unpeeled, in the whole wheat. Bake them with the chicken.

Mukmura

Chicken in Lemon Sauce

Many years ago I acquired this, my first Calcutta Jewish recipe. It came from Minnie Curlendar, whose Friday evening traditional dinners were something to behold. The table groaned with large quantities of food and that was matched in brilliance by the vivid conversation of the diners. For me it was an education in Asian generosity and Sabbath celebration.

1 chicken, 3 pounds, cut into serving pieces, giblets included, loose skin and fat removed
1 garlic clove, chopped fine
1 teaspoon minced fresh gingerroot
1 medium-size onion, chopped fine (about ¹/₂ cup)

¹/₄ teaspoon ground turmeric
1 teaspoon salt, or to taste
1 tablespoon raisins, light or dark
10 almonds, blanched in hot water, skin removed, and halved lengthwise
1¹/₄ cups water
2 to 3 tablespoons lemon juice

1. Put all the ingredients except lemon juice into a pan with ¹/₂ cup of the water. Bring to a boil over moderate heat. Cover the pan and cook for 15 minutes.

2. Uncover the pan, tilt it slightly, and *hamiss* the onion into a smooth purée. To do this, stir the small amount of sauce briskly with a wooden spoon.

3. Pour in the balance of the water, cover the pan, and continue to cook for 15 minutes more.

4. Add the lemon juice and cook for about 10 minutes, or until the chicken is tender and the sauce has thickened somewhat. Adjust the salt and lemon juice to taste.

Serve warm.

Serves 4

Chitanni

Chicken in Onion Sauce

3 tablespoons corn or peanut oil
2 cups sliced onions
1 inch of fresh gingerroot, chopped fine
3 garlic cloves, chopped fine
1 teaspoon salt, or to taste
1/2 teaspoon ground turmeric
3 cardamom pods, cracked
1 bay leaf
1/2 teaspoon chopped hot chili, fresh or dry

1 cinnamon stick, 1 inch
1 teaspoon cuminseeds
1 chicken, 3 1/2 pounds, cut into frying pieces, giblets included, loose skin and fat discarded
1 cup water
1 tablespoon tamarind paste, dissolved in 1/2 cup water
1/2 teaspoon sugar

1. Heat the oil in a pan. Add the onions, gingerroot, garlic, salt, turmeric, cardamom, bay leaf, chili, cinnamon and cuminseeds. Stir-fry the mixture for 2 minutes. Cover the pan to steam/fry over moderately low heat for 10 minutes. Then stir-fry uncovered for a minute to dissolve the moisture.

2. Add the chicken and stir well for 2 minutes. Add the water and cook, covered, over moderate heat for 30 minutes.

3. Strain the tamarind liquid through a metal sieve. Add it with the sugar and stir well. Cover the pan and cook over moderately low heat to create a thick onion sauce. Stir now and then so that it cooks evenly.

Serve warm with pilau.

Serves 6

Note: I have been told that the rule of thumb is to use double the weight of onions to that of chicken, but this seems to me too much of a good thing. The proportions noted above are enough to produce a fine onion sauce.

Variations: A 4 1/2-pound duck cut into serving pieces can also be prepared as a chitanni. The cooking time will be 15 to 20 minutes longer so as to tenderize the duck. Considerable fat will accumulate and this must be poured off before serving; or, better still, refrigerate for several hours and scoop off the congealed fat.
     Two pounds of beef or lamb, cut into 1-inch cubes, may also be

substituted for the chicken. The flavorings will be the same but the cooking time must be extended.

Cider vinegar (1¹/₂ tablespoons) and sugar (1 teaspoon) can be used instead of the tamarind liquid.

Hari Kabob
Spiced Chicken and Potatoes

12 small potatoes, 2 pounds,
  peeled
3 cups water
1 teaspoon salt
1 teaspoon crushed fresh
  gingerroot
1 teaspoon crushed garlic
1 teaspoon ground turmeric
1 teaspoon chopped fresh hot red
  chili

1 chicken, 3¹/₂ pounds, cut into
  serving pieces, giblets included,
  fat and loose skin discarded
¹/₂ teaspoon garam masala
2 bay leaves
2 cardamom pods, cracked
¹/₄ cup corn or peanut oil

1. Soak the potatoes in the water with the salt for 1 hour.

2. Add the gingerroot, garlic, turmeric and chili to the potatoes and bring the water to a boil over moderate heat. Cook for 15 minutes, or until the potatoes are nearly soft.

3. Remove the potatoes and set aside. Add the chicken to the spice broth with the *garam masala*, bay leaves and cardamom. Cook over moderate heat for 15 minutes.

4. Meanwhile, heat the oil in a wok or skillet and brown the potatoes over moderate heat until they have formed a crisp coating. Remove them from the oil and add to the chicken pot.

5. Continue to cook everything until both the chicken and potatoes are done, about 20 minutes. Remove the cover during this process so that all the liquid evaporates. This is a dry curry.

Serve warm with rice and salads.

Serves 6

Dopiaza
Spiced Chicken and Onions

Dopiaza actually means "two onions." Two onions may have been enough for the small village chickens of India, but the supermarket chickens are larger and fatter, so we use 2 cups of onions to provide a thick onion sauce.

1 teaspoon ground cuminseed
1 teaspoon ground coriander
2 tablespoons corn or peanut oil
1 chicken, 3½ pounds, cut into serving pieces, loose skin and fat discarded
2 cups chopped onions
1 teaspoon minced fresh gingerroot
1 teaspoon minced garlic
1 teaspoon ground turmeric
1 teaspoon salt, or to taste
¼ teaspoon freshly ground black pepper
½ cup chopped tomato, fresh or canned
4 whole cloves
1 cinnamon stick, 1 inch
4 cardamom pods
2 bay leaves
½ teaspoon dried hot red chili flakes
½ pound small potatoes, peeled and halved
1 cup green peas, fresh or frozen
1 cup water

1. Toast the cuminseed and coriander lightly in a dry skillet for 2 minutes, or until the aroma rises. Set aside.

2. Put the oil, chicken pieces, onions, gingerroot, garlic, turmeric, salt, black pepper and tomato in a large saucepan. Bring this to a boil over moderate heat, stir well, cover the pan, and cook for 15 minutes.

3. Uncover the pan, and stir the mixture rapidly (*hamiss*). Add the cloves, cinnamon, cardamom, bay leaves and chili flakes. Add the potatoes, peas and 1 cup water. Stir several times, cover the pot, and cook over moderate heat for 20 minutes or a bit more, until chicken and potatoes are soft.

4. Sprinkle the mixture with the toasted cuminseed and coriander and serve immediately.

Serve warm with plain rice or pilau.

Serves 4 to 6

Variation: Substitute 2 pounds boneless beef chuck cut into 1-inch cubes for the chicken. Proceed as for the chicken except the cooking time will be longer. At step 3, add 2 cups water and cook until the beef is tender and the sauce has reduced to a thick mélange.

Aloo-m-Kalla Murgi
Pot-Roast Chicken with Potatoes

This chicken and fried potatoes are traditionally served together. But once in a while, I prefer to prepare only the chicken and serve it with salads, rice and a vegetarian curry. The potatoes (Aloo-m-Kalla, see Index) make a good accompaniment to other chicken or meat dishes.

2 tablespoons corn or peanut oil
2 chickens, 3 pounds each, cut into frying pieces, giblets included, loose skin and fat discarded
2 medium-size onions, quartered
1/2 inch of fresh gingerroot, grated
2 garlic cloves, chopped fine or crushed
1/2 teaspoon ground turmeric

1 teaspoon salt, or to taste
1/2 teaspoon freshly ground black pepper
6 whole cloves
1 cinnamon stick, 3 inches, broken up
2 bay leaves
4 cardamom pods, cracked
1 cup water

1. Put the oil in a saucepan or large skillet. Place the chicken pieces in the oil, preferably in a single layer. Scatter the onions over the chicken.

2. In a bowl, mix the gingerroot, garlic, turmeric, salt, black pepper, cloves, cinnamon, bay leaves, cardamom and water together. Pour this over the chicken. Bring to a boil, cover the pan, and cook over moderate heat for 20 minutes.

3. Leave the cover slightly ajar so that the water evaporates. Turn the chicken over and brown the pieces over moderate heat for 15 minutes more, covered or not as you wish.

Serve warm.

Serves 6 to 8

Murgi Aloo Kari
Chicken and Potato Curry

Small chickens are brought in from the country to Calcutta's famous New Market, which is a huge bazaar that sells everything. The chickens are sold live and killed and dressed in the home kitchen. They weigh from 3/4 to 1 1/2 pounds and are firm of texture without much fat. Their natural flavor reminds us of clean air and country cooking.

1/2 cup chopped onion
1 teaspoon crushed garlic
1 teaspoon crushed fresh
  gingerroot
3 tablespoons corn or peanut oil
1 teaspoon ground cuminseed
1 teaspoon ground coriander
1/2 teaspoon ground turmeric
1 teaspoon salt, or to taste
1 teaspoon garam masala

1 teaspoon crushed fresh hot green
  chili
2 cups water
2 bay leaves
1 chicken, 3 pounds, cut into
  serving pieces, loose skin and fat
  discarded
1 pound potatoes, about 5 small,
  peeled, cut into 1/2-inch cubes
1 cup chopped ripe tomatoes

1. Fry the onion, garlic and gingerroot in the oil over moderate heat. When the onion is light brown, add the cuminseed, coriander, turmeric, salt, *garam masala* and chili. Stir well for 2 minutes. Add the water and bay leaves.

2. Bring to a boil and stir rapidly to smooth out the sauce (*hamiss*). Add the chicken and potatoes and cook over moderate heat for 20 minutes.

3. Add the tomatoes and simmer everything over low heat for 15 minutes, or a bit more, to reduce the sauce and cook the chicken and potatoes.

Serve warm.

Serves 6

Bamia Khuta
Sweet-and-Sour Chicken and Okra

1 chicken, 3 pounds, cut into serving pieces, loose skin and fat discarded
1 cup thin-sliced onions
1 teaspoon crushed fresh gingerroot
1 teaspoon crushed garlic
1 teaspoon salt, or to taste
1/2 teaspoon ground turmeric
2 cups water

1/2 pound okra
1/4 cup corn or peanut oil
1/2 cup chopped ripe tomato
2 tablespoons tamarind paste, soaked in 1/2 cup water for 30 minutes
1 teaspoon chopped fresh hot chili, or 1 small whole chili
1 teaspoon sugar
2 tablespoons chopped fresh mint

1. Put the chicken, onions, gingerroot, garlic, salt, turmeric and 1 cup water together into a pan. Bring to a boil over moderate heat and simmer until the liquid evaporates, about 20 minutes. Stir from time to time.

2. In the meantime, trim the ends off the okra and cut a slit 1 inch long in each pod. Heat the oil in a wok or skillet and fry the okra over moderate heat for 3 minutes. Remove and set aside.

3. Add the tomato to the chicken pan and stir-fry the mixture (hamiss) to reduce the remaining sauce to a thick paste. All the liquid should be evaporated at this stage and the chicken should begin to brown. Add the other cup of water.

4. Rub the tamarind paste and soaking water together with your fingers and strain the liquid into the chicken through a metal sieve. Bring the sauce to a boil and add the okra, chili and sugar. Cook over moderate to low heat for 10 minutes.

5. Add the mint. Adjust the sugar, should you wish a stronger sweet-sour flavor.

Serve warm. There will be plenty of sauce.

Serves 6

Murgi Cutlet
Calcutta Chicken Cutlet

Although this cutlet uses Jewish flavorings, it is probable that it was originally introduced into Indian cuisine by immigrants from Europe. It is a useful preparation for the American kitchen since it can be assembled easily. An ideal cutlet to be eaten cold at picnics.

½ cup sliced onion
2 teaspoons sliced fresh gingerroot
2 garlic cloves, sliced
1 teaspoon ground turmeric
½ teaspoon salt
¼ teaspoon freshly ground black pepper

2 whole chicken breasts, halved (4 pieces)
¼ cup flour
2 eggs, beaten
1 cup dried bread crumbs
½ cup corn or peanut oil

1. Put the onion, gingerroot, garlic, turmeric, salt and black pepper into a blender and process to a purée. Marinate the chicken pieces in this mixture for 2 hours.

2. Shake off the marinade and dip the cutlets into the flour, then into the beaten eggs, then into the bread crumbs.

3. Heat the oil in a skillet and fry the cutlets over moderately low heat for about 5 minutes on each side. The cutlets should cook slowly. Drain briefly on paper towels.

Serve warm.

Serves 4

Shoofta
Ground Chicken Barbecue

½ pound boneless chicken, ground (1 cup)
1 tablespoon chopped fresh coriander
½ cup grated onion, squeezed dry through a cloth
¼ teaspoon crushed fresh gingerroot

¼ teaspoon crushed garlic
¼ teaspoon crushed fresh hot chili
½ teaspoon salt
½ teaspoon ground turmeric
½ cup water
¼ cup corn or peanut oil

1. Mix the chicken, coriander, onion, gingerroot, garlic, chili, salt and turmeric together. Take 2 tablespoons of the mixture and roll into a firm cigar shape 4 inches long and 3/4 inch in diameter. Tap the ends flat. Continue to shape the rest of the mixture in the same way.

2. Put the *shooftas* and water in a skillet. Cover and cook over moderate heat for 3 minutes, turning them over once. Discard the water.

3. Heat the oil in the skillet and over moderate heat lightly brown the *shooftas* for 3 minutes. Drain. Serve warm as an appetizer or as an extra meat dish.

Serves 4

Variations in cooking method: Instead of frying, the *shooftas* may be broiled on metal skewers over a charcoal fire, or they may be baked in an oiled baking dish in a 350°F. oven for 15 minutes, or until done.

Variations in the meat: The *shooftas* may be made of ground beef or lamb with the same, or slightly intensified, flavorings. These variations are all traditional.

Boona Kalegi
Chicken Liver Fry

1 pound chicken livers, divided into lobes
1/2 teaspoon crushed fresh gingerroot
1/2 teaspoon crushed garlic
1/2 teaspoon salt, or to taste
1/4 teaspoon freshly ground black pepper
3 tablespoons corn or peanut oil

1. Mix everything together except the oil and let stand for 15 minutes.

2. Heat the oil in a skillet or wok and over moderate heat add the mixture. Stir-fry for 3 to 4 minutes, until the liver is just cooked through.

Serve warm.

Serves 4

Variation: Mix all the ingredients together including the oil and let stand for 15 minutes. Then thread several lobes on a metal skewer and broil over charcoal until brown and sizzling, about 5 minutes.

Gadjar Murghi Meetha
Stewed Chicken and Carrots

Meetha indicates a dish lightly seasoned with lemon and a bit of sugar for contrast—sweet-and-sour. This basic recipe is the most popular *meetha* preparation—chicken and carrots. The variations following are other compatible combinations flavored according to the basic ingredients. All make interesting additions to American menus.

2 cups shredded carrots
2 tablespoons plus 2 teaspoons corn or peanut oil
1 teaspoon crushed garlic
1 teaspoon crushed fresh gingerroot
1/4 cup sliced onion
1 teaspoon ground turmeric
1 teaspoon salt, or to taste
1/8 teaspoon freshly ground black pepper

1 chicken, 3 pounds, cut into serving pieces, including the giblets
1 cup water
2 bay leaves
4 cardamom pods
2 to 3 tablespoons lemon juice
2 teaspoons brown sugar

1. Stir-fry the carrots in the 2 teaspoons oil in a skillet over moderate heat for 3 minutes. Remove skillet from the heat and set aside.

2. Heat 2 tablespoons of oil in a large pan over moderate heat. Add the garlic, gingerroot, onion, turmeric, salt and black pepper. Stir-fry for 2 minutes. Add the chicken and brown the pieces for 3 minutes.

3. Add the water, bay leaves, and cardamom, bring to a boil, and cover the pan. Cook the chicken until nearly done, about 20 minutes.

4. Add the carrots, lemon juice and brown sugar. Stir the mixture and continue to cook over moderate to low heat for 15 minutes more to combine the flavorings and almost completely evaporate the liquid. At this stage adjust the lemon, sugar and salt if you wish a more intense flavor.

Serve warm.

Serves 6

Variations:

CHICK-PEA AND CHICKEN MEETHA

uses the same recipe, ingredients and cooking style as the basic recipe. Simply substitute a 1-pound can of cooked chick-peas, drained, for the carrots.

PUMPKIN AND LAMB MEETHA

is made with 1 pound boneless lamb, cut into 1-inch cubes, and 2 cups cubed winter squash or pumpkin. The lamb is cooked with the flavorings and 1 cup water for 1 hour before adding squash or pumpkin, lemon juice and sugar. Cook covered for another 15 minutes. Otherwise the directions are the same as for the basic recipe.

VEGETABLE MEETHA

is prepared by omitting the meat and substituting 4 cups of vegetables with the same flavorings. I would suggest a combination of carrots, *loobia* or green beans, pumpkin and okra.

Bhuna Haas, Aloo-m-Kalla

Duck Roast with Potatoes

1 duck, 4 to 4¹/₂ pounds, cut into serving pieces, loose skin and fat discarded
1 tablespoon corn or peanut oil
1 teaspoon crushed garlic
1 teaspoon crushed fresh gingerroot

¹/₂ teaspoon crushed fresh hot chili
1 teaspoon salt, or to taste
¹/₂ teaspoon ground turmeric
1 teaspoon garam masala
1¹/₂ cups water

1. Brown the duck in the oil in a large skillet over moderate heat for 5 minutes. Add the garlic, gingerroot, chili, salt, turmeric and *garam masala*. Stir well and fry for another 5 minutes.

2. Add the water, cover the skillet, and continue to cook for 1¹/₂ hours, or until the duck is tender. Turn the pieces once during this process. Should the liquid evaporate too quickly, add an extra ¹/₂ cup water.

Serve warm with the Aloo-m-Kalla (see Index). This roast does not have a sauce but the pieces will be moist and tender.

Serves 6

Hanse Mukmura
Duck with Almond, Raisin and Spice Sauce

This richly assembled *mukmura* is eaten on festival days such as Simchat Torah and the New Year. Butternut squash, pumpkin or West Indian calabasa are all firm squashes or pumpkins that can be used in this festive preparation. American ducks have a lot of fat and so it is best to prepare the *mukmura* the previous day, refrigerate overnight, and then remove and discard the congealed fat.

1 duck, 4 to 4½ pounds, cut into 8 serving pieces, loose skin and fat discarded
4 cups plus 1 tablespoon water
1 teaspoon salt
2 large onions, sliced thin (¾ cup)
2 tablespoons corn or peanut oil
½ teaspoon crushed fresh gingerroot
½ teaspoon crushed garlic
½ teaspoon crushed fresh hot green chili
½ teaspoon ground turmeric
1 cup chopped ripe tomatoes
2 cups yellow pumpkin cubes
2 tablespoons raisins
2 tablespoons blanched almonds, halved lengthwise
1 bay leaf
1 tablespoon garlic, sliced thin lengthwise
¼ cup tamarind paste, dissolved in ½ cup water and strained
2 teaspoons sugar
¼ cup fresh mint leaves

1. Cook the duck in 4 cups water with the salt over moderate heat for 45 minutes. Reserve 2 cups of the liquid.

2. Meanwhile, in another large pan, brown the onions in the oil for 2 minutes. Add the gingerroot, garlic, chili and turmeric, and fry for another 2 minutes.

3. Add 1 tablespoon water and then the tomatoes and cook for 5 minutes to combine the flavors and reduce the mixture to a purée (*hamiss*).

4. Add the pumpkin cubes and mix well. Add the cooked duck, the raisins, almonds, bay leaf, garlic slices, tamarind liquid and sugar. Stir a few times, add the reserved duck liquid, and bring everything to a boil.

5. Cook over moderate to low heat for 30 minutes, until the duck is tender and the flavorings combined. At this time adjust the salt and

sugar, if you wish, for a more intense flavor. Sprinkle in the mint leaves and stir a moment. Should the sauce reduce too much, add 1/2 cup water since the *mukmura* should have ample sauce.

Serve warm.

Serves 6 to 8

Bhuna Haas
Baked Stuffed Duck

1/2 cup diced potato
1/2 cup diced carrot
1/2 cup sliced green beans
1/2 cup green peas, fresh or frozen
1 duck gizzard, heart and liver, chopped fine
1/2 teaspoon garam masala

1/2 teaspoon minced fresh gingerroot
1/2 teaspoon minced garlic
1/2 teaspoon ground turmeric
1 teaspoon salt
1 duck, 4 1/2 pounds

1. Blanch the potato, carrot and green beans in boiling water for 2 minutes. Drain well.

2. Mix the cooked vegetables and the peas with the giblets, *garam masala*, gingerroot, garlic, turmeric and salt. Stuff the duck and sew up the opening. Prick the duck all over with a fork.

3. Put the duck in a roasting pan with no exterior seasoning, uncovered, and roast it in a 350°F. oven for about 2 hours. Pour off the accumulated fat two or three times after basting. When the duck has become tender, increase oven heat to 400°F. for 15 minutes to complete the roasting so that the skin is brown and crispy.

Serve warm, carved into slices or disjointed.

Serves 6

Variation: Pigeon is also prepared by this method. In the American kitchen, Cornish hens make an admirable substitute but should be roasted for only 1 hour.

Pacha
Stuffed Lamb Stomach

Pacha is an extremely rare preparation since no one wants to be bothered to search for the ingredients and prepare such a time-consuming dish. In Calcutta, the stomachs are purchased fresh and are meticulously cleaned and scraped in the household. The lamb (read mutton) shanks are purchased whole, with hoof and skin, and are laboriously singed, cleaned, and cut up to prepare the broth. It requires several hours of work but ultimately provides a delicious rarity.

STUFFING

2 cleaned lamb stomachs
2 cups raw rice, well rinsed
1/2 cup chopped tomato
1 tablespoon chopped coriander
1 teaspoon ground fresh gingerroot
1 teaspoon ground garlic
1/2 teaspoon black pepper
1/2 teaspoon ground fresh hot red chili
1 teaspoon ground turmeric
1/2 pound ground lamb or beef
2 teaspoons salt
3 teaspoons garam masala
3 tablespoons corn or peanut oil

BROTH

2 lamb shanks, cut into 4 pieces each
1/2 teaspoon crushed fresh gingerroot
1/2 teaspoon crushed garlic
1/4 cup sliced tomato
1 teaspoon salt
6 cups water

1. Cut the lamb stomachs into halves to make 4 pockets. (If they are large make them into 6 pockets.) Sew up each pocket on three sides, leaving one end open for the stuffing. Mix all the stuffing ingredients together.

2. Half-fill the pockets with the stuffing and sew up the fourth side, using a No. 5 or similar thickness of white thread. Set aside.

3. Prepare the soup by cooking the stuffed pockets, shanks, gingerroot, garlic, tomato and salt in 6 cups water over moderate heat for about 2 hours. Add 1 or 2 more cups water if the broth evaporates too quickly. A pressure cooker is ideal and will reduce the cooking time by half.

Serve warm. Serve the pockets, shanks and a generous amount of broth in a soup plate together.

Serves 8

Variation: Some prefer the *pacha* to be roasted dry and served without broth. Simply continue cooking the pockets and shanks until liquid has completely evaporated, about 15 minutes longer. Then brown everything in the oil that has accumulated.

Mugaz
Brain Curry

Wherever I happen to travel I always search out new recipes for brains. This recipe is particularly tasty—spicy and with a smooth texture.

1 *beef brain, 2 calf's brains or 4 lamb brains, about 1 pound*
2 *tablespoons corn or peanut oil*
1 *small onion, ground to a paste (¹/₄ cup)*
¹/₂ *teaspoon ground fresh gingerroot*
1 *small garlic clove, ground to a paste*

1 *teaspoon ground coriander*
¹/₂ *teaspoon ground cuminseed*
1 *teaspoon ground fresh hot red chili*
¹/₂ *teaspoon ground turmeric*
¹/₂ *teaspoon salt*
¹/₄ *cup chopped ripe tomato*

1. Soak the brains in cold water to cover for 30 minutes. Remove the loose membranes and drain.

2. Heat the oil in a skillet or saucepan and stir-fry the onion for 2 minutes. Add the gingerroot, garlic, coriander, cuminseed, chili, turmeric and salt. Continue to stir-fry until the mixture becomes red/brown, about 5 minutes. Add the tomato and continue to cook.

3. Add the whole brains and cook, covered, for 10 minutes. Turn the brains over and cook until the curry is dry, about 5 minutes more. Remove the pan from the heat. Cut the brains into generous-size cubes while still in the pan.

Serve warm with rice.

Serves 4 to 6

Beet Root Khuta
Sweet-and-Sour Beef and Beets

This is one Calcutta recipe that does not include their most popular spice—turmeric. Although used in most of their dishes, it is omitted here because it would discolor the rich, red sauce made by the beets.

2 tablespoons corn or peanut oil
1/4 cup chopped onion
1/4 teaspoon crushed fresh
  gingerroot
1/4 teaspoon crushed garlic
1/2 teaspoon thin-sliced fresh hot
  green or red chili
1 pound boneless beef chuck, cut
  into 1-inch cubes
1 cup water

1/2 cup chopped ripe tomato, fresh
  or canned
1 cup sliced cooked beets, with 3/4
  cup reserved liquid
1 tablespoon tamarind paste,
  dissolved in 1/4 cup water
2 teaspoons brown sugar
1/4 cup chopped fresh mint
salt (optional)

1. Heat the oil in a pan and over moderate heat brown the onion for 2 minutes. Add the gingerroot, garlic and chili, and fry for 2 minutes more.

2. Add the beef and water, bring to a boil, and cook for 1 hour.

3. Add the tomato, beets and beet liquid. Add the tamarind liquid strained through a metal sieve and the brown sugar. Continue to cook the mixture, uncovered, over low heat for 20 minutes, until the beef cubes are tender and the liquid has thickened.

4. Finally, add the mint, stir well, and cook for 5 minutes more. Add salt to taste if necessary.

Serve warm.

Serves 6

Variations: One pound lamb cubes or one 3 1/2-pound chicken cut into serving pieces, or a duck and its giblets cut into about 8 serving pieces, may be used instead of the beef.

Spiced meatballs may also be used. The meatballs (*kofta*) are flavored the same way as the Kofta Kari (see Index) and added uncooked to the curry at the same time the beets are added. The cooking time in step 1 should be reduced to 4 minutes.

Each meat requires a different length of time to cook so the *khuta* must be timed by the type of meat used. Each meat has its own intrinsic flavor, but the sweet-and-sour flavor is paramount to the dish.

Note: Lemon juice may be substituted for the tamarind should it not be easily available. Use 3 tablespoons fresh lemon juice and 1 teaspoon sugar.

Fresh beets should be cooked in their skins with sufficient water to reserve ³/₄ cup. Canned beets are eminently satisfactory.

Beef and Okra Meetha

¹/₂ pound young okra
3 tablespoons corn or peanut oil
1 teaspoon crushed fresh
  gingerroot
1 teaspoon crushed garlic
¹/₄ cup onion slices
1 teaspoon ground turmeric
2 cardamom pods
2 bay leaves

¹/₂ teaspoon salt, or to taste
¹/₈ teaspoon freshly ground black
  pepper
1 pound boneless beef chuck, cut
  into 1-inch cubes
1¹/₂ cups water
3 tablespoons lemon juice
2 teaspoons brown sugar

1. Cut a 1-inch slit into the side of each okra. Brown them lightly in the oil over moderate heat for 3 minutes. Remove and set aside.

2. In the same oil in a saucepan, lightly fry the gingerroot, garlic and onion slices over moderate heat for 2 minutes. Add the turmeric, cardamom, bay leaves, salt, black pepper and beef. Stir-fry for 3 minutes.

3. Add the water and bring to a boil. Cook the mixture, covered, until it is tender, about 1 hour.

4. Add the okra, lemon juice and brown sugar. Mix well and simmer over low heat until almost all the liquid has evaporated. Adjust the lemon, sugar and salt to taste at this time.

Serve warm.

Serves 6

Kofta Kari
Meatball Curry

MEATBALLS

1 cup grated onion, squeezed dry in a towel

1 pound ground beef

2 tablespoons fine-chopped fresh coriander

2 tablespoons fine-chopped fresh mint

1 tablespoon fine-chopped fresh hot green chili

1/2 teaspoon ground turmeric

1/2 teaspoon salt

1/2 teaspoon crushed fresh gingerroot

1/2 teaspoon crushed garlic

1 teaspoon cornstarch

1/4 cup plus 2 teaspoons corn or peanut oil

SAUCE

1/2 cup grated onion, squeezed dry in a towel

1/4 cup oil reserved from meatballs

1 teaspoon crushed garlic

1 teaspoon crushed fresh gingerroot

1 teaspoon crushed fresh hot green chili, or to taste

1 teaspoon ground turmeric

1/2 teaspoon salt

1 cup chopped ripe tomatoes, fresh or canned

1 1/2 cups water

1/2 teaspoon garam masala

1 tablespoon chopped fresh coriander

1. Mix all the meatball ingredients together, using the 2 teaspoons oil; the 1/4 cup oil is for frying. Roll into round firm balls, using 1 teaspoon of the mixture for each one. Makes 28 balls.

2. Heat the 1/4 cup oil in a skillet and over moderate heat brown the *koftas* for 2 minutes. Remove them from the oil and set aside. Reserve the oil for the sauce.

3. Make the sauce: Fry the onion in the oil in a large skillet or saucepan over moderate heat for 2 minutes. Add the garlic, gingerroot, chili, turmeric and salt, and stir-fry for 3 minutes. Add the tomatoes and stir-fry rapidly (*hamiss*) to purée the sauce. Add the water and simmer over low heat for 5 minutes.

4. Add the fried meatballs and simmer, uncovered, over low heat for 15 minutes to reduce the sauce somewhat and combine the flavorings.

5. Just before serving, sprinkle the curry with *garam masala* and the coriander.

Serve warm with other dishes such as pilau, vegetable curry, chutneys.

Serves 6

Variations: Ground lamb or ground boneless chicken, or a mixture of half lamb and half chicken, may be used in place of the beef. Prepare them in the same way or add them raw to the curry sauce and let them cook for 10 minutes before stirring so that they will not get broken up. This method uses less oil and therefore may be preferable for those on low-fat diets.

Fish and Loobia Meetha

1 pound fillets of sole, flounder or
   haddock
1/2 teaspoon ground turmeric
1 teaspoon salt
3 tablespoons corn or peanut oil
1/2 pound Chinese long beans
   (loobia)
1/4 cup sliced onion

1 teaspoon crushed gingerroot
1 teaspoon crushed garlic
1/4 cup chopped ripe tomato
2 bay leaves
2 cardamom pods
1/2 cup water
2 tablespoons lemon juice
2 teaspoons brown sugar

1. Cut the fillets into 2- to 3-inch rectangles. Rub the pieces with the turmeric and salt. Fry the pieces for 2 minutes in oil in a pan over moderate heat. Remove and set aside.

2. Cut the *loobia* into 1/4-inch diagonal slices. Lightly brown the onion, gingerroot and garlic in the same oil. Add the *loobia* and stir-fry for 3 minutes. Add the tomato, bay leaves, cardamom and water, cover the pan, and cook over moderate heat for 5 minutes.

3. Add the pieces of fish, the lemon juice and brown sugar. Do not stir since it will break up the fish, but shake the pan several times. Cover and simmer over low heat for 5 to 10 minutes, until the fish and *loobia* are cooked and the liquid has evaporated.

Serve warm.

Serves 6

Anjuli
Fish in Coconut Milk

3 tablespoons corn or peanut oil
1 pound fillets of flounder, sole or
 haddock, cut into 2-inch cubes
1 pound small eggplant, cut into
 1/4-inch-thick slices
2 cups Rich Coconut Milk (see
 Index)
1/4 cup lemon juice, or to taste
1 teaspoon salt, or to taste

1 teaspoon thin-sliced fresh hot
 green chili
1 cup cooked 1/2-inch potato
 cubes
1/2 cup onion rings, sliced thin
 from small onions
8 scallions, cut into 1/4-inch-thick
 slices

1. Heat the oil in a skillet and over moderate heat brown the fish cubes for 5 minutes. Remove with a slotted spoon and set aside.

2. Fry the eggplant slices in the same oil until soft, about 3 minutes. Drain on paper towels.

3. Pour the coconut milk into a large bowl with the lemon juice, salt and chili. Mix well. Add the other ingredients by layers starting first with the potato cubes, then the onion rings, scallions, fish cubes and the eggplant on top.

Chill briefly in the refrigerator or serve at room temperature.

Serves 4

Variation: Another method of serving is to mix all the ingredients together with the coconut milk and lemon juice. The *anjuli* served this way is spooned over hot rice.

Muchli ka Kari

Fish Curry

5 medium-size onions, chopped
  fine (2 cups)
1/4 cup corn or peanut oil
1 tablespoon crushed fresh
  gingerroot
1 tablespoon crushed garlic
2 teaspoons crushed fresh hot red
  chili
1 teaspoon salt, or to taste

1 teaspoon ground turmeric
1 cup chopped ripe tomatoes,
  fresh or canned
1/2 cup water
1 1/4 to 1 1/2 pounds whole fish
  (betki, sea bass, red snapper,
  flounder)
2 bay leaves (optional)

1. Fry the onions in the oil in a pan over moderate heat for 2 minutes. Add the gingerroot, garlic, chili, salt and turmeric. Stir-fry the mixture for 5 minutes to develop a thick paste.

2. Add the tomatoes and water and continue to stir and chop at the ingredients for 10 minutes.

3. Cut the fish into 1-inch-wide slices, including the head. Add this to the curry and simmer over low heat for 15 minutes. Baste now and then. Finally, add the bay leaves, if used, and cook for 5 minutes.

Serve warm.

Serves 4 to 6

Note: Although shrimps or prawns are not considered kosher by the traditional Calcutta Jews, the preparation would be the same for a shrimp curry. Substitute 1 pound medium shrimps, peeled, for the fish.

Muchli Kofta Kari
Fish Ball Curry

FISH BALL

2 pounds flounder, sole or haddock, chopped fine

1½ cups grated onion, squeezed dry in a towel

1 teaspoon cornstarch

½ teaspoon crushed fresh gingerroot

½ teaspoon crushed garlic

¼ teaspoon crushed fresh hot chili

½ teaspoon salt

¼ teaspoon garam masala

¼ teaspoon ground turmeric

2 tablespoons chopped fresh coriander leaves

SAUCE

3 tablespoons corn or peanut oil

½ cup grated onion, squeezed dry in a towel

1 teaspoon crushed fresh gingerroot

1 teaspoon crushed garlic

¼ teaspoon crushed fresh hot chili

¼ teaspoon ground turmeric

½ teaspoon garam masala

½ teaspoon salt

1½ cups water

¾ cup chopped ripe tomatoes, fresh or canned

2 bay leaves

1 cup green peas, fresh or frozen

1 tablespoon chopped fresh coriander

1. Mix the fish ball ingredients together. With wet hands, roll into 1½-inch balls. There should be about 25 fish balls. Set aside.

2. Heat the oil for the sauce in a pan and lightly brown the onion over moderate heat for 2 minutes. Add the gingerroot, garlic, chili, turmeric, *garam masala* and salt. Stir-fry for 2 minutes, then add 2 tablespoons water and stir down the mixture for 2 minutes more.

3. Add the tomatoes and bay leaves and continue to stir down (*hamiss*) the mixture for another 5 minutes. Add the balance of the water and the green peas. Bring to a boil and add the fish balls carefully. Do not stir. Continue to cook, uncovered, over moderate to low heat for 15 minutes to reduce the liquid and thicken the sauce.

4. Lastly, just before serving, sprinkle the curry with the coriander and stir lightly since now the fish balls will have become cooked and firm.

Serve warm.

Serves 6 to 8

Variations:

MUCHLI SEEK KABOB (FISH ON A SKEWER)
1. Use the same fish mixture as for the basic recipe. Take 2 heaping tablespoons of the fish mixture and push it on a metal skewer with wet hands. Shape a kabob 5 inches long and about 3/8 inch thick all around.

2. Grill the kabobs over charcoal, the traditional method, or in an electric or gas broiler until brown and cooked through, about 5 minutes.

Serve warm with lemon slices.

MUCHLI PAKORA (FRIED FISH FRITTER)
1. Use the same fish mixture as for the basic recipe. Prepare the round fish balls as for the curry. Flatten each ball into a round fritter about 2 inches in diameter and 1/2 inch thick.

2. Heat oil in a skillet and over moderate heat fry the fritters on both sides for 3 to 4 minutes. Drain briefly on paper towels.

Serve warm with lemon slices.

Note: Both the kabob and the fritters may be served as an appetizer with drinks or as a main course. They make delicious sandwiches for a quick lunch.

Arook
Fish and Rice Balls

SHELL

4 cups sliced scallions
1 pound fillets of flounder, sole,
   cod or similar fish
1/4 teaspoon ground turmeric
1/2 teaspoon salt
1/2 teaspoon crushed garlic

1/2 teaspoon crushed fresh
   gingerroot
2 cups raw rice, well rinsed and
   drained
2 tablespoons arrowroot powder
   or cornstarch

STUFFING

2 tablespoons corn or peanut oil
1 cup thin-sliced onion
1/2 teaspoon crushed fresh
   gingerroot
1/2 teaspoon crushed garlic
1 teaspoon salt
1 teaspoon ground turmeric

1/4 teaspoon crushed fresh hot
   chili
1/2 pound chopped fish fillets, the
   same kind as in the shell
1 tablespoon chopped fresh
   coriander

TO COOK

10 cups water
1 teaspoon salt

1 teaspoon ground turmeric

1. Grind the scallions in a processor to a smooth paste.

2. Chop the fish fillet into fine pieces. Mix it with the scallion paste, turmeric, salt, garlic, gingerroot, rice and arrowroot powder or cornstarch. This will be the dough which is to be stuffed.

3. Make the stuffing: Heat the oil in a skillet and over moderate heat fry the onion, gingerroot, garlic, salt, turmeric and chili for 3 minutes. Add the fish and stir-fry for 3 minutes more. Sprinkle with the coriander. Cool.

4. To make the *arook*, take 1/2 cup of the rice/scallion dough with wet hands and press it into the cupped fingers of your left hand. Push down firmly and smoothly into a pocket. Put 1 tablespoon of the fish stuffing into the pocket. Fold your fingers over and press again. Shape into a round ball. Prepare all the mixtures this way.

5. Bring the 10 cups of water to a fast boil in a large pan. Add salt and turmeric. With wet hands flatten the *arook* balls into slightly flattened round parabolas, 2¹/₂ inches wide and about 1¹/₂ inches thick. They should be wet and smooth. Put them into the boiling water over moderate heat and cook, covered, for 30 minutes. Remove them with a slotted spoon and serve warm.

6. To fry: The *arook* can also be fried. After boiling, cool them for 10 minutes. Deep-fry in corn or peanut oil until brown and firm, about 3 minutes. Drain on paper towels and serve warm.

Makes 8

Arook Thaheen
Spiced Fish Pancakes

1¹/₂ cups flour
1 teaspoon salt
1 teaspoon ground turmeric
1 teaspoon crushed garlic
1 teaspoon crushed fresh
 gingerroot
¹/₂ cup chopped onion
2 tablespoons chopped fresh
 coriander

¹/₄ teaspoon dried hot red chili
 flakes or fresh hot chili
1¹/₂ cups water
¹/₂ pound fillets of flounder, sole
 or similar fish, cut into about
 ¹/₄-inch cubes
¹/₂ cup corn or peanut oil

1. Mix everything together except the oil to make a relatively thin batter.

2. Heat the oil in a skillet. Use about ¹/₄ cup of the batter for each pancake, and over moderate heat brown the pancakes on both sides for 3 to 4 minutes. Drain on paper towels. The pancake-fritter should be about 3 x 4 inches in size.

Best eaten hot and crispy as a side dish.

Makes 12 pancakes

Variation: Although the fish is most popular for this pancake, other foods may be used. Substitute 3 sliced hard-cooked eggs, 1 cup ground chicken or meat, or 1 cup blanched chopped vegetables such as carrots, green beans, cauliflower and *loobia*, in any combination

Phulgobi Meetha
Dry Cauliflower Roast

3 tablespoons corn or peanut oil
1/4 cup sliced onion
1/2 teaspoon crushed garlic
1/2 teaspoon crushed fresh
  gingerroot
1 teaspoon chopped fresh hot chili
1/4 teaspoon ground turmeric
1 teaspoon salt, or to taste

1 large cauliflower, about 2
  pounds, cut into 1-inch pieces
1/2 cup water
1/2 cup chopped ripe tomato, fresh
  or canned
12 fried Kooba, see Index
  (optional)

1. Heat the oil in a saucepan or large skillet and over moderate heat fry the onion, garlic, gingerroot, chili, turmeric and salt until light brown, about 3 minutes.

2. Add the cauliflower pieces and stir-fry for 2 minutes. Add the water and tomato. Cook the mixture, covered, for 10 minutes, or until the liquid has almost evaporated and the cauliflower is softened.

3. Add the *koobas* if you are using them. Stir them into the mixture and continue to cook for 10 minutes more, or until the curry (roast) is dry.

Serve warm.

Serves 6

Mofurka
Green Leaf Fry

1 pound spinach or Swiss chard
1/2 cup water
1 tablespoon plus 2 teaspoons
  corn or peanut oil
1/2 cup chopped onion
1/2 teaspoon ground turmeric
1/2 teaspoon crushed fresh
  gingerroot

1/2 teaspoon crushed garlic
1/2 teaspoon chopped hot chili,
  fresh or dry
1/2 teaspoon salt, or to taste
2 eggs, beaten

1. Cut the spinach into coarse pieces. Bring the water to a boil in a saucepan and put in the greens. Cover the pan and cook over moderate heat for 3 minutes. Remove from the heat and keep the pan covered for about 2 minutes to ensure that the spinach has wilted. Drain and cool the spinach. Squeeze dry.

2. Heat 1 tablespoon oil in a skillet and brown the onion over moderate heat for 2 minutes. Add the turmeric, gingerroot, garlic, chili and salt. Stir well and add the greens. Stir and fry for 3 minutes to incorporate all the flavorings.

3. In another skillet, heat 2 teaspoons oil and soft-scramble the eggs. Fold them into the greens and stir-fry the mixture for 2 minutes more.

Serve hot or at room temperature for a light meal.

Serves 4

Variation: One half cup ground fish, chicken or beef can be included in the *mofurka*. Add the fish or meat when the onion is browning and continue the preparations as in the basic recipe.

Bhuna Brinjal
Fried Eggplant

1 pound eggplants, 2 or 3 small	*1 teaspoon salt*
1/4 teaspoon ground turmeric	*corn or peanut oil for frying*

1. Cut the eggplants into round 1/2-inch-thick slices. Mix with the turmeric and salt and let stand for 30 minutes. Drain off the liquid that accumulates and dry the slices on paper towels.

2. Brown the slices in oil in a skillet over moderate heat for 2 or 3 minutes. Drain briefly on paper towels.

Serve warm with any meat or vegetable dishes.

Serves 4

Brinjal Pakora
Eggplant Fritters

Pakoras are Jewish by adoption but are prepared in many Indian communities with different flavorings. Many kinds of vegetables may be used depending upon personal preference. Green beans blanched in boiling water, spinach or Swiss chard leaves, very thin slices of potato are all good choices.

EGGPLANT

1 pound eggplants, 3 or 4 small ^{1}/$_2$ teaspoon ground turmeric
1 teaspoon salt

BATTER

1 cup besan (gram or chick-pea ^{1}/$_2$ teaspoon salt
  flour) ^{1}/$_4$ teaspooon chopped fresh hot
1 cup water   chili
^{1}/$_4$ teaspoon ground turmeric   1 cup corn or peanut oil

1. Cut the eggplants into slices 4 inches long, 1^1/$_2$ inches wide and ^{1}/$_4$inch thick (estimated size). Mix the slices with the salt and turmeric and let stand for 30 minutes. Drain off the liquid that accumulates and dry the slices on paper towels.

2. Prepare a batter by mixing together the *besan*, water, turmeric, salt and chili.

3. Heat the oil in a wok or skillet. Dip the eggplant slices, one at a time, into the batter and brown them in the oil on both sides for about 3 minutes, until crisp. Drain on paper towels.

Serve warm as an appetizer with drinks or tea or at coffee hour.

Makes about 20 fritters

Variations:

ALOO PAKORA (MASHED POTATO FRITTER)

2 cups cold mashed potatoes   2 tablespoons chopped fresh
^{1}/$_4$ teaspoon ground turmeric   coriander
^{1}/$_2$ teaspooon salt ^{1}/$_2$ cup corn or peanut oil
^{1}/$_2$ teaspoon dried hot red chili   Besan Batter (see basic recipe)
  flakes, or ^{1}/$_2$ teaspoon pepper

1. Mix the potatoes, turmeric, salt, chili and coriander together into a smooth purée. Prepare a fritter by taking 1 tablespoon of the mixture and shaping a round disc 2 inches in diameter and $1/2$ inch thick. Continue with the rest of the mixture.

2. Heat the oil in a wok or skillet. Dip each fritter into the *besan* batter. Over moderate heat brown the fritter on all sides for about 3 minutes. Drain briefly on paper towels.

Serve warm.

KELA PAKORA (BANANA FRITTER)

4 firm but ripe standard-size   *$1/2$ cup corn or peanut oil*
  bananas   *Besan Batter (see basic recipe)*

1. Peel the bananas and cut them across into 4 pieces. Then slice each piece lengthwise into halves.

2. Heat the oil in a wok or skillet over moderate heat. Dip each banana slice into the *besan* batter and brown the slices in the oil on all sides for 2 to 3 minutes. Drain on paper towels.

Serve warm.

Note: In Calcutta, small bananas like those found here in Central American stores are used. The entire peeled banana may be dipped into the batter and fried, or they may be halved lengthwise.

PHULGOBI PAKORA (CAULIFLOWER FRITTER)

2 cups 2-inch cauliflowerets   *Besan Batter (see basic recipe)*
 $1/2$ cup corn or peanut oil

1. Cook the cauliflowerets in boiling water for 2 minutes. Drain and cool. Pat the cauliflower gently with a cloth towel to dry.

2. Heat the oil in a skillet or wok over moderate heat. Dip each floweret into the batter and brown in the oil for 2 to 3 minutes. Drain on paper towels.

Serve warm.

Brinjal Mahasha
Stuffed Eggplant

Here is another popular recipe with many variations. Any vegetable that can be stuffed can be used, and meat, rice and vegetables, alone or in combination, can be used for a filling. Only your imagination limits the number of mixtures to try. The tamarind liquid is sometimes replaced by lemon juice for another subtle modification. Some of the old cooks even stitch the top of the vegetable back in its original position, but that seems a bit unnecessarily complicated to me. It can be placed in position or left off entirely, according to one's taste. Try a combination of two or three different vegetables and stuffings for an attractive and pleasing menu.

1/2 pound ground beef
1 cup raw rice, well rinsed in cold water
1/2 teaspoon ground turmeric
1/4 cup chopped mint leaves
1 teaspoon crushed fresh gingerroot
1 teaspoon crushed garlic
1/2 teaspoon minced fresh hot red chili

1 teaspoon salt, or to taste
3 tablespoons oil
2 tablespoons tamarind paste
3/4 cup water
2 teaspoons sugar
6 small eggplants, 3 to 4 inches long

1. Mix the beef, rice, turmeric, mint, gingerroot, garlic, chili, salt and oil together. Set aside.

2. Soak the tamarind in the water for 20 minutes, stirring it with your fingers until it dissolves. Strain the liquid through a metal strainer and mix it with the sugar. Set aside.

3. Roll the eggplants back and forth on a firm surface several times to soften the inside pulp. Cut off the top of each one 1/2 inch below the stem and save it. Scoop out and discard the interior pulp, leaving a firm shell about 1/4 inch thick.

4. Fill the eggplants about three quarters full and press the stuffing firmly into the shells. Push the stem ends, stem first, into the stuffing to make plugs. Fit the eggplants into a saucepan or skillet just large enough to hold all of them. Cover the pan and fry over moderate to low heat for 5 minutes, or until some oil and liquid seeps out of the stuffing.

5. Pour the tamarind and sugar mixture over the eggplants. Cover the pan and cook without turning the eggplants over for about 30 minutes, or until all the liquid has evaporated. The rice will swell and fill the eggplant cavity. The stuffed vegetables can be held in a 300°F. oven for an extra 30 minutes if necessary.

Serve warm as a vegetable.

Serves 6

Variations in the Vegetables:

RED AND/OR GREEN SWEET PEPPERS
Cut the stem out in a circle of about 1½ inches. Scoop out the seeds and ribs. Fill the peppers firmly about three quarters full. Push the stem top back in and continue to cook as for the eggplants.

CABBAGE
1. Peel off about 12 large leaves and cut out 3 inches of the hard center vein of the leaf. Bring a pot of water to a boil and drop in 2 leaves at a time. Cover the pot for 1 minute, then remove the blanched softened leaves and drain them. Do this for all of the leaves.

2. Place 2 heaping tablespoons of the stuffing on each leaf and shape it into a roll 3 to 4 inches long and 1½ inches in diameter. Cook the cabbage rolls in the same manner as the other vegetables.

ONION
The onions in Calcutta are small by our standards, yet the cooks managed to peel off one layer after another until the center core was reached. I prefer to use the large Spanish onions.

1. Peel the onion and cut a 1-inch-deep incision from the stem end to the bottom. Drop the entire onion into boiling water for a minute. Remove it and carefully peel off as many layers as you can until you reach the center core.

2. Take one layer, add 1 tablespoon of stuffing, and push the 2 ends together to make an egg-shaped *mahasha*. Continue to cook these as for the other vegetables.

(recipe continues)

CUCUMBER

1. Use the large supermarket cucumbers. Peel them and cut ½ inch off each end. Cut the cucumbers lengthwise into halves and scoop out the seeds. Be certain to leave at least a ¼-inch-thick wall.

2. Fill the 2 halves of the cucumber firmly three quarters full and continue to cook as for other vegetables. The cucumbers will not have tops.

ZUCCHINI

This is not a Calcutta vegetable but it lends itself admirably to stuffing. Cut the zucchini lengthwise into halves, scoop out a center core, and stuff and cook as for the cucumber. Do not peel zucchini.

TOMATOES

Use firm, ripe tomatoes that count about 4 to the pound. Cut out the stem end, 1 inch in diameter, and scoop out seeds and pulp, leaving a firm wall. Stuff as for the sweet peppers and cook them in the same manner.

Variations in the Stuffing: Beef with rice is probably the most popular stuffing. Next would be ground chicken and rice, which is preferred by many of the Calcutta Jews.

Vegetable stuffing is also an admirable choice for vegetarians or anyone else. Green beans, carrots, green peas and raw rice are mixed with gingerroot, garlic, chili, salt, oil and turmeric as in any meat stuffing, and the mixture is used to fill the vegetable shells. Vegetables in the stuffing are chopped fine and a ratio of one quarter rice to three quarters vegetables is usual. Vegetable *mahashas* are prepared in the same manner as those using meat.

Bamia Khuta
Okra Stew with Kooba

OKRA
1/2 pound fresh okra	*2 tablespoons corn or peanut oil*

SAUCE
1/2 cup thin-sliced onion	*1 teaspoon salt, or to taste*
2 tablespoons corn or peanut oil	*11/2 cups water or chicken broth*
1 teaspoon crushed fresh gingerroot	*2 tablespoons tamarind paste, dissolved in 1/2 cup water*
1 teaspoon crushed garlic	*1 cup chopped ripe tomatoes, fresh or canned*
1/4 teaspoon ground turmeric	*1 teaspoon sugar*
1/2 teaspoon dried hot red chili flakes	*12 Koobas (see Index)*

1. Cut a 1-inch-long incision in the side of each okra. Heat the 2 tablespoons oil in a wok or skillet and over moderate heat stir-fry the okra for 3 minutes. Remove from the oil and set aside.

2. Make the sauce: Fry the onion in the oil in a pan over moderate heat for 2 minutes. Add the gingerroot, garlic, turmeric, chili and salt, and stir-fry for 2 minutes.

3. Add the water or broth and the tamarind liquid strained through a metal sieve. Simmer for 5 minutes. Add the tomatoes and sugar and continue to cook over moderate heat for 10 minutes.

4. Add the okra and put the *koobas* on top of them. Cook the stew, covered, without stirring, over low heat for 30 minutes.

Serve warm with plain rice.

Serves 6

Note: *Koobas* are delicate and should be treated carefully. The trick is to moisten the palm with cold water and roll the *kooba* with a circular motion counterclockwise which will round out the shape. Then place it on the okra. Only later, just prior to dining, when the *kooba* is firm and cooked through, can one stir the pot.

Subji Dal
Lentil and Mixed Vegetable Curry

This vegetable curry will have ample liquid although it may be quite thick. It may be served as a fine vegetable curry with rice and chutney or as an extra dish at a regular lunch or dinner.

Butternut squash, the West Indian calabasa, red or yellow pumpkins may all be used for this curry. You might also want to consider green beans, *loobia* (the Chinese long bean) or even okra, all suitably sliced. Select at least two or three of the vegetables to provide a colorful mixture.

1 cup split yellow lentils (chana ka dal)
2¹/₂ cups water
3 tablespoons corn or peanut oil
¹/₄ cup chopped onion
¹/₄ teaspoon crushed fresh gingerroot
¹/₄ teaspoon crushed garlic
¹/₄ teaspoon crushed fresh hot chili
¹/₂ teaspoon ground turmeric

¹/₂ teaspoon salt, or to taste
¹/₂ teaspoon garam masala
¹/₂ cup ¹/₂-inch cubes of yellow pumpkin or firm squash
¹/₂ cup green peas, fresh or frozen
¹/₂ cup cauliflowerets
¹/₂ cup chopped tomato, fresh or canned
1 tablespoon chopped fresh coriander

1. Rinse the lentils in cold water, then soak them in 2 cups of the water for 1 hour. Cook the lentils in the same water until they are soft but still retain a shape, about 20 minutes. Set aside.

2. Heat the oil in a large skillet or saucepan and over moderate heat fry the onion, gingerroot, garlic and chili for 2 minutes. Add the turmeric, salt and *garam masala*, and stir-fry for 2 minutes. Add the pumpkin, peas and cauliflowerets. Stir-fry them for 2 minutes.

3. Add the lentils in their liquid. Simmer the mixture over moderate to low heat for 1 minute. Add the tomato and remaining ¹/₂ cup water. Simmer for 15 minutes more. Sprinkle the coriander over all and stir.

Serve warm.

Serves 6

Bhaji
Curried Vegetables

A *bhaji* may be prepared with any number of vegetables depending upon availability in the bazaar (or supermarket) and personal tastes. Most if not all *bhajis* start with potatoes and then other vegetables are added. Cauliflower, green beans (which are called French beans in Calcutta), *loobia* (Chinese long beans), eggplant, squash or pumpkin all have their partisans. The vegetables are cut into pieces or cubes and fried with the standard flavorings.

Flavorings such as onion, gingerroot and garlic are intensified by adding fresh or dried hot chili, *garam masala* or sometimes cardamom pods with their own medicinal aroma and magic.

Bhajis appear on the table as a supplement to meat, fish and rice dishes but can stand alone for the vegetarian purist.

¹/₂ cup thin-sliced onion	*2 cardamom pods (optional)*
2 tablespoons corn or peanut oil	*1 pound small potatoes, peeled,*
1 teaspoon ground gingerroot	*cut into ¹/₂-inch cubes*
1 teaspoon ground garlic	*1 cup water*
¹/₂ teaspoon ground fresh hot chili	*2 cups 1-inch cauliflowerets*
¹/₂ teaspoon ground turmeric	*¹/₂ cup chopped ripe tomato*
¹/₂ teaspoon salt, or to taste	

1. Fry the onion in the oil in a large pan over moderate heat for 3 minutes, until it begins to turn brown. Add the gingerroot, garlic, chili, turmeric, salt, and cardamom if used. Stir-fry the mixture for 3 minutes.

2. Add the potatoes and water and cook over moderate to low heat for 15 minutes to soften the potatoes.

3. Add the cauliflowerets and tomato. Stir a bit, and let the curry cook over moderate to low heat until all the liquid has evaporated and the vegetables are soft. This is a dry curry.

Serve warm.

Serves 6

Mamoosuck
Potato Fry with Eggs

2 tablespoons corn or peanut oil
1/4 cup thin-sliced onion
1 1/2 cups julienne pieces of
  potatoes
1/2 teaspoon ground turmeric

1/2 teaspoon salt, or to taste
4 eggs, beaten
1 tablespoon chopped fresh
  coriander
2 scallions, sliced thin

1. Heat the oil in a skillet and brown the onion over moderate heat for 2 minutes. Add the potatoes, turmeric and salt and stir well. Cover the pan and cook for 3 minutes to soften the potatoes. Uncover and fry for 5 minutes longer so as to brown them.

2. Add the eggs, coriander and scallions and stir the mixture well to distribute the eggs. Cover the pan and continue to fry for 5 to 10 minutes to ensure the potatoes are cooked. Uncover and stir-fry until the mixture is dry and soft.

   Serve warm.

Serves 2 or 3

Variations:

SPINACH
1. Steam 1/2 pound spinach in 1/2 cup water over high heat for 5 minutes to wilt and partially cook the spinach. Drain well, cool enough to handle, and squeeze the spinach dry. Chop it into coarse pieces.

2. Cut enough potatoes into 1/4-inch dice to make 1 1/2 cups. Prepare the mixture by adding the potatoes to the onion and cooking for the same length of time.

3. Add and stir-fry the spinach. Add the balance of the ingredients. To intensify the flavorings you may increase the salt, coriander and scallions by half.

CHICKEN
1. Prepare 2/3 cup minced chicken breast. Cut the potatoes into 1/4-inch dice.

2. Prepare the mixture by cooking the potatoes and onion first and stir-frying with the flavorings for 5 minutes.

3. Add the chicken and continue to stir-fry until done.

BEEF

1. Grate the potatoes and fry until crisp. Put aside. In the same oil fry 1 cup sliced onions for 3 to 4 minutes.

2. In a dry skillet stir-fry $1/4$ pound beef, the onions, salt, turmeric and $1/2$ teaspoon each of gingerroot and garlic.

3. Add the crisp potatoes, $1/4$ cup water and 1 tablespoon chopped coriander. Stir-fry for 2 or 3 minutes longer and serve warm.

Aloo Dum

Spicy Whole Potatoes

Aloo dum are popular snacks but may also be served with a main dish. I find, too, that they make fine and unusual appetizers with drinks.

1 pound small potatoes (6 to 8)	*$1/2$ teaspoon crushed garlic*
3 cups water	*1 heaping tablespoon tamarind*
2 tablespoons corn or peanut oil	*paste dissolved in $1/4$ cup water*
$1/2$ teaspoon ground turmeric	*1 teaspoon ground cuminseed*
$1/2$ teaspoon crushed fresh	*1 teaspoon ground coriander*
gingerroot	*$1/2$ teaspoon salt*

1. Cook the potatoes in their skins in the water over moderate heat until soft, about 15 minutes. Drain, cool, and peel them.

2. Heat the oil in a wok or skillet and fry the potatoes over moderate heat for 3 mintues. Add the turmeric, gingerroot, garlic, the strained tamarind liquid, cuminseed, coriander and salt. Stir-fry everything until all the liquid has evaporated and only a thick sauce remains.

Serve warm with vegetarian or meat dishes.

Serves 4

Aloo-m-Kalla
Golden Deep-Fried Potatoes

The proper preparation of these famous potatoes is the yardstick by which Caluctta cooks are judged. Although much of the time the potatoes are prepared by the household servants, who also are careful of their reputation, the menus are planned and presented by the woman of the house. She is chief of the household and as such finally responsible for the standards kept.

4 pounds firm potatoes, about 24 small
2 teaspoons salt
¹/₄ teaspoon ground turmeric
corn or peanut oil, about 4 cups

1. Peel the whole potatoes evenly. Pour enough water to cover potatoes into a large saucepan. Bring the water to a boil with the salt and turmeric. Add the potatoes. Bring the water again to a boil over high heat for 1 minute. Drain and cool the potatoes. Make certain they are dry.

2. Arrange the potatoes in a low, flat 12-inch pot or wok. Cover them completely with oil. Bring this to a boil over medium to high heat, then lower heat immediately to a low simmer. Continue to simmer/fry for 1 hour, until the potatoes have formed a golden crust. Do not stir. Shake the pan once or twice during this process.

3. At this point, turn up the heat and cook them for 5 minutes longer, until they are brown. Remove the potatoes with a slotted spoon and drain them in a metal sieve or basket.

Serve immediately. The potatoes should have a crispy, firm exterior and a soft, melting interior.

Serves 6 to 8

Brinjal Bhurta
Smoked Eggplant Salad

This can be served as a salad or it may double as an appetizer to be served on toast or crackers. It does admirably when served with pappadums.

1 pound eggplants (2)
1/4 cup chopped onion
1/2 teaspoon chopped fresh hot chili

1/2 teaspoon salt, or to taste
1 teaspoon corn or peanut oil
1 tablespoon lemon or lime juice

1. Toast the eggplants over an open flame to char (smoke) the skin for about 10 minutes. This will also partially cook them.

2. Wrap the eggplants in aluminum foil and bake them in a 375°F. oven for 20 to 25 minutes, to complete the cooking process. Remove from the oven. Peel off and discard the skin. Cool.

3. Chop the tender pulp or whip it with a fork. Mix it with all the other ingredients. Refrigerate until ready to use.

Serve cool or at room temperature.

Serves 4

Beet Root ka Salata
Beet Salad

The Calcutta lemon is the small round, greenish yellow lemon-lime. It is like the Key lime of Florida and like the common lemon of Guatemala, Mexico and other Central American countries.

3/4 cup peeled thin cucumber slices

2 tablespoons chopped fresh coriander

1 small onion, sliced thin in the round

1 cup sliced cooked beets, fresh or canned

4 to 5 small ripe tomatoes, sliced in the round

1/2 teaspoon thin-sliced fresh hot chili

1 tablespoon lemon or lime juice, or to taste

1/2 teaspoon salt

1/2 teaspoon sugar

Mix everything together. Refrigerate for 1 hour before serving.

Serve cool or at room temperature.

Serves 4

Salata
Jewish Salad

6 medium-size cucumbers, peeled

2 teaspoons salt

3/4 cup cider or malt vinegar

3 tablespoons sugar

1 inch of fresh gingerroot, chopped

3 garlic cloves, chopped

2 tablespoons chopped mint

5 scallions, sliced thin

1 teaspoon chopped fresh hot chili (optional)

1. Slice the cucumbers thin. Put them in a bowl and toss them with the salt. Let stand for 20 minutes, then put them in a cotton kitchen towel and lightly squeeze out the water.

2. Bring the vinegar and sugar to a boil. Set aside to cool.

3. Mix the cucumbers, gingerroot, garlic, mint, scallions, and chili if

used, together. Mix with the vinegar and sugar and refrigerate for 1 hour before serving.

Serve with any kind of Jewish food or Indian curries.

Serves 6

Note: If you use the large supermarket cucumbers, I suggest that you halve the cucumbers lengthwise and scoop out and discard the seeds. Cut cucumbers into half-moons.

The *salata* may be prepared one day in advance, which simply intensifies the flavor.

Shulgum
Pickled Turnips

The turnip (*Brassica rapa*) used for this pickle is the small white turnip with a purple ring around the stem end. Some people like to color it with beet liquid (liquid from canned beets may be used), but this is optional. This pickle will keep for several weeks, becoming stronger-flavored the longer it is kept.

3 teaspoons salt
1 cup water
2 tablespoons strong beet liquid
   (optional)

4 medium-size white turnips,
   about ¹/₂ pound

1. Dissolve the salt in the water, and mix in the beet liquid if used. Peel the turnips and cut them into round slices ¹/₄-inch thick.

2. Put them in a narrow-necked glass jar and pour the brine over to cover. It will probably be necessary to put a heavy object such as a small glass in the neck of the bottle to hold the turnips under the brine.

3. Set aside at room temperature for 48 hours. Refrigerate for 2 days more before using.

Serve with any kind of Indian food.

Makes 1¹/₂ cups

Bamia Pickle
Pickled Okra (Lady's-Fingers)

*¼ pound fresh young okra
(about 20 small pods)*
2 teaspoons minced garlic
*2 teaspoons minced fresh
gingerroot*

*2 teaspoons minced coriander
leaves*
¾ cup cider vinegar
1 tablespoon sugar

1. Cut a 1-inch incision into the side of each okra.

2. Mix the garlic, gingerroot and coriander together. Stuff each okra with about ¼ teaspoon or a bit more of this mixture.

3. Warm the vinegar in a small saucepan and dissolve the sugar in it. Cool.

4. Fit the stuffed okra tightly into a jar large enough to contain the total number. Pour the vinegar/sugar over so that it covers the okra. Cover the jar and keep it at room temperature for 24 hours. Refrigerate the pickle for a week before using.

Serve with any kind of Indian food.

Makes 1 cup

Jharak Lemboo
Lemon Pickle

This pickle does not have to be refrigerated. I have used some that is 6 months old and without doubt it could stand for up to 1 year without deteriorating. The color darkens to a rich brown with age.

5 or 6 small lemons   *2 to 3 tablespoons coarse salt*

1. Cut a 1-inch crisscross through the tip of the lemons. Rub the other end lightly against a grater to bruise the skin on each lemon

2. Thoroughly rub each lemon with the salt.

3. Put lemons in a glass jar large enough so that one can shake them up or turn them as they mature. Liquid will accumulate during the pickling process.

4. Place the jar in the sun (a sunny window will do) for 2 weeks. The longer one allows the lemons to pickle, the more intense the flavor. The lemons will change color and become darker as the liquid accumulates.

Serve the lemons cut into pieces with both meat and vegetable curries.

Dhania Chutney
Coriander Chutney

1 large bunch of fresh coriander, about 4 ounces	*1 tablespoon sliced fresh hot green chili*
1 garlic clove, sliced	*¹/₄ cup lemon juice, or to taste*
1 inch of fresh gingerroot, sliced and peeled	*1 teaspoon salt*

1. Wash the coriander and cut the bunch into slices.

2. Purée all ingredients together in a food processor to make a relatively smooth paste.

Chill and serve with any type of Jewish food.

Makes ¹/₂ cup

Variation: Add to the coriander mixture ¹/₄ cup peeled fresh coconut pieces or 2 peeled and sliced large Granny Smith apples. Purée and chill.

Halba (Hilbeh)
Fenugreek Chutney

Halba, a unique chutney in India, imparts an exotic addition to Calcutta food. It is known by some members of the community as Jewish paste. *Halba* can be prepared in advance of a celebration and may be refrigerated for not more than 1 week.

2 tablespoons fenugreek powder
2¼ cups or more of cold water
¼ cup chopped fresh coriander
1 teaspoon chopped fresh
  gingerroot

1 garlic clove
½ teaspoon chopped fresh hot
  green chili (optional)
3 tablespoons lemon juice
½ teaspoon salt, or to taste

1. Mix the fenugreek and 1 cup water together until it is smooth. Let the mixture stand for 10 minutes. The water will rise to the top. Carefully pour off the water without disturbing the fenugreek. Repeat this procedure with another cup of water. This will remove the slightly bitter taste of fenugreek.

2. Chop the coriander, gingerroot, garlic and chili together. Purée this to a smooth paste with the lemon juice and salt.

3. Add the purée to the fenugreek with ¼ cup water and mix well. Fenugreek swells to many times its original bulk and develops a very firm consistency. If it becomes too firm, simply add 1 or 2 teaspoons cold water and mix well.

Serve with any type of Calcutta Jewish food.

Makes ½ cup

Pudeena

Sweet-and-Sour Mint Chutney

1 tablespoon tamarind paste
1/4 cup water
1 cup loose fresh mint leaves,
   without stems
1 cup fresh coriander leaves,
   without stems

1 small onion, halved
1 teaspoon chopped gingerroot
1 teaspoon chopped garlic
1/2 teaspoon sugar
1/4 teaspoon salt
1 teaspoon sliced fresh hot chili

1. Soak the tamarind in the water for 30 minutes. Mix together with your fingers. Strain and reserve the liquid. Discard the pulp and seeds.

2. Place all the ingredients including the tamarind liquid in a processor, and process to a smooth paste. Refrigerate this smooth, green chutney.

Serve cool or at room temperature.

Makes 1 cup

Coriander and Mint Chutney

This mint chutney has almost the same ingredients as the previous recipe, but the lemon juice and smaller amounts of ginger and garlic make it milder and give it quite a different flavor.

1 cup fresh coriander leaves
1 cup fresh mint leaves
1/2 teaspoon salt
1/2 teaspoon minced fresh
   gingerroot

1/2 teaspoon minced garlic
1/2 teaspoon sliced fresh hot chili
2 tablespoons lemon or lime juice

Process everything into a smooth, green purée. Refrigerate.

Serve cool or at room temperature.

Makes 1 cup

Tomatar Chutney
Tomato Chutney

1 pound ripe tomatoes, 4 or 5
  medium-size
1 tablespoon coriander leaves,
  ground to a purée
1/4 teaspoon crushed fresh
  gingerroot

1/4 teaspoon crushed garlic
1/4 teaspoon salt
1/2 teaspoon sugar
1 tablespoon lemon or lime juice

1. Char the skin of the tomatoes over an open flame until slightly black. Peel off and discard the skin. Grind the tomatoes to a smooth purée in a processor or through a food mill.

2. Thoroughly mix the tomato purée, coriander, gingerroot, garlic, salt, sugar and lemon juice together. Refrigerate for 1 hour.

Serve cool or at room temperature.

Makes 1 1/2 cups

Tomatar Zelata
Jewish Tomato Relish

1 1/2 pounds ripe tomatoes, about
  6
6 scallions with green tops, sliced
1 teaspoon sliced fresh hot green
  chili

1 teaspoon salt, or to taste
1/4 cup lemon juice
2 teaspoons sugar

1. Pour boiling water over the tomatoes and let stand for 1 minute, then drain and peel. Chop tomatoes into coarse pieces and drain out the liquid through a metal sieve.

2. Mix this tomato mush with the scallions, chili, salt, lemon juice and sugar. Refrigerate and serve cold within 3 days.

Makes 2 cups

Variation: Should you not want to use the hot chili, substitute 1/2 teaspoon freshly ground black pepper.

Preserved Garlic and Ginger

¹/₄ pound garlic
¹/₄ pound fresh gingerroot

¹/₄ cup corn or peanut oil

1. Peel and wipe dry the garlic and the gingerroot. Cut into slices.

2. Grind garlic and gingerroot separately in a food processor. Mix them together, add the oil, and process into a smooth paste.

3. Store the mixture in a jar with a tight cover in the refrigerator. The mixture will remain usable for at least 2 months.

Use with any sort of Jewish dishes or as an ingredient in Indian curries where equal amounts of garlic and gingerroot are called for.

Kaka

Caraway Seed Biscuit

4 cups flour
4 teaspoons baking powder
¹/₄ teaspoon salt
1 teaspoon sugar

1 tablespoon caraway seeds
2 eggs, beaten in 1 cup water
¹/₂ cup corn or peanut oil

1. Mix the flour, baking powder, salt, sugar and caraway seeds together.

2. Add the egg/water mixture and the oil. Mix into a firm dough that can be handled easily.

3. On a floured board, roll out the dough into long cigars and shape 3-inch circles. Put them on a lightly greased cookie sheet. Bake in a 350°F. oven for 35 to 40 minutes, or until light brown.

Cool the biscuits and store them in a jar or a can with a tight cover.

Makes about 30

Sambusak
Cheese Turnovers

SAMBUSAK PASTRY

2 cups flour
1/4 teaspoon salt
1/4 teaspoon sugar
1 teaspoon baking powder

1/4 pound (8 tablespoons)
  margarine or butter
1/3 to 1/2 cup cold water, as
  needed

FILLING

4 ounces Cheddar or mozzarella
  cheese
4 ounces feta cheese

2 eggs, beaten
1/2 teaspoon freshly ground black
  pepper

1. Mix the flour, salt, sugar and baking powder together. Add the margarine by rubbing or cutting it into the flour. Add enough of the water to prepare a moist but firm dough. Knead it for a minute to smoothness, wrap it in aluminum foil, and refrigerate for 1 hour or more.

2. Grate the cheeses together in a processor, add the eggs and black pepper, and mix to a rather smooth consistency.

3. Break the dough into walnut-size pieces and roll them into round balls. Roll out the balls into 3¹/₂- to 4-inch circles. Put 1 heaping teaspoon of the cheese mixture into the center of each circle. Fold pastry over into half-moon shapes and press the edges together firmly. To seal the edges, I suggest that the lower edge of the dough be moistened with a wet finger.

4. Heat oven to 400°F. Put the turnovers on an ungreased cookie sheet, and bake for 30 to 40 minutes. Remove and cool. They are best served warm but may be served at room temperature.

Makes 20 turnovers

Note: The *sambusak* freeze well. Cool, place in a plastic bag, and freeze. To serve again, defrost for 1 hour and warm briefly in a 375°F. oven.

Badam Sambusak
Almond Turnovers

¹/₂ cup blanched almonds
¹/₄ cup sugar
1 or 2 drops of rosewater
  (optional)

1 recipe Sambusak Pastry (see
  preceding recipe)

1. Grind the almonds coarse in a processor. Mix with the sugar, and rosewater if used.

2. Prepare the pastry the same way as for the cheese turnovers, and fill with the almond mixture. Bake in a 375°F. oven for 15 to 20 minutes, or until light brown.

Makes 20 turnovers

Variation: Freshly grated coconut or pistachio nuts with sugar and rosewater may also be used as fillings for the *sambusak*.

Agar-Agar Dessert

5 or 6 strands of agar-agar, 12
  inches to each strand, cut into
  4-inch pieces
2 cups water

¹/₂ cup sugar
1 tablespoon Rich Coconut Milk,
  see Index (optional)
¹/₄ teaspoon rosewater (optional)

1. Soak the agar-agar in 2 cups water for 2 hours.

2. Bring this to a boil over moderate heat and stir constantly to dissolve the agar-agar. Add the sugar, mix well, and remove from the heat.

3. Add the coconut milk, and rosewater if used. Pour into a glass dish to cool. Refrigerate the dessert for several hours, until it becomes firm. (It will be like a very stiff gelatin.) Cut into 1-inch diamond shapes. Serve with tea or coffee after dining.

Makes about 20 pieces

Luzeena
Coconut Fudge

4 cups freshly grated coconut
2 cups sugar

¹/₄ teaspoon cardamom seeds, crushed

1. Stir-fry together the coconut, sugar and cardamom in a wok or large dry skillet over low heat. Stir continuously as a liquid begins to develop.

2. Continue to stir-fry, with a wooden spoon, until the coconut has browned, about 20 minutes.

3. Turn out the coconut quickly into a glass pie dish and press the fudge firmly to make a smooth surface. Cut the fudge into 2- to 3-inch diamond-shaped pieces while the coconut is still warm. Cool well and store in a glass jar or metal container.

Makes about 20 pieces

Variation: With a cold, wet hand, take 1 heaping tablespoon of the cooled but still soft fudge and press it into a round ball 1 inch in diameter. Set aside on wax paper. Continue to make round balls from the rest. Cool and store.

Dol Dol

Coconut Creamy Fudge

Here again the origin of a food is in question. The *dol dol* probably came from Cochin, yet it has been prepared and served in Jewish homes for generations regardless of its culinary origin. It is a very popular sweet served with morning coffee or afternoon tea and any time after dinner. Because it is made with coconut rather than cow's milk it does not conflict with the dietary laws forbidding the use of cow's milk with meat dishes.

6 cups Rich Coconut Milk (see Index)
1½ cups rice flour

1½ cups sugar
1 teaspoon rosewater (optional)

1. Mix the coconut milk, rice flour and sugar well together in a large saucepan. Bring this to a boil over moderate heat, then turn heat to low. Stir continuously to prevent burning and continue to simmer the mixture for 30 to 40 minutes. The mixture will reduce to a thick paste and the coconut oil will rise, giving a shiny appearance to the surface.

2. When the *dol dol* comes away from the sides of the pan toward the end of the cooking, add the rosewater if used and stir it into the mixture for 5 minutes more.

3. Turn out the *dol dol* into a glass or metal pan about 6 x 9 inches or a bit larger. Smooth over the surface. The fudge should be 1½ to 2 inches thick. Cut the fudge into generous diamond-shaped pieces.

Turn out the fudge pieces from the pan and serve at room temperature.

Makes about 20 pieces

Note: The *dol dol* is fragile and should be eaten the same day, or at most the next day, after it is made. It should not be refrigerated for longer than 1 day.

Apam
Bread Pudding with Coconut Milk

I would hazard a guess that this recipe has European, perhaps British, origins since it is not essentially Indian or Calcutta Jewish. However it came into being, it has certainly become a popular addition to this particular cuisine.

4 cups water
4 cups freshly grated coconut
1 loaf (1 pound) day-old white bread, crust removed
1/2 cup sugar, or to taste

4 eggs, beaten
1/2 teaspoon vanilla extract
1/4 cup sliced blanched almonds
1/4 cup white or dark raisins

1. Bring the water to a boil with the grated coconut. Remove the pan from the heat immediately. Cut the bread into 2-inch pieces and add to the coconut mixture. Mix well.

2. Stir in the sugar. Add the eggs, vanilla, almonds and raisins. Mix well.

3. Pour into a buttered heatproof glass or metal baking dish large enough so that the mixture is not more than 2 inches deep. Bake in a 375°F. oven for 30 minutes, or until golden brown.

Serve warm, cut into generous diamond-shaped pieces.

Serves 6 to 8

Nankathai
Butter Cookies

1/2 pound (16 tablespoons) butter or margarine
2/3 cup sugar
1 egg yolk
1 teaspoon vanilla extract
2 tablespoons corn or peanut oil

2 1/2 cups flour
1 teaspoon baking powder
1/2 teaspoon baking soda
1/4 teaspoon salt
1/3 cup ground almonds (optional)

1. Cream butter and sugar together. Add the egg yolk, vanilla and oil and mix well.

2. Sift the flour, baking powder, baking soda and salt together. Add this to the butter mixture. Fold in the almonds if used. Form into a soft dough.

3. Take 1 heaping teaspoon of the mixture for each cookie and roll into a ball. Press them slightly to make round flat discs about 1/2 inch thick. Place all the discs on a lightly oiled cookie sheet, spacing them about 2 inches apart. Bake in a 350°F oven for 20 to 25 minutes, or until lightly browned.

Cool well and store in an airtight tin.

Makes 30

Koleecha
Coconut Cookies

2 cups coconut shreds   *1/2 cup sugar*
1/4 cup milk   *1 cup semolina* (soojee)
6 tablespoons butter or margarine *poppy seeds*

1. Moisten the coconut in the milk for 5 minutes. Cream the butter and sugar together. Add the semolina and the coconut/milk mixture and mix well.

2. Take 1 heaping teaspoon of the mixture and shape a firm, round ball. Flatten it slightly, and sprinkle a few poppy seeds on top. Place rounds on an oiled cookie sheet. Bake in a 350°F oven for 20 to 25 minutes, or until golden brown.

Cool well and store in an airtight container.

Makes 20 cookies

Halek
Date Syrup for Passover

I prepare this syrup several times during the year and serve it on ice cream or sherbet. It always creates a sensation because of the rich, natural flavor of the dates. The burnished amber color and thick consistency make the *halek* a unique and exotic syrup for daily or Passover purposes. If serving at Passover, add 1/2 cup chopped walnuts to 1 cup *halek*, and serve for spooning over matzoh. This is the Calcutta Passover haroseth, Sephardic style.

2 cups pitted dates   **4 to 5 cups water**

1. Put the dates in a saucepan and pour in enough of the water to cover them completely. Bring this to a boil and remove the pan from the heat immediately. Do not stir.

2. Let the mixture cool for about 2 hours. Line a mixing bowl with a towel. Pour into the towel about 1 cup of the date mixture. Lift up the towel by its 4 corners and squeeze out the liquid gently. Twist the towel and continue to squeeze until all the liquid has been extracted. Empty the towel and set the pulp aside for another purpose. Repeat this step with all of the dates and liquid.

3. Bring all of the squeezed syrup to a boil over moderate heat. Turn heat down to low. Simmer the mixture for about 20 minutes or a bit more, or until the syrup has reduced by one third. During the early part of the simmering, remove the scum that collects on the top to produce a clear, dark syrup.

4. The syrup will be cooked enough when a few drops will form a soft ball in cold water. It should have the same consistency as maple syrup. When ready, cool the syrup, then pour it into a bottle which can be refrigerated, covered, for several months.

Makes 1 cup

Panir
Jewish Plaited Cheese

The famous white salt cheese, formerly used in making *sambusak* and just for eating out of hand, is becoming difficult to find. Nahoums in Calcutta no longer make it because of the scarcity of rich whole milk, and also because there is less demand. Therefore this recipe is included as the record of a lost tradition.

1 whole rennet capsule, or ½   *salt*
  teaspoon rennet powder
5 quarts whole milk at room
  temperature

1. Dissolve the rennet in ½ cup of milk, then mix it into the rest of the milk in a large container. Let it stand to solidify for 4 to 6 hours. It will become firm faster in warm weather than in cold.

2. Pour the firm milk into a cloth bag and spread it into a rectangle about 1 inch thick. Put a heavy weight on the bag to press out the liquid and leave it for about 30 minutes.

3. Have a pot of boiling water ready. Remove the cheese from the bag and cut it into 4 large squares. Dip each square into the hot water, then pull the cheese into long strips. Take 3 or 4 strands of the cheese and plait it by crossing the strands one over the other.

4. Rub the twisted cheese generously with salt and put the plaits in a bowl. Prepare salt water in the proportion of 1 tablespoon salt to 1 cup cold water, and pour it over the cheese. The cheese should be covered with salt water and refrigerated. In this manner, it will keep for several weeks.

Kaddus

Sacramental Wine

This recipe is also included more for the record than because it is expected to be much in demand. In the early days of the Jewish Calcutta community, homemade wine was commonplace. Now it is the exception. The proportions used were 1 pound of raisins to 1 quart of water.

seedless raisins
water

1. Rinse the raisins and put them with the water in a clean, covered pottery or stone jar. Keep at room temperature. Stir the mixture daily and occasionally rub the raisins gently between your fingers.

2. Allow 21 days for fermentation but remember that this wine was made in Calcutta, with its steaming daily heat. Taste the mixture as it matures to ensure that it is not turning sour. At the end of the 21 days strain the mixture, pressing the raisins gently, and pour the wine into a fresh jar.

TO MAKE VINEGAR:
Return the raisins to the jar or crock with 2 cups water. Let it ferment until the vinegar stage has been reached. I am told that a most delicious vinegar is produced this way.

The Anglo-Indian Kitchen

I am always astonished at the quantity and variety of Indian foods. The vastness of the subcontinent, the different racial and religious groups and the sheer numbers of people cooking and eating, almost guarantee that everything edible will ultimately be eaten in one delicious concoction or another.

As soon as one finishes investigating one regional cuisine, another surfaces and is too inviting to be ignored. I have been tempted by one set of kitchens after another and haven't yet come to the end.

Now I am cooking with the Anglo-Indians of Calcutta, where I made my home some years ago and where I return each year. The Anglo-Indians are the Eurasians, of mixed Indian and English blood, who have evolved into a racial group of their own and with a cuisine that reflects their origins. When Job Charnock established the East India Company in 1690 in what is now Calcutta, it was the beginning of the British Colonial period and with a little literary license could reasonably be called the beginning of the Anglo-Indian kitchen.

The cooking is hearty and spicy, with more than a touch of British Colonial ideas married to the wonderful Indian flavorings and cooking techniques. It should be pointed out that we are concentrating on Anglo-Indians of Calcutta and that the Anglo-Indians of Bombay and in Bangalore-Mysore of the south have their own specialties based upon their own regional and familial preferences.

English ideas and expressions crop up in these recipes, such as one which cautions us to use "good English vinegar." There are recipes for cutlets, sausages, potato mince, bread pudding and gooseberry jam and they are cooked in a "handy," which is a saucepan. Breads and biscuits are part of the English heritage, and a Christmas cake is *de rigueur* for the Anglo-Indian holiday. But in Calcutta, chutneys, pickles, curries, kabobs take their place beside the British recipes and so reveal the hand of India. The spices and especially the hot chili are common here as they are in every cooking style in India. Anglo-Indian cooking uses everything with assurance and ingenuity.

Keema Kari
Ground Beef Curry

3 tablespoons corn or peanut oil
1/4 cup sliced onion
1 teaspoon ground fresh
  gingerroot
2 garlic cloves, ground to a paste
1/2 teaspoon dried hot red chili
  flakes
1/4 teaspoon ground turmeric
1 pound ground beef
2 tablespoons chopped fresh mint

1 teaspoon salt, or to taste
1 cup potato cubes
1/2 cup water
4 whole cloves
2 cardamom pods, cracked
1 cinnamon stick, 1 inch
1 medium-size tomato, quartered
1/2 cup green peas, fresh or frozen
1 tablespoon chopped fresh
  coriander

1. Heat the oil in a pan and over moderate heat brown the onion for 2 minutes. Add the gingerroot, garlic, chili flakes and turmeric and fry for 1 minute.

2. Add the beef, mint and salt and stir-fry for 3 minutes. Add the potatoes, stir for a minute and add the water, cloves, cardamom and cinnamon. Cover the pan and cook for about 10 minutes.

3. When the potatoes are almost soft, add the tomato and green peas. Cover the pan and cook over low heat for 10 minutes more, until the liquid has evaporated. Scatter the coriander over the top and stir for a moment.

Serve warm with rice, *dal* or bread.

Serves 6

Glassy
Sweet Mango Beef

Why Glassy? The word is English but its application to this curried dish is mysterious. Somewhere along the line the preparation was named but its origin has been lost.

4 small potatoes, 3/4 pound,
  peeled and halved
3 cups water
1/4 cup corn or peanut oil
1 teaspoon ground fresh
  gingerroot
2 garlic cloves, ground to a paste
1/4 teaspoon freshly ground black
  pepper
1/2 teaspoon salt, or to taste

2 tablespoons ground onion
1 pound beef chuck, cut into slices
  1/4 inch thick, 3 inches long and
  1 inch wide
1/2 cup chopped tomato, fresh or
  canned
1 small hot green chili, a 1-inch
  slit cut in the side
1 tablespoon sweet mango chutney

1. Boil the potatoes in 2 cups water over moderate heat for 10 minutes. Drain well.

2. Heat the oil in a pan and lightly brown the potatoes over moderate heat for 3 minutes. Remove them and set aside.

3. Add the gingerroot, garlic, black pepper, salt and onion to the oil and stir-fry over moderate heat for 2 minutes. Add the beef and continue to stir-fry until the color changes, about 3 minutes. Add 1 cup water, bring to a boil, and cook, covered, for 30 minutes.

4. Add the browned potatoes, tomato, chili and mango chutney. Cook until the meat is tender and the sauce has reduced by half, about 20 minutes.

Serve warm with Indian or European bread.

Serves 4

Shami Kabob
Stuffed Beef Fritter

These are admirable appetizers to serve with drinks. On the other hand they may be eaten as a side dish with other Indian foods.

MEAT

1 pound beef, cut into 1-inch cubes
1/2 pound yellow split lentils (chana ka dal)
4 small hot green chilies, sliced
1 teaspoon sliced fresh gingerroot
2 cardamom pods, broken up

1 cinnamon stick, 1 inch, broken up
4 whole cloves, broken up
1/2 teaspoon salt, or to taste
2 cups water
2 eggs, beaten

STUFFING

1/4 cup minced onion
1 tablespoon chopped fresh mint

1/4 teaspoon salt
1 tablespoon lime juice

1/2 cup corn or peanut oil

1. Cook the meat, lentils, spices and salt together in the water for 1 hour, or until the meat is tender and nearly all the liquid has evaporated. The mixture should still be moist.

2. Process the mixture into a smooth paste with the eggs. Set aside.

3. Make the stuffing: Mix onion, mint, salt and lime juice together and set aside.

4. Take 1 heaping tablespoon of the meat mixture and roll it into a ball. Push a deep pocket into the center and fill it with about 1 teaspoon of the stuffing. Roll it up again into a ball and then slightly flatten it into a round disc about 3/8 inch thick. Shape all the meat mixture and stuffing in the same fashion.

5. Heat the oil in a wok or skillet and brown the kabobs over moderate heat for 2 minutes. Drain on paper towels and serve warm.

Makes 10 kabobs

Brinjal (Baigain)
Stuffed Eggplant Cutlet

My household cook, during those Calcutta years, prepared these egg-plant cutlets in large numbers for buffets. They were always greeted with much applause because of their flavor and crispy preparation.

6 small eggplants (1½ pounds)	1 teaspoon salt
2 cups water	¼ teaspoon freshly ground black
½ cup plus 2 tablespoons oil	pepper
¼ cup minced onion	2 eggs, well beaten
1 pound ground beef	¾ cup bread crumbs
¼ cup minced fresh mint	
1 teaspoon minced fresh hot green chili	

1. Cut the eggplants lengthwise into halves. Bring the water to a boil in a large pan and lay the halves, flesh side down, in the water. Cover the pan and cook for about 3 minutes, or until the eggplants have softened but are still firm. Do not overcook. Remove them and drain well on towels. Scoop out the partially cooked pulp, leaving a wall about ½ inch thick. Chop the pulp into coarse bits.

2. Heat 2 tablespoons oil in a skillet and fry the onion for 2 minutes. Mix the beef, mint, chili, salt and black pepper together and add it to the onion. Stir-fry until the meat changes color, about 3 minutes. Add the eggplant pulp and mix well. Turn out the mixture and cool.

3. Stuff the eggplant shells to the top. Spread about 1 tablespoon beaten egg over each eggplant half. Sprinkle over this 1 tablespoon bread crumbs and pack it down firmly over the egg.

4. Pour the ½ cup oil into a skillet over moderate heat. Carefully place the eggplant halves, egg side down, into the oil. Fry for 3 minutes, turn over, and brown the skin side for 1 minute. Drain on paper towels briefly.

Serve warm with other dishes.

Serves 6

Dhorma
Stuffed Squash in Coconut Milk

The original recipe calls for snake gourd, which is nicknamed "snake oil" by the Anglo-Indians. It is a long snakelike gourd with a hollow center, making it a natural vegetable to be stuffed. Zucchini and cucumbers both make good substitutes.

4 zucchini or large cucumbers
  (1½ pounds)
1 tablespoon corn or peanut oil
1 pound ground beef
2 teaspoons chopped parsley
2 teaspoons chopped mint

1 tablespoon minced fresh
  gingerroot
½ teaspoon salt, or to taste
½ teaspoon minced fresh hot
  green chili

SAUCE
¼ cup corn or peanut oil
2 teaspoons ground fresh
  gingerroot
1 garlic clove, crushed to a paste
1 teaspoon dried hot red chili
  flakes
½ teaspoon salt, or to taste
½ teaspoon ground turmeric

2 cups Rich Coconut Milk (see
  Index)
4 cardamom pods, cracked
1 cinnamon stick, 2 inches,
  broken into halves
4 whole cloves
4 bay leaves

1. Cut the zucchini lengthwise into halves. Scoop out the centers, leaving a wall ¼ inch thick. You are left with boat-shaped pieces.

2. Heat the oil in a skillet and add the beef, parsley, mint, gingerroot, salt and chili. Stir-fry the mixture for 3 minutes so that it is cooked and dry.

3. Cool for a minute, then firmly pack the mixture into the zucchini halves.

4. For the sauce, heat the oil in a pan and stir-fry the gingerroot, garlic, chili flakes, salt and turmeric in the oil over moderate heat for 2 minutes. Add the coconut milk, cardamom, cinnamon, cloves and bay leaves. Bring to a boil and simmer, uncovered, stirring frequently, for 5 minutes.

5. Add the stuffed zucchini to the coconut milk mixture and cook for 10 minutes.

Serve warm with rice.

Serves 6

Korma Curry
Chicken, Lamb or Beef in Yogurt Sauce

1 cup plain yogurt
2 pounds boneless lamb, cut into 1-inch cubes, or 2 pounds boneless beef chuck, cut into 1-inch cubes, or 1 chicken, 3 pounds, cut into frying pieces, loose skin and fat discarded
1/4 cup corn or peanut oil
1 pound potatoes, 4 medium, peeled and halved
1/4 cup thin-sliced onion
1 tablespoon ground fresh gingerroot

1 tablespoon ground garlic
1/2 teaspoon dried hot red chili flakes
4 cardamom pods, cracked
4 whole cloves
1 cinnamon stick, 3 inches, broken into halves
4 bay leaves
1 teaspoon salt, or to taste
2 cups water
1/4 cup Crispy Onions (see Index) for a garnish

1. Mix the yogurt and meat together and marinate for 15 minutes.

2. Heat the oil in a pan and cook the potatoes over moderate heat for 5 minutes, until they are light brown. Remove them and set aside.

3. Add the onion slices and stir-fry them for 2 minutes. Add the gingerroot, garlic and chili flakes and stir-fry for 2 minutes.

4. Add the meat, cardamom, cloves, cinnamon and bay leaves and stir-fry for 3 minutes. Add the salt and water, cover the pan, and cook over moderate heat until the meat is almost tender, about 40 minutes.

5. Add the browned potatoes and continue to cook until everything is done. The sauce will have reduced substantially since this is a dry curry.

Serve warm, sprinkled with the crispy onions and accompany with a pilau made with 2 cups rice and 1 cup green peas.

Serves 6 to 8

Kofta Kari
Meatball Curry

2 pounds ground beef
2 tablespoons fresh mint leaves, ground to a paste
1/4 cup onion slices, ground to a paste
1 tablespoon ground fresh hot green chili
1 teaspoon garam masala
1 teaspoon salt, or to taste
1/2 cup soft bread crumbs, soaked in water and squeezed dry
3 tablespoons corn or peanut oil
1 pound potatoes, 4 medium-size, peeled and halved

1 tablespoon sliced fresh gingerroot
2 garlic cloves, sliced
1/2 teaspoon dried hot red chili flakes
1/4 teaspoon ground turmeric
4 tablespoons water
1/4 cup chopped onion
3 bay leaves
2 cups Rich Coconut Milk (see Index)

1. Mix the beef with the mint, ground onion, chili, *garam masala*, salt and bread crumbs, and shape into balls 1 1/2 inches in diameter. Press firmly. Set aside. Makes 20 balls.

2. Heat the oil in a skillet and lightly brown the potatoes over moderate heat for 5 minutes. Remove potatoes from the oil and set aside.

3. Grind the gingerroot, garlic, chili flakes, turmeric and 2 tablespoons water together in a processor to make a smooth paste. Set aside.

4. Make the sauce: Using the same oil in which the potatoes were fried, brown the chopped onion over moderate heat for 3 minutes, adding the bay leaves toward the end. Add the spice paste and stir-fry for 1 minute, then add the rest of the water and stir well. Add the potatoes and continue to stir-fry for 2 minutes.

5. Add the coconut milk and bring the sauce to a boil. Place the meatballs carefully in the pan and cook without stirring, to prevent breaking up the meat, for 5 minutes. Shake the pan back and forth.

6. Simmer the curry, uncovered, over low heat for 15 minutes, testing the potatoes to insure they are soft.

Serve warm with pilau or plain rice.

Serves 8

Bandagobi Bada
Stuffed Cabbage Rolls

3 cups water
12 large cabbage leaves
5 tablespoons corn or peanut oil
1/4 cup fine-chopped onion
1 1/2 pounds ground beef
2 tablespoons chopped fresh mint
1 teaspoon salt, or to taste
1/2 teaspoon freshly ground black pepper

1/2 teaspoon ground fresh gingerroot
1 garlic clove, ground to a paste
1/2 teaspoon ground coriander
1/2 teaspoon ground turmeric
2 eggs, beaten
1 tablespoon flour
1/2 to 3/4 cup bread crumbs

1. Bring the water to a boil in a pan over moderate heat. Add the cabbage leaves a few at a time, cover the pan, and heat leaves for 2 minutes to soften them. Remove leaves and set aside. Prepare all the leaves this way.

2. Heat 1 tablespoon oil in a skillet and fry the onion lightly over moderate heat for 1 minute. Add the beef, mint, salt, black pepper, gingerroot, garlic, coriander and turmeric. Stir-fry until the beef changes color and the mixture is dry. Cool and set aside.

3. Put 2 heaping tablespoons of the beef mixture in the center of a cabbage leaf. Fold the leaf into a tight roll 1 inch in diameter. Prepare all the leaves and filling in this way.

4. Beat the eggs and flour together into a batter. Heat the balance of the oil, 4 tablespoons, in a skillet. Dip each roll into the batter, then into the bread crumbs. Brown them in the oil over moderate heat for about 3 minutes. Add more oil if necessary. Drain the crisp rolls on paper towels.

Serve warm.

Serves 6

Vindaloo
A Spicy Two-Meat Stew

Vinegar is a preservative and therefore the *vindaloo* may be kept in the refrigerator for several days before using. In fact, the flavors are intensified if the *vindaloo* is eaten one or two days after cooking. Warm slightly before serving.

In the extraordinary hot climate of Calcutta, making *vindaloos*, which were made with vinegar but without a drop of water, was a method of preserving food where refrigeration was not available. Some of these dishes, such as those prepared with shrimps or prawns, were bottled, kept on the kitchen shelf and used as a condiment with rice. This archaic method is probably not followed now since refrigeration is more common but it was no doubt the system during the Colonial period.

The *vindaloo* requires that a substantial amount of oil be used in the preparation. For our purposes and without compromising the flavor, I have suggested that the excess oil be poured off before dining.

Toasting and grinding whole spice seeds is the old-time method and very effective in deriving the most flavor. However, I have also lightly toasted ground spices, which is an improvement over using them directly from the container.

This recipe is one prepared by the Bhatia Christians of Calcutta, a group of Anglo-Indians who have intermarried with Bengali Indians.

1 tablespoon coriander seeds	4 garlic cloves, ground to a paste
1 tablespoon poppy seeds (kus kus)	1 pound boneless pork, cut into 2-inch cubes
1 tablespoon red mustard seeds	1 pound boneless beef chuck, cut into 2-inch cubes
1 tablespoon cuminseeds	
1/2 cup corn or peanut oil	1 teaspoon salt, or to taste
2 tablespoons dried hot red chili flakes	1 cup water
1 tablespoon ground fresh gingerroot	1/2 cup vinegar

1. Lightly toast the coriander, poppy seeds, mustard seeds, and cuminseeds in a dry skillet for 2 or 3 minutes until the aroma is released. Grind the seeds in a processor to a fine powder. Set aside.

2. Heat the oil in a pan and add all the toasted dry spices, the chili, gingerroot and garlic. Stir-fry over moderately low heat for 2 minutes.

Add the meats and salt and stir continuously for 10 minutes as the meat browns.

3. Add the water, cover the pan, and cook until the meats are tender, about 1 hour.

4. When the meats have been fully tenderized, add the vinegar and continue to cook until the vinegar evaporates and the oil has risen. This is an indication that the vindaloo is ready. At this stage, all the oil may be poured off before serving.

Serve warm with plain white rice and *masoor dal.*

Serves 6

Beja

Brain Curry

1 beef brain, soaked in cold water for 30 minutes and well drained, membrane removed
1 1/2 cups water
2 tablespoons corn or peanut oil
2 tablespoons thin-sliced onion
1/4 teaspoon ground turmeric
1 teaspoon ground fresh gingerroot

1 garlic clove, ground to a paste
1/2 teaspoon dried hot red chili flakes
1/2 teaspoon salt, or to taste
1/4 cup loosely packed fresh coriander leaves

1. Cook the brain in 1 cup water in a covered pan over moderate heat for 10 minutes. Drain. Cool and cut the brain into 6 to 8 pieces. Set aside.

2. Heat the oil in a pan and fry the onion over moderate heat for 2 minutes. Add the turmeric, gingerroot, garlic, chili flakes and salt. Stir-fry for 2 minutes.

3. Add the brain and 1/2 cup water, cover the pan, and cook for 10 minutes, or until the liquid evaporates. Do not stir since it may break up the brain pieces, but shake the pan back and forth to mix. Add the coriander leaves and shake the pan to combine with the brain pieces.

Serve warm with rice, salads, chutney and a vegetable curry, if you wish.

Serves 4

Sausage Curry

The sausages we use are European but the remainder of the recipe is very much Indian. A felicitous combination. The hot Italian-style sausages work very well in this curry.

1 pound hot Italian-style sausage
1¼ cups water
2 tablespoons corn or peanut oil
1 tablespoon sliced onion
1 teaspoon ground fresh gingerroot
1 garlic clove, ground to a paste
½ teaspoon dried hot red chili flakes

1 tablespoon ground onion
¼ teaspoon ground turmeric
½ teaspoon salt, or to taste
3 small potatoes, about ½ pound, peeled and halved
¾ cup chopped ripe tomatoes, fresh or canned
2 tablespoons chopped fresh coriander

1. Poke 3 holes in each sausage with a fork and put them in a pan with ¼ cup water. Cook over moderately low heat for about 15 minutes, or until all the liquid evaporates and the sausages are lightly browned. Set aside.

2. Add the oil to the same pan and brown the sliced onion over moderate heat for 2 minutes. Add the gingerroot, garlic, chili flakes, ground onion, turmeric and salt. Stir-fry for 2 minutes.

3. Add the potatoes, mix well, and add 1 cup water. Cover the pan and cook over moderate heat for 10 minutes.

4. Cut the sausages lengthwise into halves and add them with the tomatoes to the pan. Cover, and cook until the potatoes are soft and the sauce has reduced by half. Add the coriander and stir for a moment.

Serve warm with Coconut Rice or Rice and Lentils (see Index) and pappadums.

Serves 6

Jal Frazi
Chicken and Potato Hash

Jal frazi is a popular leftover chicken dish and one that could also utilize roast beef or pork cooked previously and cubed. It is often served with the Sweet, Hot and Sour Red Pumpkin (see recipe), plain rice and *dal*.

2 tablespoons corn or peanut oil
2 cups potato cubes
1/2 teaspoon salt, or to taste
1/4 cup thin-sliced onion
1/2 teaspoon dried hot red chili flakes

2 cups cooked chicken, cut into 1/2-inch cubes
1 teaspoon minced fresh gingerroot
3 tablespoons water

1. Heat the oil in a large skillet and over moderate heat fry the potatoes with the salt for 5 minutes to brown them lightly. Remove and set aside.

2. In the same oil, fry the onion for 2 minutes, or until light brown.

3. Add the chili flakes and stir-fry for 1 minute. Add the chicken, potatoes and gingerroot and mix well. Add the water, cover the skillet, and cook for 5 minutes to soften the potatoes completely.

4. Remove the cover and stir-fry rapidly for 2 minutes to brown and dry the hash.

Serve warm.

Serves 4

Murgi Malai

Chicken in Rich Coconut Milk

This curry is a winner—an assortment of spices and seasonings laced together by the coconut milk and reduced to a thick gravy.

1/4 cup corn or peanut oil
3 small potatoes, about 1/2 pound, peeled and halved
1 medium-size onion, chopped fine (1/2 cup)
2 garlic cloves, crushed to a paste
2 teaspoons ground fresh gingerroot
2 teaspoons crushed dried or fresh hot red chili
1 teaspoon white poppy seeds
1/4 teaspoon ground turmeric

1 teaspoon salt, or to taste
1 chicken, 3 pounds, cut into serving pieces, including the giblets, loose skin and fat discarded
4 cardamom pods, cracked
1 cinnamon stick, 3 inches, broken into halves
4 whole cloves
2 bay leaves
2 cups Rich Coconut Milk (see Index)

1. Heat the oil in a pan and lightly brown the potatoes over moderate heat for 5 minutes. Remove them and set aside.

2. Brown the onion in the same oil for a minute. Add the garlic, gingerroot and chili and stir-fry for a minute. Add the poppy seeds, turmeric and salt and stir-fry for 2 minutes more.

3. Add the chicken pieces and brown them in the oil for 10 minutes, adding the cardamom, cinnamon, cloves and bay leaves.

4. Pour in the coconut milk, bring to a boil and simmer everything together over low heat for 20 minutes.

5. Return the potatoes to the pan and cook for 15 minutes more, or until the chicken and potatoes are tender and the liquid reduced to a thick gravy.

Serve warm with rice and salad.

Serves 6

Haas Aur Bhass
Duck and Bamboo Shoots

Fresh bamboo shoots are available in the markets around Calcutta during the monsoon season. All bamboo shoots are edible but not all are palatable so one has to choose carefully. The raw bamboo shoot is peeled and sliced and must be cooked longer than the canned variety. Canned bamboo shoots are readily available here.

1 duck, 4 to 4¹/₂ pounds
2 tablespoons minced fresh gingerroot, crushed to a paste
4 garlic cloves, crushed to a paste
2 teaspoons dried hot red chili flakes
1 teaspoon ground turmeric

2 teaspoons salt, or to taste
1 teaspoon garam masala
1 cup water
4 cups Rich Coconut Milk (see Index)
2 pounds canned bamboo shoots, cut into julienne

1. Cut the duck into 16 pieces. Include the giblets. Discard loose skin and fat.

2. Mix everything together except the coconut milk and bamboo shoots. Put into a pan and bring to a boil over moderate heat. Cover the pan and cook until the water evaporates, about 25 minutes. Continue to stir-fry in the melted fat for 5 minutes more to brown the duck.

3. Add the coconut milk and cook over moderate heat, uncovered, basting frequently, for about 20 minutes. The oil will rise to the top.

4. At this point add the bamboo shoots and cook for 5 minutes more. Pour off as much fat as possible.

Serve warm with white rice.

Serves 6

Haas Roast
Duck Roast

1½ pounds potatoes, peeled and cubed
1 duck liver
3 tablespoons corn or peanut oil
1 teaspoon freshly ground black pepper
3 teaspoons salt, or to taste

1 tablespoon chopped fresh mint
½ cup green peas, fresh or frozen
1 duck, 4½ pounds
3 inches of fresh gingerroot, chopped fine
2 cups water

1. Cook the potatoes in water and mash them.

2. Fry the duck liver in 1 tablespoon of the oil over moderate heat for 3 minutes. Cool and cut it into ¼-inch cubes.

3. Mix the potatoes, liver, black pepper, 1 teaspoon of the salt, the mint and green peas together. Use this mixture to stuff the duck, and sew it up.

4. Rub the stuffed duck with half of the gingerroot. Heat the rest of the oil in a pan and brown the duck over moderate heat for 10 minutes. The duck should develop a deep brown color.

5. Add the water to the pan as well as the balance of the gingerroot and salt (2 teaspoons). Cook, covered, over moderate heat for about 45 minutes, turning the duck over now and then. Cook until the duck is tender and the water has evaporated.

6. Brown the duck in the accumulated fat for 10 minutes more. Discard as much fat as possible.

Carve the duck and serve warm with the stuffing.

Serves 6

Haas Ka Vindaloo
Duck Vindaloo

Vindaloo is a classic dish of the Anglo-Indian community. It can be prepared with pork, chicken or beef but in my opinion, duck is the best.

Since there is so much fat in American ducks, I suggest that the *vindaloo* be prepared a day in advance, refrigerated overnight, and the congealed fat removed the next day. Warm the duck for 10 minutes before serving.

1 inch fresh gingerroot, sliced
4 garlic cloves, sliced
3 teaspoons dried hot red chili
*   flakes*
1/4 teaspoon mustard seeds
1/2 cup cider vinegar

1 duck, 4 1/2 pounds, cut into 8
*   serving pieces, giblets included,*
*   loose skin and fat discarded*
1 teaspoon ground turmeric
2 teaspoons salt, or to taste
1/2 cup water

1. Grind together in a processor the gingerroot, garlic, chili flakes and mustard seeds into a paste. Lubricate the mixture with 1 tablespoon vinegar during this process.

2. Marinate the duck pieces and giblets with the paste, turmeric and salt for 1 hour.

3. Put the duck and marinade, the balance of vinegar and the water, in a roasting pan, cover, and cook over moderately low heat for about 1 1/2 hours, or until the duck is tender and all the liquid has evaporated. Skim off and discard as much fat as possible.

Serve warm with rice, chutneys, salad and vegetable curries.

Serves 6

Muchli Moolu

Fish and Gravy

This is a richly seasoned dish that combines two of the most popular foods available in tropical Calcutta, fish and coconut.

1/4 cup corn or peanut oil	1 tablespoon ground garlic
2 pounds fillets of sole, flounder, or similar fish, cut into 2-inch squares	1/2 teaspoon ground turmeric 3 cups Rich Coconut Milk (see Index)
1/4 cup onion slices	1 teaspoon salt, or to taste
1/2 cup onion slices, ground to a paste	4 whole hot green chilies, slit 1 inch down the center

1. Heat the oil in a pan and fry the fish cubes over moderate heat for 2 minutes. Remove the fish and set aside.

2. Pour off half of the oil. Fry the sliced onions in the balance of the oil over moderate heat until light brown. Add the onion paste, garlic paste and turmeric. Stir-fry for 2 minutes. Add the coconut milk and bring to a boil, stirring frequently.

3. Add the salt, chilies and fish cubes. Continue to cook and baste over moderate heat for 10 minutes to reduce the sauce to one fourth of the original volume.

Serve warm with rice and other dishes.

Serves 6 to 8

Khuta Meetha Lal Khadoo
Sweet, Hot and Sour Red Pumpkin

This vegetable dish, easily assembled and full of flavor, is ideal for a rainy day when the monsoon rains are pouring down and no one is stirring from the house.

2 tablespoons corn or peanut oil
1/4 cup thin-sliced onion
1 teaspoon ground fresh gingerroot
1 garlic clove, ground to a paste
1/2 teaspoon dried hot red chili flakes
1/4 teaspoon ground turmeric
1/2 teaspoon salt

1 teaspoon sugar
1 pound red pumpkin or butternut squash, peeled, cut into 1/2-inch cubes
1/4 cup water
1 heaping tablespoon tamarind paste, soaked in 1/2 cup water for 30 minutes and strained

1. Heat the oil in a pan and over moderate heat fry the onion for 2 minutes until light brown. Add the gingerroot, garlic, chili flakes, turmeric, salt and sugar. Fry for 1 minute.

2. Add the pumpkin cubes and stir-fry for 1 minute. Add the water, cover the pan, and cook until the pumpkin is softer but still firm. Add the tamarind liquid and stir-fry until the liquid has nearly evaporated. A small amount of sauce should remain.

Serve warm with rice.

Serves 4

Variation: One can also add 1/2 cup small, fresh shrimps, peeled and deveined, to the pumpkin. Fry the shrimps in 2 teaspoons oil for 2 minutes, long enough for them to change color. Add them to the pumpkin with the tamarind liquid and stir-fry until everything is well combined and the liquid has nearly evaporated.

Boona Kichri
Rice and Lentils

1 cup moong dal
3 tablespoons corn or peanut oil
1/2 cup thin-sliced onion
2 cups raw rice, well rinsed and
  drained
1 cinnamon stick, 2 inches

4 cardamom pods, cracked
4 whole cloves
3 bay leaves
1 teaspoon salt
3 1/2 cups water

1. Brown the lentils in a dry skillet over moderately low heat for 5 minutes until they reach a rich brown color. Do not scorch. Rinse under cold water and drain well.

2. Heat the oil in a pan, add the onion and crisp the slices over moderate heat. Remove half of the onion and set aside.

3. Add the rice and lentils together to the pan and stir-fry with the cinnamon, cardamom, cloves, bay leaves and salt for 3 minutes.

4. Add the water and bring to a boil. Reduce heat to low, cover the pan, and cook for 12 to 15 minutes. It may be necessary to add a little more water to soften the rice. This is a dry dish in which each grain of rice is separate. Stir once toward the end of the process.

Serve warm garnished with the rest of the crispy fried onions. Serve with Jal Frazi or Vindaloo (see recipes).

Serves 6

Nariel Ka Bhat
Coconut Rice

3 tablespoons corn or peanut oil
1/4 cup thin-sliced onion
2 cups raw rice, well rinsed and
  drained
4 cardamom pods, cracked
4 whole cloves

1 cinnamon stick, 2 inches
3 bay leaves
1/2 teaspoon salt
1/4 teaspoon ground turmeric
3 1/2 cups Rich Coconut Milk (see
  Index)

1. Heat the oil in a pan and over moderate heat fry the onion until golden brown and crispy, about 3 minutes. Remove half of the onion and set aside as a garnish.

2. Add the rice and stir-fry for 2 minutes. Add the cardamom, cloves, cinnamon, bay leaves, salt and turmeric; stir well.

3. Add the coconut milk. Bring to a boil, turn heat to low, cover the pan, and cook for 12 to 15 minutes. The rice should be dry and soft. You may also at this stage put the rice into a 350°F. oven and bake for 15 minutes. This will develop a crisp, brown bottom to the rice.

Serve warm, sprinkled with the crispy onions.

Serves 6

Tomatar Bhat
Tomato Rice

This is an attractive pink rice with substantial flavor and spice. It goes well with any kind of Anglo-Indian food.

2 tablespoons corn or peanut oil
1 cup thin-sliced onions
1 teaspoon dried hot red chili flakes
2 cups raw rice, rinsed and well drained
1 cardamom pod, cracked
2 whole cloves
1 cinnamon stick, 1 inch
3¹/₂ cups water
1 cup fine-chopped ripe tomatoes
¹/₄ cup Crispy Onions (see Index)
1 tablespoon chopped coriander

1. Heat the oil in a pan and cook the sliced onions and chili flakes over moderate heat for 2 minutes or until onions are light brown.

2. Add the rice, cardamom, cloves and cinnamon and stir-fry for 3 minutes.

3. Add the water, bring to a boil, turn the heat to low, and cover the pan. When the rice is half cooked, about 4 minutes later, add the tomatoes and stir. Cover the pan and complete the cooking.

Serve warm, garnished with the crispy onions and chopped coriander.

Serves 6

Bali Chow

Sour and Hot Tomato Chutney

2 pounds medium-size ripe
 tomatoes
2 tablespoons chopped fresh
 gingerroot
1 tablespoon chopped garlic
1 tablespoon dried hot red chili
 flakes

²/₃ cup cider vinegar
¹/₂ cup corn or peanut oil
1 teaspoon salt
1 tablespoon nappey, bottled
 shrimp paste (see Note)

1. Rinse the tomatoes and wipe them dry. Cut into quarters.

2. Soak the gingerroot, garlic and chili flakes in ¹/₂ cup vinegar for 15 minutes. Process to a smooth paste.

3. Heat the oil in a pan over low heat and add the paste, the balance of the vinegar and the salt. Stir-fry for 1 minute. Add the tomatoes and *nappey*. Simmer over low heat, stirring continuously with a wooden spoon, for 20 to 25 minutes, until the oil rises to the top and the tomatoes are reduced to a coarse paste.

4. Cool for 1 hour. Bottle the chutney in glass jars. Refrigerate for 24 hours and use with any Indian food. Will keep refrigerated for several months.

Makes 2 to 3 cups

Note: Nappey (the name used in Calcutta) is a Burmese and Indonesian essence of shrimp that is used in cooking to give the flavorings greater depth. I prefer to use the Lee Kum Kee brand, bottled in Hong Kong. It is a concentrated paste. It should be refrigerated after opening.

Tomatar Chutney
Sweet Tomato Chutney

3 tablespoons tamarind paste
²/₃ cup cider vinegar
2 pounds medium-size ripe
  tomatoes, quartered
1 tablespoon ground fresh
  gingerroot
3 garlic cloves, ground to a paste

2 teaspoons ground fresh hot
  green chili
4 cardamom pods, whole
4 whole cloves
2 inches of cinnamon stick, broken
  up
1 cup sugar

1. Soak the tamarind paste in ¹/₄ cup vinegar for 30 minutes to dissolve it. Strain the liquid through a metal sieve; discard seeds and fiber.

2. Simmer the tomatoes in the balance of the vinegar in a large pan over moderate heat for 5 minutes. Add the gingerroot, garlic, chili, cardamom, cloves and cinnamon. Mix well with a wooden spoon. Add the tamarind liquid and sugar and mix again.

3. Continue to stir everything together over moderately low heat for 5 minutes. The chutney will become thick. Cool completely. Bottle the chutney. It can be refrigerated for several months.

Makes about 3 cups

Note: This chutney is prepared in Calcutta without any water so that it can be stored on the pantry shelf rather than in the refrigerator. Using water would destroy the preserving capacity of the vinegar.

Pudeena Chutney
Mint Chutney

1 cup loosely packed fresh mint
  leaves
1/2 teaspoon minced fresh
  gingerroot
1 garlic clove, chopped fine
1/2 teaspoon minced fresh hot
  green chili

2 teaspoons tamarind paste,
  dissolved in 1 tablespoon water,
  strained
1/4 teaspoon salt
1/4 teaspoon sugar

1. Coarse-grind the mint in a processor.

2. Add the gingerroot, garlic, chili, tamarind liquid, salt and sugar. Grind to a relatively smooth paste but do not overprocess.

Serve at room temperature with any kind of Anglo-Indian food.

Makes 1 cup

The
Parsi
Kitchen

*I*ndia is the culinary Great Earth Mother of Asia. All who enter her boundaries are welcomed, sometimes absorbed, always changed as she holds the new arrivals to her bosom and introduces the new spices and seasonings that the Indian genius has perfected. Those who come from other lands bring with them their national dishes, which are then married to the new gamut of spices according to personal and regional preferences. So it was with the Parsis, the ancient Persians who migrated to India.

The Parsis are Zoroastrians and follow the religion of their prophet, Zarathushtra, who preached that there was only one God, Ahura Mazda. The sun and fire light up his teachings, which promote "good thoughts, good words, good deeds."

The disintegration and collapse of the Persian Empire occurred when the Arabs overthrew the rulers in 651 A.D.. The Parsis, who could no longer follow their ancient religion, fled to India. They settled down in Gujerat Province, where Bombay is the principal city, as farmers, weavers, carpenters. Initially they were rural people before they became urbanized in Bombay and then in Calcutta. Adherence to their religion centered around the Fire Temple for prayer and the Towers of Silence where their bodies were deposited after death.

Parsi dishes are not carbon copies but an amalgamation of ideas and techniques perfected over the centuries and frozen in time. The cooking leans on fish and other seafood, poultry and especially mutton (lamb). Beef is not eaten out of respect for the Hindu ruler, the Raja of Sanjan, who gave them refuge.

Eggs are prepared with gusto and imagination and are eaten frequently. Vegetables are given short shrift by people who are essentially meat eaters. Hot chilies are lavishly used. Their classic dish, Dhan Sak, described in this chapter, is world class.

This community, which is probably the most Westernized in India, is now estimated to be 85,000 persons, principally situated in Bombay district, and a small group of about 1200 in Calcutta. It was there that I systematically recorded these recipes, in one of India's extraordinary racial communities.

The outlook for the future of this closely knit community does not appear good. There are those who feel it inevitable that they will eventually be absorbed by the sea of humanity around them and lose their group identity, which has been waning since the departure of the British in 1947. Therefore, I felt compelled to make a record of their distinctive cuisine while it is still possible to find the traditional cooks and their recipes.

Tomatar Ras Ne Chawal
Tomato Soup and Rice

1 chicken, 3 pounds, cut into serving pieces, loose skin and fat discarded
6 cups water
1 teaspoon salt, or to taste
3 tablespoons corn or peanut oil
1 cup onion chunks, ground to a paste

1 teaspoon ground fresh gingerroot
1 teaspoon ground garlic
1/2 teaspoon ground cuminseed
1/2 teaspoon dried red chili flakes
1/2 cup homemade tomato purée

1. Cook the chicken in the water with the salt over moderate heat for 20 minutes.

2. Heat the oil in a skillet and over moderate heat fry the onion paste for 3 minutes. Add the gingerroot, garlic, cuminseed and chili flakes. Stir-fry the mixture for 3 minutes more.

3. Add this spice mixture to the chicken pot with the tomato purée and simmer over moderately low heat for 20 minutes more. Adjust the salt if necessary.

Serve hot with plain white rice, which may be added to the soup if wanted.

Serves 6

Variations: In place of the chicken, use 1 pound boneless beef or lamb cut into 1-inch cubes. Follow the same directions as for the chicken but cook the meat longer, about 1 hour or until tender. Then add the spice mixture and cook until done.

Meatballs may also be used to good account. Use 1 pound ground beef or lamb mixed with 1/2 teaspoon salt. Shape the balls 1 1/2 inches in diameter. Bring the water and salt to a rolling boil and drop in the meatballs one by one. Cook for 5 minutes, then add the spice mixture and tomato purée. Cook for 20 minutes more.

Note: A simple tomato purée may be prepared with 1 cup of sliced ripe tomatoes and 1/2 cup water. Cook in a covered pan over moderate heat for 15 minutes. Process to a purée in a blender.

Murghi Na Farcha
Fried Chicken

1 cup oil
2 teaspoons ground fresh
  gingerroot
2 teaspoons ground garlic
1 teaspoon dried hot red chili
  flakes
1 teaspoon ground cuminseed

2 teaspoons salt, or to taste
1 chicken, 3 pounds, cut into
  serving pieces, loose skin and fat
  discarded
1 cup water
4 eggs, separated
1/2 cup bread crumbs

1. Heat 1/4 cup oil and fry the gingerroot, garlic, chili flakes, cuminseed and salt over moderate heat for 1 minute. Add the chicken pieces and brown them for 5 minutes.

2. Add the water, cover the pan, and cook until the chicken is tender and nearly all the liquid has evaporated, about 30 minutes. Cool the chicken in the pan.

3. Just before dining, beat the egg whites until stiff. Beat the yolks and fold them into the whites. Coat each piece of chicken with the thick gravy in the pan. Dip the chicken into the bread crumbs and then into the beaten egg.

4. Heat the remainder of the oil (3/4 cup) in a skillet and over moderate heat fry the chicken pieces until crispy brown on all sides. Drain briefly on paper towels.

Serve warm, with potato chips or French fries.

Serves 4

Note: The chicken pieces may be coated with the bread crumbs several hours in advance of dining, and refrigerated. When ready to serve dip chicken pieces into the egg and brown in the oil.

Chicken Vindaloo
Hot Chicken with Mustard and Potatoes

2 teaspoons sliced garlic
2 teaspoons sliced fresh hot red
  chili
2 teaspoons ground cuminseed
1 teaspoon mustard seeds
1 teaspoon black peppercorns
1 teaspoon ground turmeric
1/4 cup cider vinegar
1/2 cup corn or peanut oil

1 cup onion slices, ground to a
  paste
1 chicken, 3½ pounds, cut into
  serving pieces, loose skin and fat
  discarded
1 teaspoon salt, or to taste
1 cup water
2 pounds potatoes, 8 small, peeled
  and halved

1. Grind the garlic, chili, cuminseed, mustard seeds, peppercorns and turmeric together in a processor with 2 tablespoons of the vinegar, which acts as a lubricant.

2. Heat 1/4 cup oil in a pan and fry the onion paste over moderately low heat until light brown. Add the ground spices and continue to fry the mixture until it turns reddish and has a "crumbled" look.

3. Add the chicken and cook for 10 minutes to brown it. Add the balance of the vinegar, the salt and 1 cup water. Continue to cook for 25 minutes, or until the chicken is tender and the sauce quite thick.

4. During this time, cook the potatoes in sufficient water until they are soft but still firm. Drain well and cool.

5. Crisp-fry the potatoes in 1/4 cup oil for about 10 minutes. Add them to the chicken for the last 5 minutes of cooking time. Shake the pan to mix the potatoes with the chicken and sauce.

Serve warm.

Serves 6

Papeta, Green Peas Ma Murghi
Chicken with Green Peas and Potatoes

The English words, "green peas," are included in the Indian title because the Parsis are quite Westernized and use many English words for Western products.

7 tablespoons corn or peanut oil
1 cup onion slices, ground to a paste
2 teaspoons ground fresh gingerroot
2 teaspoons ground garlic
1 teaspoon dried hot red chili flakes
1 chicken, 3 pounds, cut into serving pieces, loose skin and fat discarded

1 teaspoon salt
2 cups water
1 teaspoon garam masala
1 pound fresh or frozen green peas
2 pounds potatoes, 8 small, peeled and halved

1. Heat 3 tablespoons of the oil in a pan and brown the onion paste for about 5 minutes. Add the gingerroot, garlic and chili flakes and stir-fry over moderate heat for 2 minutes. Add the chicken pieces and brown everything together for 5 minutes.

2. Add the salt and 2 cups water, cover the pan, and cook until the chicken is tender and the sauce has thickened.

3. Add the *garam masala* and cook uncovered for 5 minutes more.

4. As the chicken cooks, blanch the peas briefly in water and drain well. Set aside.

5. Cook the potatoes in water until they are almost tender, about 10 minutes. Drain well and cool for several minutes. Heat remaining 4 tablespoons oil in a wok or skillet and over moderate heat fry the potatoes until they are crisp and brown.

Use both the peas and potatoes as a garnish around the perimeter of the serving dish with the curried chicken.

Serves 4

Variation: The *papeta* may be made with duck too. The cooking time is longer but the flavoring is essentially the same.

Murghi Kari
Chicken Curry, Parsi Style

This curry may be prepared early in the day and warmed up, but not boiled, just before serving. To prevent it being too oily, pour off as much oil as possible at the end of step 2, just before the coconut milk is added.

4 tablespoons corn or peanut oil	2 teaspoons salt, or to taste
½ cup ground onion	1 chicken, 3½ pounds, cut into
2 teaspoons ground fresh	frying pieces, loose skin and fat
gingerroot	discarded
2 teaspoons ground garlic	1 cup chopped tomatoes, fresh or
2 teaspoons dried hot red chili	canned
flakes	1 pound potatoes, 4 medium-size,
2 teaspoons ground coriander	peeled and quartered
2 teaspoons ground cuminseed	1½ cups water
2 teaspoons poppy seeds	1 cup Rich Coconut Milk (see
1 teaspoon ground turmeric	Index)

1. Heat the oil in a pan and fry the onion paste over moderate heat until light brown. Add the gingerroot, garlic, chili flakes, coriander, cuminseed, poppy seeds and turmeric. Stir-fry for 3 minutes as the mixture turns reddish brown.

2. Add the salt and chicken and fry for 5 minutes, turning the pieces around several times. Add the tomatoes, potatoes and water. Cover the pan and cook until potatoes and chicken are done, about 30 minutes.

3. When the sauce has thickened at the end of the cooking time, add the coconut milk, stir for a minute, and remove pan from the heat.

Serve warm with white rice.

Serves 6

Murghi Curry Ek Sau Badam
Chicken Curry with 100 Almonds

This old recipe is made only on special occasions. The almonds and coconut milk produce a rich thick sauce; the 100 almonds of the title indicate the luxurious quality of the dish. The price of almonds in Calcutta is exorbitant for most people who would want to prepare the curry.

3 tablespoons corn or peanut oil
1 cup chopped onions, ground to a paste
2 teaspoons ground fresh gingerroot
2 teaspoons ground garlic
2 teaspoons dried hot red chili flakes
1 teaspoon ground turmeric
1 teaspoon salt, or to taste

1 chicken, 3 pounds, cut into serving pieces, loose skin and fat discarded
1/2 cup water
100 almonds (about 3/4 cup), blanched and ground to a paste in a processor
1 1/2 cups Rich Coconut Milk (see Index)

1. Heat the oil in a pan and stir-fry the onion paste over moderate heat until it is light brown, about 3 minutes. Add the gingerroot, garlic, chili flakes, turmeric and salt. Stir-fry until the mixture has turned a reddish color, about 10 minutes.

2. Add the chicken and brown it for 5 minutes. Add the water and cook in a covered pan for 25 minutes to tenderize the chicken.

3. Add the almond paste, stir well, and cook over moderately low heat for 5 minutes.

4. Add the coconut milk and simmer for 5 minutes, basting frequently. Remove it from the heat.

Serve warm with rice, *dal* and chutney.

Serves 6

Kaju Ma Murgi
Chicken and Cashews

India was a famous source of cashew nuts for many years. For best quality, I prefer to buy unroasted cashews and bake them in a 350°F. oven for 10 minutes, then turn off the heat and let them stand for 10 minutes more. The fresh roasted taste is worth this extra trouble.

2 tablespoons corn or peanut oil
3 medium-size onions, cut into thin slices (1½ cups)
2 teaspoons ground fresh gingerroot
2 teaspoons ground garlic
2 teaspoons dried hot red chili flakes
1 teaspoon salt, or to taste

1 teaspoon ground cuminseed
1 chicken, 3 pounds, cut into serving pieces, loose skin and fat discarded
1 cup water
3 tablespoons tomato paste
1 teaspoon sugar
½ cup lightly roasted cashew nuts

1. Heat the oil in a pan and fry the onion slices over moderate heat until golden brown, about 5 minutes. Add the gingerroot, garlic, chili flakes, salt and cuminseed. Stir-fry for 2 minutes.

2. Add the chicken and brown the pieces for 5 minutes. Add the water and cook, covered, until the chicken is almost tender, about 25 minutes.

3. Add the tomato paste, sugar and cashew nuts and cook for 10 minutes more. The chicken should be tender and the sauce thickened.

Serve warm with French fried potatoes.

Serves 6

Murghi Maivalahan
Baked Chicken Shreds

Maivalahan translates from the Gujerati language as "my darling."

1/4 cup corn or peanut oil
2 teaspoons ground fresh
  gingerroot
2 teaspoons ground garlic
1 teaspoon dried hot red chili
  flakes
1 chicken, 3 pounds, cut into
  serving pieces, loose skin and fat
  discarded

1 cup onion slices, ground to a
  paste
1/2 teaspoon salt
1 1/2 cups water
1 tablespoon raisins
1/2 cup Crispy Onions (see Index)
1/2 cup dairy sour cream
4 whole eggs

1. Heat the oil in a pan and stir-fry the gingerroot, garlic and chili flakes for 2 minutes. Add the chicken and brown for 5 minutes. Add the onion paste and salt and fry for 2 minutes.

2. Add the water, mix well, cover the pan, and cook until the chicken is tender and the sauce thickened, about 30 minutes.

3. Cool the chicken and reserve the sauce. Shred the meat into long threads. Discard the fat and bones. Mix the shreds with the reserved spice sauce.

4. Put half of the chicken and sauce in a baking dish about 9 inches round. Sprinkle over all with 1/2 tablespoon raisins and 1/4 cup of the crispy onion. Pour all the sour cream over this layer. Repeat with another layer of chicken, raisins and onion. Break the eggs carefully into 4 depressions made in the surface of the chicken. Bake in a 350°F oven for 15 minutes so that the eggs just set.

Serve warm.

Serves 4 to 6

Variation: Instead of placing the whole eggs on the surface of the chicken, another method is to beat the eggs into a froth and pour it over the chicken. Then bake for 15 minutes.

Keemo Papeto
Beef Mince and Potatoes

3 tablespoons corn or peanut oil
1 medium-size onion, chopped fine
  (1/2 cup)
1 teaspoon ground garlic
1 teaspoon ground fresh
  gingerroot
1 teaspoon dried hot red chili
  flakes
1/2 teaspoon ground turmeric

2 tablespoons tomato paste
1/2 teaspoon salt
1 teaspoon ground cuminseed
1 pound ground beef
1/2 pound potatoes, peeled and cut
  into julienne (2 cups)
1/2 cup fresh or frozen green peas
1/2 cup water

1. Heat the oil and fry the onion over moderate heat for 3 minutes, or until light brown. Add the garlic, gingerroot, chili flakes and turmeric. Stir-fry for 1 minute. Add the tomato paste, salt, cuminseed and beef, and stir-fry for 2 minutes.

2. Add the potatoes, green peas and water and cook, covered, for 10 minutes to reduce the sauce and tenderize the ingredients.

   Serve warm with rice and *dal*.

Serves 4

Sali Boti
Kabob on a Stick

1 pound boneless lamb, cut into
  1-inch cubes
1/4 teaspoon ground turmeric
1/4 teaspoon freshly ground black
  pepper
1 teaspoon ground fresh
  gingerroot
1 teaspoon ground garlic

1 teaspoon salt
1 1/2 cups water
1 pound potatoes, 4 medium-size,
  unpeeled
1 medium-size onion
2 eggs, beaten
1/2 cup bread crumbs
oil for deep-frying

1. Cook the lamb, spices, garlic and salt in the water in a covered pan over moderate heat until the lamb is tender but firm and the water has nearly evaporated. Remove the lamb and set aside.

2. Cook the whole potatoes until soft but firm. Cool them, peel, and cut into 1-inch cubes.

3. Cut the onion into halves and separate the layers.

4. Assemble the kabobs on a skewer in this order: first slip on a cube of potato; then a cube of lamb and a layer of raw onion; then potato cube, lamb cube, onion; then a third layer, ending with potato.

5. Dip the skewer into the beaten eggs, then roll it in the bread crumbs; shake off the excess. Heat oil in a skillet and brown the kabobs over moderate heat on all sides for about 3 minutes. Drain on paper towels.

Serve warm on the skewer.

Makes 8

Variations: Lamb or chicken liver can be used instead of the boneless lamb. First, marinate the liver with the same flavorings used to cook the lamb for 4 hours. Stir-fry in oil for 2 minutes, then cool. Thread the potato, liver and onion on a skewer as for the lamb. Dip into eggs and crumbs and deep-fry.

Cubes of uncooked chicken may also be used. Marinate in the flavorings for 4 hours. Stir-fry in oil for 2 minutes and assemble as for the lamb.

Bheeda Ma Gos
Lamb and Lady's-Fingers

Lady's-fingers is the common name for okra in Calcutta, or in any part of India for that matter.

The green papaya is used in India because it is a meat tenderizer; it is used for the local beef and mutton which are usually rather tough. For your cooking, the use of the papaya is optional.

½ cup corn or peanut oil
1½ cups thin-sliced onions
1 teaspoon ground fresh gingerroot
1 teaspoon ground garlic
1 to 2 teaspoons dried hot red chili flakes, or to taste
3 bay leaves
1 teaspoon salt, or to taste

1 pound boneless lamb, cut into 1-inch cubes
½ cup tomato purée
¼ cup grated green papaya (optional)
1 cup water
1 pound fresh okra, cut into 1-inch pieces

1. Heat the oil in a wok or skillet and add the onions to prepare onion crisps. Fry over moderately low heat for about 10 minutes, or until the onions turn light brown. Remove onions from the oil and set aside. Remove all the oil and reserve it.

2. Place the onions in a clean pan. Add the gingerroot, garlic, chili flakes, bay leaves and salt. Over moderate heat stir-fry the mixture for 3 minutes. The onions will provide the oil needed.

3. Add the lamb and stir-fry for 2 minutes. Add the tomato, the papaya if used, and the water. Cook, covered, for about 30 minutes to tenderize the lamb.

4. In a wok or skillet, heat 2 tablespoons of the reserved oil and stir-fry the okra for 5 minutes. Add okra to the lamb stew and cook the mixture over moderately low heat for 15 minutes more.

Serve warm. Serve with bread, chapatis, salads and chutneys. Rice is not usually served with this dish.

Serves 6

Note: If you like to have a natural tenderizer on hand, the papaya is a good choice. Grate it and dry it in the sun or oven and store the powder in a jar with a tight cover.

Jardalu Ma Gos
Lamb with Apricots

1/4 cup corn or peanut oil
1 cup sliced onions
1 teaspoon ground fresh gingerroot
1 teaspoon ground garlic
1 teaspoon ground fresh hot red chili
2 pounds boneless lamb, cut into 1-inch cubes

1 cup fine-chopped onions
1 teaspoon salt, or to taste
1 cinnamon stick, 3 inches, broken into halves
1 cup water
1/2 pound dried apricots, soaked in 1 cup water for 4 hours
2 to 3 cups French fried potatoes

1. Heat the oil in a pan and crisp-fry the sliced onions over moderate heat for about 10 minutes. Remove all the oil except 1 tablespoon. Leave the onions in the pan.

2. Add the gingerroot, garlic and chili and brown them over moderate heat for 2 minutes. Add the lamb, chopped onions, salt and cinnamon stick and stir-fry for 3 minutes.

3. Add the water and cover the pan. Cook for about 45 minutes, or until the lamb is almost tender.

4. Add the apricots and soaking liquid and cook over moderately low heat for 15 minutes.

5. Add the French fries. Shake the pan back and forth several times but do not stir.

Serve warm.

Serves 6 to 8

Khato Mitho Keemo
Sweet-Sour Minced Lamb

3 tablespoons corn or peanut oil
1/2 cup fine-chopped onion
1 teaspoon ground fresh
  gingerroot
1 teaspoon ground garlic
1 teaspoon dried hot red chili
  flakes
1/2 teaspoon ground turmeric

1/4 cup tomato paste
1 teaspoon salt, or to taste
1 teaspoon ground cuminseed
1 pound boneless lamb, ground
3/4 cup water
1 teaspoon sugar
1 tablespoon cider vinegar
1/2 cup fresh or frozen peas

1. Heat the oil in a saucepan or skillet and fry the onion over moderate heat until light brown. Remove all but 1 tablespoon oil.

2. Add the gingerroot, garlic, chili, turmeric, tomato paste, salt and cuminseed. Stir-fry for 1 minute. Add the lamb and stir-fry until the pink color disappears, about 2 minutes.

3. Add the water and cook for 5 minutes. Add the sugar, vinegar and peas and stir-fry for 5 minutes more.

Serve warm with rice and *dal.*

Serves 4 to 6

Note: One cup of uncooked julienne potato straws may be added instead of the peas. The potatoes are added at the same time as the sugar and vinegar and cooked for 5 minutes, or until tender.

Gravy Ma Cutlace
Lamb Cutlets with Tomato Gravy

GRAVY

2 pounds ripe tomatoes, chopped
1/4 cup chopped onion
1/2 teaspoon ground fresh
  gingerroot
1/2 teaspoon ground garlic
1 teaspoon salt

2 whole cloves
1 cinnamon stick, 1 inch
1 tablespoon butter
1/2 teaspoon flour
1 tablespoon vinegar
1 tablespoon brown sugar

GROUND LAMB CUTLETS

2 pounds boneless lamb, ground
1 teaspoon ground fresh
  gingerroot
1 teaspoon ground garlic
1/2 teaspoon salt, or to taste
1/2 teaspoon minced fresh hot
  green chili
1/4 teaspoon ground turmeric

1 teaspoon ground coriander
1 teaspoon ground cuminseed
1 scallion, green part only, sliced
  thin
1/4 cup chopped fresh coriander
2 eggs, beaten
1 cup bread crumbs

1/2 cup corn or peanut oil

1. Cook the tomatoes, onion, gingerroot, garlic, salt, cloves and cinnamon stick together in a covered pan over moderately low heat for 15 minutes to make a thick gravy.

2. Heat the butter in a skillet and stir in the flour over moderate heat. Add this to the tomato gravy and stir well. Add the vinegar and brown sugar and simmer over moderately low heat for 5 minutes. Set aside.

3. Mix the cutlet ingredients together except for the bread crumbs and oil. Shape oval cutlets that are about 1/4 inch thick and 3 inches long. Cover with bread crumbs. Prepare all the meat this way.

4. Heat the oil in a skillet and over moderate heat brown the cutlets on both sides for 3 or 4 minutes. Drain briefly on paper towels.

Serve warm with the tomato gravy.

Serves 6

Beja Na Cutlace
Brain Cutlets

1 pound lamb brains, 4
1 cup water
1/2 teaspoon ground fresh
   gingerroot
1/2 teaspoon ground garlic
1 tablespoon minced fresh
   coriander

1/2 teaspoon salt
1/2 teaspoon minced fresh hot
   green chili
1/4 cup minced onion
1 cup bread crumbs
1 egg, beaten
1/4 cup corn or peanut oil

1. Pull off the loose membranes from the brains. Poach the brains in plain water in a covered pan for 5 minutes. Drain.

2. Chop the brains into coarse pieces. Add the gingerroot, garlic, fresh coriander, salt, chili and onion. Mix well. Prepare oval cutlets 3 inches long and 1/2 inch thick. Dip the cutlets into the egg, then press into the bread crumbs.

3. Heat the oil in a skillet and brown the cutlets over moderate heat for 2 minutes on each side. Drain on paper towels.

Serve warm.

Makes 6 cutlets

Masala Ni Kalegi
Liver and Spice

Traditionally, this is prepared with lamb liver but chicken livers are more easily available in our supermarkets. Chicken gizzards, trimmed of the tough lining, could be used also. The cooking time should then be extended and 1/2 cup more water should be added.

3 tablespoons corn or peanut oil
2 medium-size onions, sliced thin
  (1 cup)
1 tablespoon ground fresh
  gingerroot
1 tablespoon ground garlic
1 teaspoon ground cuminseed
1 teaspoon ground coriander
1/2 teaspoon ground turmeric
1 to 2 teaspoons dried hot red
  chili flakes

3 bay leaves
1 teaspoon salt, or to taste
1/2 cup water
1 pound chicken or lamb liver, cut
  into 1-inch pieces
2 tablespoons cider vinegar
1 teaspoon sugar
1 tablespoon chopped fresh
  coriander

1. Heat the oil in a saucepan or large skillet and brown the onions over moderate heat for 3 minutes. Add the gingerroot, garlic, cuminseed, coriander, turmeric, chili flakes, bay leaves and salt. Stir-fry for 2 minutes, adding 1 tablespoon water to lubricate the mixture.

2. Add the liver pieces and stir-fry for 2 minutes. Add the balance of the water. Cook until the water has evaporated. Add the vinegar and sugar and stir-fry for 2 minutes. This is a dry fry.

Serve warm, garnished with the coriander, as an appetizer or a main dish.

Serves 6

Masoor Ma Jeeb
Tongue and Lentils

3 lamb tongues, about 1 pound
3 cups water
1 cup masoor dal, soaked in
   water for 2 hours and drained
1 cup chopped scallions
1/2 cup chopped ripe tomato, or 3
   tablespoons tomato paste
1 teaspoon ground garlic
1 teaspoon ground fresh
   gingerroot
1/2 teaspoon ground turmeric
1 teaspoon ground cuminseed
1 teaspoon ground coriander
1/4 cup Crispy Onions (see Index)
1 teaspoon salt, or to taste
1 fresh hot green chili (optional)
2 tablespoons corn or peanut oil

1. Simmer the tongues in the water for about 30 minutes. Remove the tongues but reserve the water. Pull off the skin and cut the tongues into 1/2-inch-thick slices.

2. Return the tongues to the pan and reserved water with all the other ingredients. Bring to a boil and cook, covered, over moderate to low heat until the *dal* and tongues are soft, about 1 hour. Stir the mixture together now and then.

Serve warm with Kachumbar (salad) and Gor Amli Ni Kachumbar (tamarind chutney) and breads.

Serves 6

Patra Ni Machi

Fish in Banana Leaves

Although the Parsis use banana leaves, most of us will have to use aluminum foil. I saw a simple home version of the steaming process in a Parsi home. A coarsely woven basket was placed over a pot of boiling water. The fish packets were put in and the basket covered with a kitchen cloth. It steamed very efficiently with this makeshift equipment.

The *patra* is now served as a first course or as an appetizer, but originally it was prepared only for Parsi weddings or other festivities.

COCONUT CHUTNEY

1 coconut, with the hard brown shell
1 cup loosely packed fresh coriander leaves
4 small hot green chilies, seeds and stems removed

1 tablespoon sugar
1/2 teaspoon salt
2 tablespoons lemon juice

1 pound fillets of flounder, sole, scrod or red snapper

1. Open the coconut and discard its water. Remove the meat and trim off the brown skin. Grate the meat, all of it, in a processor or by hand.

2. Add the coriander, chilies, sugar, salt and lemon juice. Grind all together into a coarse paste. This is the "chutney" and as such may be used as a straightforward table condiment with any Parsi dish as well as in the following recipes.

3. Cut the fish into 8 more or less equal pieces about 3 inches square. Put 1 heaping tablespoon of the chutney over a piece of fish to cover it. Cut 16 strips of aluminum foil 2 inches wide and 8 inches long. For each piece of fish, make a cross with 2 strips of the foil, put the fish and chutney in the center and fold over one strip and then the other. Or use rectangles of the foil to make bundles. Tie with a string.

4. Steam the bundles in a Chinese-style steamer for 30 minutes.

Unwrap bundles and serve warm.

Serves 4 to 6

Variations:

FRIED STUFFED FISH

1 pound whole sea bass, red snapper or similar fish
¹/₂ cup Coconut Chutney (see basic recipe)

3 tablespoons corn or peanut oil

1. Make 2 deep diagonal slashes 2 inches apart on each side of the fish. Stuff the slashes as deep as you can with 1 heaping teaspoon of the chutney. Stuff the fish cavity with the balance.

2. Heat the oil in a skillet and over moderate heat fry the fish on each side until cooked through, about 6 minutes.

Drain briefly on paper towels and serve warm.

Serves 4

CRUMB-FRIED FISH

1 pound fillets of flounder, sole or scrod
1 cup Coconut Chutney (see basic recipe)

1 cup toasted bread crumbs
2 eggs, beaten
¹/₂ cup corn or peanut oil

1. Cut the fish into 8 pieces, about 3 inches square. Cover one side of a piece with 1 heaping tablespoon of the chutney and press it down firmly. Dip the fish carefully into the crumbs (this will hold in the chutney) and then into the beaten eggs. Sprinkle both sides with remaining crumbs.

2. Heat the oil in a skillet and over moderate heat fry the fish for 2 or 3 minutes on each side, or until brown and crisp. Drain briefly on paper towels.

Serve warm as an appetizer or as a first course.

Serves 4

CHUTNEY CHEESE FRITTER

8 slices of mozzarella cheese,
* about 3 x 2 inches*
1 cup Coconut Chutney (see basic
* recipe)*

2 eggs, beaten
1 cup toasted bread crumbs
¹/₂ cup corn or peanut oil

1. Cover one side of a slice of cheese with 1 heaping tablespoon of the chutney. Press it down all over the surface. Dip the cheese into the crumbs, then into the beaten egg, then again into the crumbs.

2. Heat the oil in a wok or skillet and over moderate heat fry the cheese for 2 minutes on each side, or until crisp brown. Drain on paper towels.

Serves 4

Patio
Fish Curry

Pomfret is the fish used in this dish by the Parsis, but large prawns or shrimps may also be used. My own preference would be fillet of flounder, sole, scrod or similar fish. Hard-cooked eggs, peeled and whole, are also prepared with the same sauce as the *patio*. Use 10 eggs with this recipe.

4 tablespoons corn or peanut oil
1 tablespoon besan (*chick-pea flour*)
1 cup onion slices, crushed to a paste
6 garlic cloves, crushed to a paste
1 teaspoon ground cuminseed
1 cup grated coconut, ground to a paste

2 cups water
2 teaspoons dried hot red chili flakes
1 teaspoon salt, or to taste
1 cup chopped peeled tomatoes, processed to a purée
2 pounds fish fillets, cut into 3-inch pieces, or the whole fish cut into 2-inch-wide slices

1. Heat the oil in a pan and fry the *besan* over moderate heat for 2 minutes. Add the onion slices, garlic and cuminseed and stir-fry for 2 minutes.

2. Add the coconut paste and stir-fry for 1 minute. Add ½ cup of the water to prevent sticking. Stir well as you add the chili flakes, salt, tomato purée and the balance of the water, 1½ cups. Cook for 10 minutes, stirring frequently. Notice that the oils will rise to the top.

3. Add the fish slices, cover the pan, and simmer until the fish is cooked, from 10 to 15 minutes.

Serve warm with Kitchree Patio (see Index).

Serves 6

Sahs

Fish in Egg Sauce

1/4 cup corn or peanut oil
2 cups thin-sliced onions
2 teaspoons ground fresh
  gingerroot
2 teaspoons ground garlic
1 teaspoon ground turmeric
2 teaspoons dried hot red chili
  flakes
2 teaspoons ground cuminseed
2 cups water

2 cups fine-chopped tomatoes
1 teaspoon salt
2 teaspoons sugar
1 pound fillets of flounder, scrod
  or sole, cut into 3-inch strips
  about 1/4 inch thick
1 tablespoon chopped fresh
  coriander
3 eggs, beaten
3 tablespoons cider vinegar

1. Heat the oil in a pan and brown the onions over moderate heat for 3 minutes. Add the gingerroot, garlic, turmeric, chili flakes and cuminseed. Stir-fry over moderately low heat for 3 minutes. Add 1/2 cup of the water and stir for another minute.

2. Add the tomatoes, salt and sugar and simmer the mixture for 10 minutes.

3. Add the balance of the water, 1 1/2 cups, and bring to a boil. Add the fish and the coriander. Simmer the mixture over low heat for 10 minutes more.

4. Beat the eggs and vinegar together and add to the fish. Remove the pan from heat and tilt it back and forth several times to incorporate the vinegar into the sauce, which will thicken.

Serve immediately with Kitchree (see Index).

Serves 6

Variations: The *sahs* can be prepared with breast of chicken. Cook the chicken strips in place of the fish for 25 minutes. Then add the egg and vinegar mixture.

Cubes of lamb may also be used, but these will have to be cooked for 1 hour in order to be tender. Continue all the steps as for the fish.

Large prawns or shrimps, peeled and deveined, are an excellent substitute for the fish. The same steps and timing will serve.

Masala Ni Tarelli Machi
Spiced Fried Fish

Any sort of fillet of fish will work here, but my own preference would be flounder, scrod, sea bass or even baby shark.

1 pound fillets of fish, cut into 3-
  inch pieces
1 tablespoon ground garlic
1/2 teaspoon ground cuminseed
2 teaspoons ground fresh hot
  green chili

1/4 teaspoon ground turmeric
1 teaspoon salt
2 teaspoons lemon or lime juice
1 egg, beaten
1/4 cup corn or peanut oil

1. Marinate the fish slices in everything except the oil for 3 to 4 hours.

2. Heat the oil in a skillet and fry the fish over moderate heat for about 4 minutes. The fish should be light brown and crisp outside but still moist inside. Drain on paper towels.

Serve warm.

Serves 4

Prawn Patio
Sweet-and-Sour Prawns

This prawn dish is traditionally served at weddings, birthdays and other auspicious occasions.

The original recipe that I was taught in Calcutta called for 1 cup of oil, which seemed excessive for our tastes. It was explained that in order to produce the proper color and texture of the *patio*, the onions and other seasonings must be fried with sufficient oil. Frying the onions with so much oil appeared to produce a sort of "crumb" look as the onions were reduced to minute pellets or crumbs in the oil and a characteristic reddish color appeared just before the prawns and water were added. However, it seems to me much healthier and just as satisfactory to use the smaller amount of oil.

4 tablespoons corn or peanut oil
1 cup onion slices, ground to a paste
2 teaspoons ground cuminseed
2 teaspoons ground garlic
2 to 3 teaspoons dried hot red chili flakes
½ teaspoon ground turmeric
1 teaspoon salt, or to taste
2 pounds prawns, peeled and deveined
½ cup water
3 tablespoons cider vinegar
1 tablespoon sugar, or a bit less to taste

1. Heat the oil in a skillet or saucepan and fry the onion paste over moderate heat until light brown. Add the cuminseed, garlic, chili flakes, turmeric and salt. Stir-fry for 5 minutes as a red color develops.

2. Add the prawns and water and cook over moderately low heat for 5 minutes. Add the vinegar and sugar and mix well. Cook for 5 minutes more to thicken the sauce somewhat.

Serve warm with white rice and plain *dal.*

Serves 6

Prawn Vindaloo
Hot Prawns

A *vindaloo* is a hot spicy dish, with very little sauce, usually served with *dal* and white rice to lessen the intensity of the spice flavorings. Although it should be hot, it should not be strong enough to anesthetize the taste buds.

1 tablespoon sliced garlic
1 tablespoon sliced fresh hot red chili
2 teaspoons ground cuminseed
1 teaspoon mustard seeds
1 teaspoon black peppercorns
1 teaspoon ground turmeric
1/4 cup cider vinegar

1/4 cup corn oil
1 cup onion slices, ground to a paste
2 pounds prawns or large shrimps, peeled and deveined
1/2 cup water
1 teaspoon salt

1. Grind the garlic, chili, cuminseed, mustard seeds, peppercorns and turmeric together in a processor with 2 tablespoons of the vinegar to act as a lubricant.

2. Heat the oil in a pan and fry the onion paste over moderately low heat until light brown. Add the ground spices and continue to fry the mixture until it turns reddish, with a "crumbled" look.

3. Add the prawns and cook, stirring frequently, for 10 minutes. Add the balance of the vinegar, the water and salt and continue to simmer, uncovered, for 5 minutes more. There will be very little sauce.

Serve warm.

Serves 6

Variation: The prawn *vindaloo* can be prepared as a proper pickle, which means that it is a bottled (or refrigerated) condiment used now and then with other foods as an adjunct to the meat or fish dishes being served. Should you wish to prepare this as a pickle, follow the instructions, but omit the onions and the water and cook the prawns separately in 2 tablespoons of oil before adding them to the mixture.

Kitchree
Rice and Lentils

6 tablespoons butter or margarine
1 cup raw rice, rinsed and drained well
3/4 cup lentils (masoor dal), rinsed and drained
1 teaspoon salt
4 bay leaves
1 teaspoon garam masala
1 teaspoon ground turmeric
3 cups chicken broth or water
1/4 cup Crispy Onions (see Index)

1. Melt the butter in a pan and add the rice and lentils. Stir-fry over moderate heat for 2 minutes. Add the salt, bay leaves, *garam masala* and turmeric, and stir well for 2 minutes.

2. Add the broth and bring to a boil. Turn heat to low and simmer, covered, for 15 minutes, or until rice and lentils are dry and soft.

3. Remove from the heat and let stand covered for 10 minutes more.

Serve warm, sprinkled with the crispy onions.

Serves 6

Kitchree Patio
Lentil and Vegetable Rice

The *kitchree* is usually served with Patio, Fish Curry (see Index). However, it stands on its own merits and may be served with any type of Parsi curry.

2 cups raw rice, well rinsed
1/4 cup red lentils, rinsed
1/4 cup Crispy Onions (see Index)
1/2 teaspoon ground turmeric
1 teaspoon ground coriander
1 teaspoon salt
1 tablespoon corn or peanut oil
3 whole cloves
3 bay leaves
1/2 teaspoon whole cuminseeds, lightly toasted in a dry skillet
1/2 cup 1/2-inch potato cubes
1/4 cup thin-sliced green beans
1/2 cup thin-sliced okra, fried in 1 teaspoon oil for 2 minutes
3 1/2 cups water

1. Put everything together in a pan. Bring to a boil over moderate heat, then reduce to low heat, cover the pan, and cook for about 15 minutes. Stir once or twice during this time. Should the rice appear too dry, add 1 or 2 tablespoons water. Cook until soft.

2. Remove pan from the heat and keep it covered for another 15 minutes before serving.

Serve warm.

Serves 6

Dahi Ni Kadhi
Yogurt Curry

2 cups plain yogurt
1/2 cup water
1 tablespoon corn or peanut oil
1/4 teaspoon whole black mustard
  seeds
1 tablespoon besan (chick-pea
  flour)
1/2 teaspoon minced fresh
  gingerroot

1/2 teaspoon minced garlic
1/8 teaspoon ground turmeric
1/4 teaspoon ground cuminseed
1/4 teaspoon salt
1 teaspoon chopped fresh
  coriander (optional)

1. Beat the yogurt and water together. Set aside.

2. Heat the oil in a pan and over moderate heat fry the mustard seeds until they pop open. Add the *besan* and stir-fry for 1 minute.

3. Add the gingerroot, garlic, turmeric, cuminseed and salt and stir-fry for 2 minutes. Remove pan from the heat for 3 minutes.

4. Add the yogurt/water, mix well, and simmer over low heat for 3 minutes. Do not boil since this may curdle the curry.

Sprinkle with coriander and serve warm to spoon over rice or vegetables.

Serves 4 to 6

Tarkari Nu Bafat
Vegetable Stew

There are several old cookbooks writen in Gujerati, the language of the Parsis. Some of the books are of a previous century and have never been completely translated to reveal the origins of the cooking. The *tarkari* is one of these old recipes.

2 tablespoons corn or peanut oil
1 cup chopped onions
1/2 teaspoon ground gingerroot
1/2 teaspoon ground garlic
1/2 teaspoon ground turmeric
1 teaspoon dried hot red chili
  flakes
2 teaspoons ground coriander
1 teaspoon ground cuminseed
1 teaspoon salt
1/2 cup water

6 small pickling onions
2 small potatoes, cut into 1-inch
  cubes
12 green beans, cut into 2-inch
  pieces
1 cup Rich Coconut Milk (see
  Index)
1 medium-size ripe tomato, cut
  into 1/2-inch cubes (1 cup)
1 cup green peas, fresh or frozen

1. Heat the oil in a pan and fry the onions until brown, about 5 minutes. Add the gingerroot, garlic, turmeric, chili flakes, coriander, cuminseed and salt. Stir-fry for 2 minutes.

2. Add the water, pickling onions, potatoes and green beans. Cook over moderate heat until the water evaporates, about 15 minutes.

3. Add the coconut milk, tomato and peas and cook over moderately low heat for 10 minutes, basting frequently so that the coconut milk does not separate.

Serve warm.

Serves 6

Ravayu (Vegnu)
Stuffed Eggplant

This recipe may be prepared one day in advance and refrigerated; warm it briefly before serving.

1 pound small eggplants, 5 or 6
3/4 cup fine-chopped onions
1/4 cup fine-chopped ripe tomato
1/2 teaspoon salt, or to taste
1/4 cup grated fresh coconut
   (optional)
1 teaspoon ground turmeric
2 tablespoons chopped fresh
   coriander

1 teaspoon ground coriander
1/2 teaspoon ground cuminseed
1/2 cup coarse-chopped shrimps
3 tablespoons corn or peanut oil
2 teaspoons sugar, dissolved in 2
   tablespoons cider vinegar

1. Slice through each eggplant from the round end to within 1 inch of the stem. Make a quarter turn and slice again to divide eggplant into 4 parts held together at stem ends. You can now scoop out about a quarter of the pulp from the eggplant sections, leaving a hollow for the stuffing.

2. Mix together the onions, tomato, salt, coconut, turmeric, fresh and ground coriander, cuminseed and shrimps. Stuff each eggplant with some of the mixture and press it back together.

3. Put the oil in a baking dish or skillet large enough to hold the eggplants. Place them horizontally in the oil. Cover the dish. Bake in a 350°F. oven for 45 minutes, or until vegetables are soft. Or cook them on top of the stove for 30 minutes.

4. At the end of the baking or cooking, sprinkle the sugar/vinegar mixture over all and cook for 10 minutes more.

Serve warm.

Serves 4

Aloo Pur Anda

Potatoes and Eggs, Peasant Style

1/4 cup corn or peanut oil
2 medium-size onions, sliced thin
(1 cup)
1 tablespoon ground fresh
gingerroot
1 tablespoon ground garlic
1 tablespoon minced fresh hot
green chili

1 teaspoon salt, or to taste
2 pounds potatoes, peeled and cut
into 1-inch squares 1/4 inch
thick
2 tablespoons chopped fresh
coriander
6 whole eggs

1. Heat the oil in a skillet and lightly brown the onions over moderate heat for 3 minutes. Add the gingerroot, garlic, chili and salt, and stir-fry for 2 minutes.

2. Add the potato squares and stir-fry for 1 minute. Cover the pan and cook the mixture over moderately low heat for 10 minutes, or until the potatoes are soft. Sprinkle with the coriander.

3. Pour the mixture into a well-greased 9-inch baking dish and make 6 round indentations spaced apart. Carefully break an egg into each hollow. Bake in a 350°F oven for 15 minutes to set the eggs.

Serve warm as a first course.

Serves 6

Note: This is a classic Parsi dish using vegetables, with an egg on top. Another method is to prepare the potatoes in a skillet, as before, add the eggs, cover the pan and continue to cook on top of the stove for 10 minutes more to set the eggs.

Tarkari Ni Akoori
Scrambled Vegetables and Eggs

Akoori, a Gujerati word, is translated as, "a mixture." This recipe is an old one not usually remembered in recent years but nevertheless traditional and delicious. This is another example of the Parsi love affair with eggs. Vegetarians will certainly like this as a main dish.

3 tablespoons corn or peanut oil
1 cup coarse-chopped onions
¹/₂ teaspoon ground fresh gingerroot
¹/₂ teaspoon ground garlic
¹/₄ teaspoon freshly ground black pepper
¹/₂ teaspoon ground turmeric
1 teaspoon salt, or to taste
1 teaspoon dried hot red chili flakes, soaked in 1 tablespoon water

1 small ripe tomato, chopped
2 tablespoons freshly grated coconut (optional)
1 cup green peas, fresh or frozen
1 cup cooked ¹/₄-inch potato cubes
1 cup okra slices, stir-fried in 1 tablespoon oil for 3 minutes
¹/₂ cup loosely packed chopped fresh coriander leaves
8 eggs, beaten

1. Heat the oil in a pan and brown the onions over moderate heat for 2 minutes. Add the gingerroot, garlic, black pepper, turmeric, salt, chili flakes, tomato and coconut. Stir-fry the mixture for 3 minutes.

2. Add the peas, potato cubes and okra and mix well. Remove pan from the heat and cool the mixture slightly for 2 minutes.

3. Mix the coriander and eggs together. Put the stew over moderate heat again and stir-fry for 2 minutes. Pour in the eggs and scramble everything together until the eggs have set and dried. Do not overcook.

Serve warm as a main or side dish.

Serves 6

Pora
Parsi Omelet

4 eggs, beaten
1/4 cup chopped onion
2 tablespoons chopped fresh
  coriander
1 teaspoon chopped fresh hot
  green chili
1/2 teaspoon ground fresh
  gingerroot

1/2 teaspoon ground garlic
1/2 teaspoon ground turmeric
1 teaspoon ground cuminseed
1/2 teaspoon salt, or to taste
2 tablespoons corn or peanut oil

1. Mix all the ingredients together except the oil.

2. Heat the oil in a skillet and over moderate heat prepare individual omelets with about 1/4 cup of the egg mixture for each. Brown the omelets lightly on each side.

Serve warm as a breakfast dish. Also, it makes a very good sandwich with fresh bread, for picnics or anytime.

Serves 4

Bheeda Per Eda
Eggs on Lady's-Fingers

This dish may also be baked in a 350°F. oven for 15 minutes, rather than steamed. It may be prepared for 6 or 8 persons, with the same amount of flavoring and vegetables but allowing 1 egg per person. It is an admirable starter for a dinner or a fine luncheon dish by itself.

3 tablespoons corn or peanut oil
1 pound okra, cut into 1/4-inch-
  wide slices
1 cup thin-sliced onions

1/2 teaspoon ground turmeric
1/2 teaspoon hot red chili flakes
1 teaspoon salt, or to taste
4 whole eggs

1. Heat the oil in a skillet and fry the okra and onions together over moderate heat until they are soft, about 10 minutes.

2. Add the turmeric, chili flakes and salt, and stir-fry for 1 minute. Pour the mixture into a baking dish big enough so that the vegetables will be about 1 inch deep. Make 4 depressions in the mixture and drop 1 egg carefully into each depression.

3. Steam the dish over hot water in a Chinese-style steamer for 10 minutes to set the eggs.

Serve warm by scooping out a portion of the okra with 1 egg per person.

Serves 4

Akoori
Spiced Scrambled Eggs

This is a breakfast or lunch preparation that is quick and easy, yet rather exotic.

2 tablespoons corn or peanut oil
1/2 cup chopped onion
1 teaspoon ground fresh gingerroot
1 teaspoon ground garlic
1/2 teaspoon salt, or to taste

1/4 cup chopped ripe tomato
1/2 teaspoon ground turmeric
3 tablespoons chopped fresh coriander
4 eggs, beaten

1. Heat the oil in a skillet and lightly brown the onion over moderate heat. Add the gingerroot, garlic and salt and stir-fry for 2 minutes.

2. Add the tomato and continue to stir-fry for 1 minute. Lastly, add the turmeric, coriander and eggs. Scramble the mixture according to your preference from creamy soft to well done.

Serve warm.

Serves 4

Ravo

Cream of Wheat Sweet Dessert

1/4 pound (8 tablespoons) butter
  or margarine
2 cups semolina (soojee), or
  Cream of Wheat
2 cups milk
1/2 cup sugar
2 eggs, well beaten

1 teaspoon Three-Spice Mix (see
  Index)
1 tablespoon raisins
20 almonds, blanched, cut into
  1/4-inch pieces and lightly
  browned in oil

1. Melt the butter in a pan over moderately low heat. Add the semolina and toast it very lightly for about 3 minutes, stirring continuously. Do not discolor by overtoasting.

2. Add the milk as you continue to stir. Add the sugar and stir until the mixture is smooth. Remove the pan from the heat for 2 minutes to cool slightly.

3. Add the eggs and stir them quickly into the mixture. Return the pan to low heat, cover, and cook the *ravo* for 10 minutes more. Let it stand covered off the heat for 10 minutes longer.

4. Turn out in a serving dish and sprinkle with the spice mix, raisins and almonds.

Serve warm.

Serves 6 to 8

Note: The *ravo* may be eaten at room temperature but is better when still warm. You may also warm the *ravo* briefly in the oven prior to serving.

Malido
Whole-Wheat Butter Halwa

The *malido* is a rich, crumbly dessert prepared for special occasions such as birthdays, festivals or any other joyous time.

¹/₄ pound (8 tablespoons) butter or margarine
20 almonds, blanched and coarse-chopped
2 tablespoons raisins
3 cups whole-wheat flour
2 cups sugar
2 cups water
6 eggs, beaten until creamy
1 teaspoon caraway seeds
2 teaspoons Three-Spice Mix (see Index)
3 tablespoons maraschino cherries, chopped

1. Heat 2 teaspoons butter in a skillet and brown the almonds and raisins lightly for 2 minutes. Set aside as a garnish.

2. Melt the rest of the butter in a pan, add the flour, and stir continuously over moderately low heat to toast lightly for 2 minutes. Set aside.

3. Dissolve the sugar in the water in a saucepan and bring to a boil over moderately low heat. Simmer for 5 minutes to thicken the syrup. Pour it into the flour mixture and stir until smooth. Cool for a minute.

4. Add the beaten eggs. Mix well together.

5. Put the mixture (*halwa*) over moderately low heat and stir continuously for several minutes until it comes away from the sides of the pan. Stir in the caraway seeds and spice mix. Cover the pan and let the *halwa* cook over *very low* heat for 10 minutes.

6. Turn the *halwa* out into a serving dish and sprinkle with the almonds, raisins and cherries.

Serve warm.

Serves 8

Bhakras
Parsi Cookies

The *bhakra* is actually a cookie doughnut with a soft center. The original recipe, the old-time method, is to use "snake juice," which is a country concoction of palm toddy, a lightly fermented drink from the palm tree. Since this is not available these days, baking powder and yogurt are substituted to provide a similar result.

3 eggs, beaten
1 cup sugar
3 tablespoons butter, melted
1 cup plain yogurt
3 cups flour
1 teaspoon Three-Spice Mix
(recipe follows)

1 teaspoon caraway seeds
1/8 teaspoon salt
1/2 teaspoon baking powder
12 almonds, blanched and coarse-
chopped
1 cup corn or peanut oil (or
more) for deep-frying

1. Mix the eggs and sugar together. Add the butter, yogurt, flour, spice mix, caraway seeds, salt, baking powder and chopped almonds. Mix everything into a firm dough. Cover the dough, or put it into a plastic bag, and rest it, unrefrigerated, overnight.

2. Dust a board with flour. Roll out the dough to 1/4-inch thickness. With a cookie cutter cut out pancakes 2 1/2 inches in diameter.

3. Heat the oil in a wok or skillet and over moderate heat fry the cookies, turning them over once, until light brown. Drain on paper towels.

Serve as a coffee or tea hour snack.

Makes about 20

Note: Resting the dough overnight and using the yogurt and baking powder mixture both influence the fermentation and leavening and also the flavor.

Elichi-Jaifal No Masalo
Three-Spice Mix

This is a typical Parsi spice mix used principally for cookies and desserts.

1 tablespoon ground cardamom   1½ teaspoons ground mace
1 tablespoon grated nutmeg

Mix everything together and store in an airtight jar.

Nankhatai
Classic Cookies

1 pound butter or margarine, at
   room temperature
1 pound sugar (2 cups)
2 pounds flour (6 cups)

1 teaspoon grated nutmeg
¼ teaspoon salt
2 teaspoons baking powder

1. Cream the butter until smooth. Add the sugar and cream well together.

2. Mix the flour, nutmeg, salt and baking powder together. Add this to the butter mixture. Knead (mix) into a firm dough.

3. Take a large walnut-size piece and shape it into a ball. Flatten the ball into a cookie about ½ inch thick. With the tines of a fork, make 2-inch-long lines on the surface of the cookie for decoration. Continue to shape cookies with remaining dough.

4. Bake in a 350°F. oven for 15 minutes, or until cookies are light tan in color.

Store in a tin with a tight cover.

Makes about 20 cookies

Sev

Vermicelli Sweet

Sev is served on special occasions such as the Navjot (Parsi initiation ceremony) for boys and girls. It is one of the most popular desserts.

Calcutta's New Market has a corner where the vermicelli is sold in 3-foot-high heaps. One heap is of vermicelli that has been browned in a baker's oven; the other heap is the plain or unbaked version. Both are of the thinnest, most fragile, hairlike noodles—a sight to behold.

6 tablespoons butter or margarine
6 ounces maiden's hair vermicelli,
 the very thinnest
1 cup water
5 tablespoons sugar
3 teaspoons rosewater

8 almonds, blanched and sliced
 thin lengthwise
2 tablespoons raisins
2 teaspoons corn or peanut oil
¹/8 teaspoon grated nutmeg

1. Melt the butter in a skillet or saucepan. Add the vermicelli and brown it in the butter over moderately low heat for 2 minutes. Add the water, sugar and rosewater and continue to simmer and stir for 20 minutes to evaporate the liquid.

2. Brown the almonds and raisins in the oil, separately, over moderately low heat for 1 minute. Set aside.

3. Coat a heatproof glass pie plate with butter. Pour in the vermicelli mixture. Sprinkle with the nutmeg and the almonds and raisins. Steam over hot water in a Chinese-style steamer for 15 minutes.

Serve immediately, warm.

Serves 4

Korha No Murambo
White Pumpkin Conserve

This is an all-purpose jam that is served at weddings and other festivities as an accompaniment to the meat, fish and rice dishes. It is a sweet fruit chutney with a light flavor of cardamom.

The conserve may also be eaten for breakfast on toast or as an accompaniment to curries. It is compatible with any type of Indian food.

2 pounds white pumpkin	3 cups sugar
10 cashew nuts	2 cups water
10 almonds, blanched	1 tablespoon lemon or lime juice
20 pistachio nuts	1 teaspoon cardamom seeds
2 teaspoons corn or peanut oil	

1. Peel the pumpkin and remove the seeds. Grate the white pulp and lightly squeeze it in a towel to remove excess liquid.

2. Cut the nuts into coarse pieces and lightly fry them in the oil for 2 minutes. Remove and set aside.

3. Mix the pumpkin, sugar and water together in a pan. Bring to a boil and simmer over moderately low heat for 15 minutes. Add the lemon juice and cardamom seeds.

4. Continue to simmer for about 45 minutes, or until the liquid has evaporated and the pumpkin is a light tan color and has thickened.

Serve cool, garnished with the chopped nuts. The conserve may be refrigerated for 1 or 2 weeks.

Makes 1 quart

Dhan Sak
The Lentil, Lamb, Rice, Kabob and Salad Classic

For a grand finale, I would like to present the Dhan Sak— "the wealth of 7 pulses"—a classic Parsi preparation head and shoulders above the standard Indian preparations. It is the traditional Sunday dinner—served in the middle of the day for health's sake—as well as the preferred menu for special occasions and favored guests. It is considered by some to be a "heavy" meal, but that is probably because it is eaten in such great quantities. The flavorings, on the other hand, though of normal strength for the Parsis, I found dynamic. I would suggest that the measures of the spices given here (traditional amounts) be cut considerably or checked by frequent tastings until an acceptable level of spiciness is reached.

Beer makes a fine accompaniment.

The recipes here serve 8 persons. In a typical family-style way, the table is laden with serving dishes holding the lamb cubes with the spicy lentil/pumpkin purée, the lamb kabobs, the spiced rice, fresh vegetable salad and the onion and coriander chutney. Each dish has its own part to play in bringing out the full flavor of the whole production, and it should be prepared as a complete menu.

It may be prepared in stages, cooking the kabobs the day before and preparing the relish, for instance, as well as cooking the lamb, ready for reheating just before dinner. It is certainly wise to check out the ingredient list and to make up a supply of fresh *sambhar* and mix up equal amounts of the cuminseed, coriander and chili flakes for later use in the purée. Here is the recipe for *sambhar*, which is used in other recipes as well.

Sambhar

1 teaspoon fenugreek powder
1 teaspoon salt
1 teaspoon turmeric
1 teaspoon asafetida

2 teaspoons dried hot red chili
    flakes
2 teaspoons corn or peanut oil
1/4 teaspoon dry mustard

Mix all together and store in a dry, cool place.

Lamb in Lentil and Pumpkin Purée
For Dhan Sak

2 pounds boneless lamb, cut into
1-inch cubes

1 eggplant, ½ pound, cut into 2-
inch cubes

1 cup yellow squash or pumpkin
cubes

½ cup sliced onion

1 pound yellow lentils (dal),
rinsed

¼ cup chopped fresh mint

½ cup loosely packed chopped
fresh coriander

1 tablespoon chopped fresh hot
green chili

2 teaspoons salt, or to taste

1½ teaspoons ground turmeric

6 cups water

SPICE MIX

¼ cup corn or peanut oil

2 tablespoons sambhar *spice
mixture (see preceding page)*

2 tablespoons cuminseed/
coriander/chili flakes, mixed

1 tablespoon ground fresh
gingerroot

1 tablespoon ground garlic

1. Mix everything except the spice mix together in a large pan. Bring to a boil and cook over moderate heat until the meat is tender, about 1 hour. Remove the meat and set aside.

2. Whip the remaining liquid and vegetables into a purée.

3. Heat the oil in a wok or skillet and over moderately low heat stir-fry the spice mix ingredients for about 5 minutes. The mixture will expand to a thick consistency and will be reddish brown.

4. Add spice mixture to the vegetable purée and simmer the mixture over moderately low heat for 10 minutes.

5. Return the lamb to the pan and cook for 5 minutes more.

Serve warm with the Dhan Sak.

Serves 8

Dhan Sak Chawal
Spiced Rice for Dhan Sak

2 cups raw rice, well rinsed
4 cups water
6 cardamom pods
4 bay leaves
6 whole cloves

1 cinnamon stick, 1 inch
2 teaspoons salt, or to taste
3 tablespoons corn or peanut oil
1 teaspoon cuminseeds
3 teaspoons sugar

1. Put the rice, 3½ cups of the water, cardamom, bay leaves, cloves, cinnamon and salt in a pan.

2. Heat the oil in a skillet and brown the cuminseeds over moderately low heat for a moment. Add the sugar to caramelize as the mixture turns dark brown. Add this to the rice pan. Rinse out the skillet with the remaining half cup of water and add to the rice pan. Bring to a boil.

3. Turn the heat down to very low and simmer, covered, until dry, about 15 minutes.

Serve warm with the Dhan Sak.

Serves 8

Dhan Sak Na Kabob
Lamb Kabob for Dhan Sak

½ pound lamb, ground (1 cup)
1 teaspoon ground fresh
   gingerroot
1 teaspoon ground garlic
¼ cup thin-sliced scallions, green
   part only
¼ cup chopped fresh coriander
½ teaspoon salt
½ teaspoon chopped fresh hot
   green chili
¼ teaspoon ground turmeric

1 teaspoon ground coriander
1 teaspoon ground cuminseed
½ teaspoon dried hot red chili
   flakes
1 teaspoon sambhar powder
   (optional, see Index)
2 eggs, beaten
1 cup mashed potatoes
1 cup toasted bread crumbs
1 cup oil or more for deep-frying

1. Mix everything together except the bread crumbs and oil. Prepare balls 1½ inches in diameter. Roll them in the crumbs and set aside.

2. Heat the oil in a wok or skillet and over moderate heat fry the kabobs for 3 to 4 minutes, or until the outer surface is crisp. Drain on paper towels.

   Serve with the Dhan Sak.

Makes 20 kabobs

Variation: The lamb and potato kabobs are the combination traditionally served with the Dhan Sak. However, a most popular variation is also prepared by substituting 1 cup of small shrimps, chopped fine, for the lamb, using the same flavorings as for the lamb.

Note: These kabobs will also serve admirably as appetizers with drinks or any other time.

Kachumbar
Fresh Salad Served with Dhan Sak

1 cup cubes of ripe tomato
1/2 cup chopped onion
1 medium-size cucumber, peeled, halved vertically and seeds removed, sliced into half-moons

1/4 cup chopped coriander leaves
1/2 teaspoon salt
lettuce, sliced into thin strips
radishes
lime slices

1. Mix the tomato cubes, onion, cucumber, coriander and salt together.

2. Place the salad on a bed of lettuce strips. Garnish with radishes, either sliced or made into flowers. Serve with the lime slices.

Each diner uses as much lime juice as he wants.

Serves 8

Gor Amli Ni Kachumbar
Special Relish for Dhan Sak

1/3 cup brown sugar
2 tablespoons tamarind paste, soaked in 1/4 cup water for 30 minutes, strained
1/4 cup chopped onion

1/4 cup chopped fresh coriander leaves
1 teaspoon minced fresh hot green chili
1/8 teaspoon salt

Mix everything together. Serve with the Dhan Sak.

Serves 8

The
Hindu
and
Muslim
Kitchens
of
Kashmir

There is a special magic in the word Kashmir that conjures up a land of great beauty. In the northwest corner of India, surrounded by the spectacular snow-covered Himalaya mountains, filled with lakes and streams and blessed with a rich soil, Kashmir has enchanted poets and peasants for centuries—"pale hands I love beside the Shalimar."

It is in the ancient capital, Srinagar, founded by the Emperor Asoka in the third century B.C., that our introduction to the people and the cooking begins. The great Dal Lake and the Jhelum River surround the capital city, providing vistas of unsurpassed beauty. The tall, slender Lombardy poplars introduced by the British, and the weeping willows, lend an air of mystery and provide romantic, misty reflections in the water and distant silhouettes in the countryside.

The Moguls endowed the city with exotic architecture and designed the Shalimar and other gardens on the shore of the lake for their ladies as an escape from the dusty, penetrating heat of Delhi, their capital.

Kashmir had been overrun by a succession of invaders via those natural funnels into India, the mountain passes from Iran and Afghanistan. The resulting population is made up of an Indo-Aryan type of people with a strong Caucasian element that produces tall, fair people with blue eyes. Kashmiris are both Hindu and Muslim.

Nowadays, houseboats ply the lakes and rivers for the tourists while the *shikara* (low-slung canoes) swoop through the water carrying passengers smoking their hookahs, salesmen hawking their incomparable handicrafts, loads of wood and *nadru*, the long slender tubes of the edible lotus roots dug from the lake bottom.

It is an added attraction that one of the most beautiful regions in India also produces one of the most delectable and original cuisines.

Kashmir has the highest protein intake of any region in India. The cool, invigorating climate and altitude of 6500 feet accounts for great demand for meat. When one mentions meat in Kashmir, it automatically refers to mutton. Beef is not eaten and in fact the slaughter of cows is forbidden.

Chicken, duck, eggs, milk and yogurt are other foods in daily use. *Panir*, the firm white country cheese, is used in many ways in the cooking.

191

The four temperate seasons operate here. When winter arrives with the first snow, the tourists disappear, a bitter chill is in the air, and one looks forward to an early spring and the reappearance of flowers, fruits and vegetables.

During the autumn, when I recently visited Srinagar, cabbage, cauliflower, turnips of several varieties, kohlrabi and the giant white radish were available everywhere—popular winter vegetables that can be stored.

Kashmir is famous for its fruits and nuts. Peaches, apricots, several kinds of apples, cherries and strawberries are produced in quantity with their natural flavors intact, untouched by chemical miracles. Walnuts and almonds are grown and sold all over India.

Most of the spices used in Kashmiri cooking are brought in from the hot, tropical regions of India where they are grown. Green and black cardamom pods, cinnamon, fennel, cloves, cuminseed, coriander, black pepper, hot red chili and turmeric are the most popular spices. These and onion, garlic, fresh and dried gingerroot are used with a generous hand.

There is no doubt in my mind, after living in India and cooking Indian food for more than twenty-five years, that the cuisine of Kashmir is one of the most inventive and imaginative to be found.

This is especially evident at wedding feasts and other festive occasions. At such a time professional cooks are hired. They are expensive and in great demand, especially during the wedding months of June, July and August (depending upon what the family astrologer indicates as an auspicious date). The guest list is long and the menu lavish.

The traditional menu for Hindu weddings is planned with four meat dishes and from twelve to thirty vegetarian dishes, depending upon available money and the size of the guest list. Also, a rice dish (see Shadi Pilau) and a sweet dish. Portions of all foods are generous.

The traditional Muslim wedding emphasizes meat dishes, and there may be ten to twelve or more. The limiting factor is the amount of money available for this event. Each four persons are allotted 1 pound of Basmati rice (see Shadi Meetha Pilau), 4 kilos of assorted meat dishes, 1 kilo of yogurt, 1 pound of *Halwah* and a small plate of mint and/or walnut chutney. *Kahava*, the tea made with sugar, almonds, cardamom and cinnamon, is *de rigueur* at the wedding.

However, Kashmiri home cooking is relatively simple and the cooking equipment unsophisticated. Foot-high kerosene stoves, a frying pan or two, several pots to cook rice and curries and the *kerai* (wok), which may be the most useful utensil of all, can produce almost any type of dish. In addition, there is the round stone mortar with a wooden pestle that reduces whole spices to powder and vegetables and meat to smooth purées. Simple kitchen equipment is all that is necessary to prepare any Kashmiri culinary invention.

The American kitchen will be able to reproduce the enticing Kashmiri cooking with ease. Our food processors, automatic rice cookers, modern stoves and good lighting make it just that much easier. All the spices and seasonings are available in Asian food shops and most supermarkets.

Dagith Maz
Ground Lamb with Mushrooms

Dagith means "pounding" since the lamb is traditionally pounded in a mortar. However, it is not pounded or ground as fine as in other Kashmiri meat dishes so our standard ground lamb is acceptable.

2 tablespoons corn or peanut oil
1 cup chopped onions
4 garlic cloves, chopped
1 pound lamb, ground
1/2 cup chopped tomato, fresh or canned
1/2 teaspoon ground turmeric
1/4 teaspoon freshly ground black pepper

1 teaspoon salt
4 cardamom pods, cracked
2 whole cloves
1/2 cup water
1/2 pound small whole fresh mushrooms

1. Heat the oil in a wok or skillet and over moderate heat fry the onions and garlic until golden, about 3 minutes. Add the lamb and stir-fry until the meat changes color.

2. Add the tomato, turmeric, black pepper, salt, cardamom and cloves. Stir-fry rapidly for 2 minutes. Add 1/4 cup water and continue to stir-fry.

3. Add the well-rinsed mushrooms and remaining 1/4 cup water, cover the pan, and cook over moderately low heat for 10 minutes.

Serve warm with rice and other dishes.

Serves 6

Variations: Ground chicken with both white and dark meat may be used instead of the lamb and green peas instead of mushrooms. Therefore, one could use chicken and mushrooms; chicken and green peas; lamb and green peas; or lamb, mushrooms and green peas—all good combinations.

Kara Masala
Lamb in Coriander

My Kashmiri cook said that the origin of this recipe is Pakistani. But political boundaries have nothing to do with regional foods that move back and forth across lines wherever they may be on a map. This lamb dish has all the earmarks of a proper Kashmiri concoction—spicy, vivid and made with lamb, their most popular meat.

3 tablespoons corn or peanut oil
2 cups thin-sliced onions
2 teaspoons minced fresh gingerroot
4 whole cloves
1½ pounds lamb shank or shoulder, cut into 3-inch pieces including bone

½ teaspoon ground cardamom
½ teaspoon ground turmeric
½ teaspoon freshly ground black pepper
2 teaspoons ground coriander
1 cinnamon stick, 1 inch
1 teaspoon salt, or to taste
1½ cups water

1. Heat the oil and brown the onions and gingerroot over moderate heat for 3 or 4 minutes. Add the cloves and lamb and stir-fry the mixture for 5 minutes. Add the cardamom, turmeric, black pepper, coriander, cinnamon and salt.

2. Add the water, cover the pan, and cook for about 45 minutes, or until the lamb is tender and almost all the liquid has evaporated, leaving a thick brown sauce.

Serve with rice or Indian breads.

Serves 4

Tupa
Lamb with Dumplings

The *tupa* is a dish from the region of Ladakh, inhabited principally by Tibetans. Although I learned this dish in Srinagar and it is to be found in Kashmir, it cannot be considered a traditional Kashmiri preparation.

LAMB

2 tablespoons corn or peanut oil
1 cup fine-chopped onions
3 garlic cloves, chopped fine
1 teaspoon minced fresh
  gingerroot
1 pound boneless lamb, cut into
  1-inch cubes
1/2 teaspoon ground turmeric

1/2 teaspoon freshly ground black
  pepper
1/2 teaspoon ground cuminseed
1/2 teaspoon ground cardamom
1/4 teaspoon dried hot red chili
  flakes
3 cups water

DUMPLINGS

2/3 cup whole-wheat flour (ata)

2 to 3 tablespoons water

1. Heat the oil in a pan and fry the onions, garlic and gingerroot over moderate heat until brown. Add the lamb and brown for 5 minutes, adding 2 tablespoons water to prevent burning.

2. Add the turmeric, black pepper, cuminseed, cardamom and chili flakes, and stir-fry for 2 minutes. Add the balance of the water and cook, covered, for 40 minutes, or until the lamb is tender.

3. Mix the flour and water together to prepare a firm dough. Roll out 1 or 2 long cigars about 3/4 inch in diameter. Pinch off 1/2 inch, roll it into a ball, and press it lightly to flatten out into a round, flat dumpling about 1/4 inch thick. Continue to shape dumplings from the rest of the dough.

4. Add the dumplings to the lamb, cover the pan, and cook over moderately low heat for 15 minutes. Total cooking time for lamb and dumplings is about 1 hour.

Serve warm. Traditionally nothing else is served with the *tupa* but I find that plain rice is most compatible.

Serves 4

Maz Dupiaza
Lamb Shank in Onion Gravy

LAMB

1½ pounds lamb shank, cut into 2-inch pieces, including bone

1 cup minced onions

4 garlic cloves, chopped fine

1½ cups water

GRAVY

1 tablespoon corn or peanut oil

1 tablespoon minced onion

½ cup plain yogurt

½ teaspoon freshly ground black pepper

1 teaspoon salt, or to taste

½ teaspoon ground cinnamon

4 cardamom pods, cracked

2 whole cloves

½ cup water

1. Cook the lamb, 1 cup onions and the garlic in 1½ cups water for about 20 minutes, or until nearly all the liquid has evaporated.

2. Make the gravy: Heat the oil in a skillet and brown the onion until crisp. Add onion and oil to the lamb. Cook the mixture over moderately low heat, adding the yogurt in a steady stream. Stir continuously so that the yogurt does not curdle.

3. Add the black pepper, salt, cinnamon, cardamom, cloves and ½ cup water to the pan and continue to stir over heat for 3 minutes. Cover the pan and cook until the lamb is tender, about 30 minutes. Should the gravy dry out too quickly, add another ½ cup water and continue to cook. The sauce should be thick and spicy.

Serve warm with other dishes.

Serves 4

Matz
Meatballs

MEATBALLS

1 pound boneless lamb, cut into
  cubes
1/4 teaspoon freshly ground black
  pepper

1/2 teaspoon salt
1/2 teaspoon ground cardamom
1 egg white, lightly beaten
oil for frying

SAUCE

1 1/2 cups thin-sliced onions
1 inch of fresh gingerroot, chopped
  fine
1/4 teaspoon dried hot red chili
  flakes

1 1/4 cups water
1 teaspoon ground turmeric
1 teaspoon salt, or to taste

1. Grind the lamb in a processor until it is smooth. Add the black pepper, salt and cardamom, mix well, and then incorporate the egg white.

2. Prepare 12 meatballs 1 1/2 inches in diameter. Heat the oil in a wok or skillet and brown the meatballs on all sides for about 2 minutes. Set aside. Remove all but 3 tablespoons oil.

3. Add the onions and gingerroot to the oil and over moderate heat stir-fry until brown and crisp. Do not burn. Push the onions and gingerroot to one side and add the chili. Stir quickly and add 1 tablespoon water, stirring the entire mixture together.

4. Add the turmeric and salt and 1/4 cup water. Stir-fry rapidly, then add the balance of the water and the meatballs. Stir for a minute and cook over moderately low heat until nearly all the liquid has evaporated, about 15 minutes. A thick brown sauce will result.

Serve warm with white rice and other dishes.

Serves 6

Note: Originally the large kitchen mortar and pestle were used to pound the lamb for about 15 minutes, just enough to shred it but not to pulverize it.

Variations: The meatballs as produced by the Hindu community include whole dried apricots, one placed in the center of each meatball. The apricot is first soaked for several hours and cooked in lightly sweetened water until just soft. It is then pushed into the center of the lamb and the meatball is deep-fried. The sauce is the same as given here. The browned meatballs without the sauce make admirable appetizers.

The mixture can also be shaped into kabobs to be cooked over charcoal for 3 minutes, then browned in hot oil. Use about 2 table-spoons of the lamb mixture for these Seek Kabobs. Serve with lemon quarters and Indian bread.

Kaliya
Spicy Lamb

This is a typical lamb (mutton) dish served at Hindu weddings. Note the absence of hot chili and a reliance on aromatic fennel seed, cuminseed and cardamom for flavoring. Garlic is generously used.

1½ pounds lamb, shank or ribs
*   with bone, cut into 3-inch pieces*
2 cups water
1 teaspoon ground turmeric
1 teaspoon ground fennel seed
1 teaspoon ground cuminseed
½ teaspoon ground cardamom
¼ teaspoon minced fresh
*   gingerroot*

1 teaspoon salt
3 garlic cloves, sliced thin,
*   browned in oil and pounded to*
*   a paste in a mortar*
3 bay leaves
¼ cup plain yogurt

1. Cook the lamb in the water with the turmeric, fennel, cuminseed, cardamom, gingerroot, salt, garlic and bay leaves in a covered pan over moderate heat until tender, about 45 minutes.

2 Add the yogurt, stir well, and cook over moderately low heat for 5 minutes more.

Serve warm.

Serves 4

Harissa
Meat and Rice Mélange

Harissa means a rapid, firm stirring (with a wooden spoon) that shreds the meat and combines all the ingredients. The same word *harissa* in Tunisia, where I have also studied the cuisine, refers to the very hot chili condiment used in cooking and at table. A curious coincidence.

Very few households prepare the *harissa*, but there are a small number of restaurants in the old bazaar area of Srinagar that prepare it in large quantities. Beginning in the very early hours of the morning, they chop, cook, stir the food and stoke the wood or charcoal fires. Hungry diners of the working class line up for their *harissa* and in a very short time all is gone. It is impossible to locate a portion later in the morning.

My cook would buy several portions and return home to warm it up later for lunch. The restaurant style includes far more rice than the home recipe. Nonetheless, it is one of the most delicious preparations in a style of cooking that has many extraordinary dishes.

1 pound boneless lamb, cut into 1-inch cubes
1 pound boneless chicken, light and dark meat, cut into 2-inch pieces
1/3 cup raw rice
10 whole cardamom pods, cracked
1 teaspoon ground fennel seed
1 teaspoon ground cinnamon
1 1/2 teaspoon ground ginger, or 1 teaspoon ground fresh gingerroot

1/4 teaspoon ground cuminseed
4 whole cloves
1/2 teaspoon salt
1/2 pound onions, about 3, sliced thin, fried in oil until golden, then processed to a paste
4 cups water

GARNISH

2 tablespoons chopped onion
1 tablespoon corn or peanut oil

2 Seek Kabobs for each person (see Variations, preceding recipe)

1. Put all the ingredients except the garnish together in a pan and bring to a boil. Cook covered over very low heat for 2 hours, or until the meat is very tender and almost all the liquid has evaporated. About 1/4 cup liquid may remain.

2. Stir the mixture firmly with a wooden spoon to shred the meat, for 3 to 4 minutes. Do not mash the meat.

3. Fry the 2 tablespoons of chopped onion in the oil in a skillet over moderate heat until light brown; set aside. Serve generous portions of the *harissa*, garnished with the fried onion and *seek kabobs*.

Serve with bread or chapatis.

Serves 4 to 6

Ab Ghosh
Lamb in Milk Sauce

LAMB

1 pound boneless lamb, cut into 2-inch pieces	*6 cardamom pods, cracked*
1½ cups water	*1 teaspoon fennel seeds, tied up in cheesecloth*
1 teaspoon salt	*2 whole cloves*
¼ teaspoon freshly ground black pepper	*1 teaspoon ground cuminseed*

MILK SAUCE

2 teaspoons corn or peanut oil	*1½ cups milk*
2 scallions, white part only, cut lengthwise	*1 cinnamon stick, 2 inches*
	½ teaspoon ground cuminseed

1. Cook the lamb in the water with the salt, black pepper, cardamom, fennel, cloves and cuminseed over moderate heat until the lamb is tender and most of the liquid has evaporated, about 45 minutes.

2. Make the milk sauce: Heat the oil in a pan and fry the scallions until crisp. Add the milk, cinnamon and cuminseed and cook over moderately low heat for 10 minutes to reduce the milk by about a quarter.

3. Add the lamb and its sauce and simmer the mixture over moderately low heat for 15 minutes more.

Serve warm with rice and other dishes.

Serves 6

Gustaba
Lamb Balls in Yogurt Sauce

This is one of the great classic dishes of Kashmir. The result depends on the method of pulverizing the lamb and the length of time it takes to do so. It is a production! The lamb pieces are beaten with a wooden mallet on a rectangular stone until the meat begins to change color. Now and then a few drops of water are sprinkled over the meat to accelerate the breakdown of the fibers. Tough fibers are removed and discarded.

What is left after *two hours* of pounding is a silky smooth paste which is then mixed with the other ingredients. The *gustaba*, when cooked, has a light rubbery texture that is unique in the cooking of India or anywhere else for that matter. A modern processor does this more quickly and just as efficiently. One should not underprocess the lamb since the texture depends upon a complete breakdown of the fibers.

LAMB

*1 pound boneless leg of lamb, cut
    into 1-inch cubes
    seeds from 3 cardamom pods
1/4 teaspoon freshly ground black
    pepper*

*1/2 teaspoon salt
1 egg white, lightly beaten*

BROTH

*5 cups water
1/2 teaspoon ground cuminseed
1 teaspoon salt*

*1 cinnamon stick, 1 inch
4 cardamom pods, cracked*

YOGURT SAUCE

*2 tablespoons corn or peanut oil
4 scallions, white part only, sliced
    thin
1 cup plain yogurt
1/2 teaspoon salt, or to taste*

*1 cup reserved broth
3 stalks of fresh mint
1 tablespoon Scallion Paste (see
    Index)
1/2 teaspoon ground cuminseed*

1. Pulverize the lamb in a processor for at least 5 minutes. The meat should be silky. Add the cardamom seeds, black pepper, salt and egg white and stir these in by hand.

2. Moisten your hands with cold water. Take about 1/2 cup of the lamb and shape into a large ball. There should be 4 to 6 balls, 2 inches in diameter.

3. Bring the water to a boil with the cuminseed, salt, cinnamon stick and cardamom pods. Add the lamb balls (*gustaba*) one at a time and cook over moderate heat for 10 minutes. Remove the foam that rises to the surface so that there will be a clear, spiced broth. Remove the lamb balls and set aside. Reserve 1 cup broth.

4. Make the sauce: Heat the oil in a pan and lightly brown the scallions. Add the yogurt and stir continuously over moderate heat to prevent the yogurt separating. Add the salt and continue to stir for 2 minutes.

5. Add the reserved cup of broth and the lamb balls, the mint, scallion paste and cuminseed. Continue to cook over moderately low heat for 10 minutes to thicken the sauce. Remove the mint stalks.

Serve warm with rice.

Serves 4

Rista

Small Lamb Balls in Spice Sauce

Both *rista* and *gustaba* may be prepared at the same time. The lamb is pulverized in the same manner and the lamb balls both large and small are cooked in a broth. At this stage, the preparations take different routes, the *rista* with a vivid sauce and the *gustaba* with a milder yogurt sauce.

A walk around the old quarter of Srinagar, the capital city of Kashmir, or past public restaurants in the early hours of the morning will make you aware of a characteristic and constant pounding noise. The lamb (mutton) is being pulverized with a wooden mallet on a stone platform, as *rista* and *gustaba* are being prepared for the day. This takes hours.

When the meat is not being pounded, spices are being broken down from the seeds and bark to a powder. Pulverizing your own spices guarantees that you will have pure spice rather than the adulterated powdered ones from the bazaar.

1 recipe lamb balls (gustaba)
1 recipe broth for gustaba
2 tablespoons corn or peanut oil
6 scallions, white part only, sliced thin
1/2 teaspoon dried hot red chili flakes
1/4 cup water
1/2 teaspoon ground cinnamon
1/4 teaspoon freshly ground black pepper
1 teaspoon ground turmeric
1/2 cup plain yogurt
1 tablespoon Scallion Paste (see Index)
1 cup reserved broth
1 teaspoon cuminseeds, lightly toasted in a dry skillet

1. Shape lamb balls by taking 1 tablespoon of the meat and rolling it to 1 inch in diameter. Cook them in the same broth as used in the *gustaba* for 10 minutes. Remove the balls and set aside. Reserve 1 cup of broth. Makes 12 *rista*.

2. Heat the oil in a pan and lightly brown the scallions for about 3 minutes. Add the hot chili and stir-fry for a minute. Add the water and stir rapidly for another minute.

3. Add the cinnamon, black pepper, turmeric, yogurt and scallion paste, stirring rapidly to incorporate all the ingredients. Add the broth, the

lamb balls and the cuminseeds. Continue to cook over moderately low heat for 15 minutes.

Serve warm with rice and other dishes.

Serves 6

Tabac Maz
Browned Lamb Chops

This is a classic Kashmiri preparation; the meat is traditionally browned in a tightly covered clay pot that rests in a bed of charcoal. When one side of the lamb is browned, it is turned over and browned dry on the other side. Kashmiri homes do not have ovens.

A variation on the method used in this recipe, which would be closer to the old charcoal tradition, would be to put *ghee* (clarified butter) in the bottom of a heatproof glass baking dish. Line up the chops in a single layer in the dish and tightly cover it. Bake in a 375°F. oven for 10 minutes, then turn the chops over and bake on the other side for 10 minutes longer.

1 pound lamb chops, shoulder or rib	*¹/₂ teaspoon ground fennel seed*
1 cup water	*2 whole cloves*
1 cinnamon stick, 2 inches, halved	*¹/₂ teaspoon ground turmeric*
6 cardamom pods, cracked	*1 teaspoon salt*
¹/₂ teaspoon freshly ground black pepper	*2 tablespoons corn or peanut oil*

1. Cook the lamb in the water with all the spices and the salt until it is tender and the liquid has evaporated, about 20 minutes over moderately low heat.

2. Heat the oil in a skillet and over moderate heat brown the lamb on both sides for about 4 minutes. The chops should be dry and crisp.

Serve warm with rice, chutney and side dishes of vegetables.

Serves 4

Shami Kabob
Spiced Lamb Patties

The kabobs may be served as a side dish or as an appetizer with drinks. My Kashmiri cook used a stone mortar and wooden pestle to grind the spices, lentils and meat. This is an indispensable kitchen implement where modern electric gadgets do not exist.

After the lamb and *dal* were cooked and dry, he pounded the mixture in the mortar for 15 minutes, until it was completely pulverized. The resulting kabobs were the best I had eaten, crisp and brown on the outside, light and smooth on the inside.

²/₃ *cup yellow lentils (chana ka dal), well rinsed*

1 pound boneless lamb, cut into 1-inch cubes

2 teaspoons chopped fresh gingerroot

4 cardamom pods, cracked

1¹/₂ cups water

2 whole cloves

¹/₂ teaspoon freshly ground black pepper

¹/₂ teaspoon ground cuminseed

1 cinnamon stick, 3 inches, broken up

1 teaspoon salt, or to taste

1 teaspoon dried hot red chili flakes

1 egg

oil for frying

1. Cook everything except the egg and oil together in a covered pan over moderately low heat until the lamb and lentils are tender, about 30 minutes. Cook until the liquid has evaporated. The mixture should be dry.

2. Grind this in a processor until smooth and light. Add the egg and mix well. Prepare patties 2¹/₂ inches in diameter and ¹/₂ inch thick.

3. Heat 3 tablespoons oil in a skillet and brown the kabobs over moderate heat for 2 minutes on each side. Add more oil as needed. Drain kabobs briefly on paper towels.

Serve warm with Indian breads.

Makes 12 kabobs

Rogan Jhosh
Aromatic Red Lamb

Rogan means "red color" and *jhosh* means "heat," a red hot lamb dish. When I was taught this preparation in Kashmir, dried red chilies were boiled in water for a few minutes and strained. The liquid was added to the lamb. Ginger and pepper intensified the vivid heat in the sauce.

The red cockscomb flowers are commonly found in Kashmiri gardens, and the fresh or partially dried heads are purchased in the bazaar. The deep maroon heads, the color of beets, are cooked in water and the resulting red color is added to the lamb. The liquid has no flavor and is only used as a coloring agent.

3 tablespoons corn or peanut oil
2 pounds boneless leg of lamb, cut into 2-inch cubes
4 garlic cloves, chopped fine
1 cup chopped onion
1½ cups cockscomb liquid (optional), or 1 teaspoon paprika dissolved in ¾ cup water
1 teaspoon ground turmeric
2 teaspoons salt, or to taste

2 teaspoons ground cinnamon
1 teaspoon freshly ground black pepper
½ teaspoon dried hot red chili flakes
2 teaspoons ground cardamom
2 teaspoons ground fennel seed
2 whole cloves
½ teaspoon ground ginger
1 cup plain yogurt
⅔ cup Scallion Paste (see Index)

1. Heat the oil in a pan and brown the lamb over moderate heat, adding the garlic. Stir-fry for 5 minutes. Add the onion and continue to fry for 10 minutes as a gravy forms. Add the cockscomb liquid or paprika water and continue to cook for 5 minutes.

2. All together add the turmeric, salt, cinnamon, black pepper, chili flakes, cardamom, fennel, cloves and ginger. Cover the pan and cook for 30 minutes.

3. Now add the yogurt, ¼ cup at a time, stirring continuously to form the sauce. Add the scallion paste and stir for 5 minutes more. The lamb should be tender and the sauce red and thick.

Serve warm with rice.

Serves 6

Shadi Pilau

Sweet Rice with Dry Fruit (Wedding Rice)

This rice is served at Hindu weddings. It is not a dessert but is eaten with meat dishes. The recipe I learned in Kashmir called for 2 cups sugar, which was too much, even though the sugar of India does not have the intensity of sweetness of our refined table sugar. But the amount of sugar is still your personal preference.

Coconut, called copra in Kashmir, is used as a garnish for sweet dishes as well as in this rice. It is the ripe, dry coconut with a hard brown husk that is used. The coconut meat is cut into thin 2-inch slices.

4 cups water
6 bay leaves
1/2 teaspoon ground turmeric, or a few threads of saffron
2 cups raw Basmati rice, well rinsed

2 tablespoons corn or peanut oil or ghee
1 cup sugar
1/2 cup coconut slivers
2 tablespoons white raisins
8 dates, seeded and halved

1. Boil the water, bay leaves and turmeric together over moderate heat for 3 minutes. Add the rice and cook for 6 minutes. Pour off all remaining water.

2. Heat the oil and pour it into the rice. Mix well. Add the sugar, coconut, raisins and dates, and mix again. Cover the pan.

3. Bake in a 350°F. oven for 20 minutes. The cover must be a tight fit to steam the rice. Do not uncover, but shake the pan back and forth several times during the baking process.

Serve warm with other wedding dishes.

Serves 6

Shadi Meetha Pilau
Sweet Wedding Rice

This sweet rice is not a dessert but is served with meat and vegetable dishes at Muslim weddings and on other special occasions.

¹/₂ cup sugar
3 cups water, or as needed
2 tablespoons corn or peanut oil
¹/₄ cup thin-sliced onion
*2 cups raw Basmati rice, well
  rinsed and drained*

¹/₄ cup coconut slivers
1 tablespoon light or dark raisins
*10 blanched almonds, halved
  lengthwise*
*1 tablespoon shelled pistachios
  (optional)*

1. Dissolve the sugar in the water and bring to a boil over moderate heat. Remove from heat and set aside.

2. Heat the oil in a pan and lightly brown the onion. Add the rice and stir-fry for 2 minutes. Add the sugar water, bring to a boil, and immediately reduce heat to low. Cover the pan.

3. After 5 minutes add the coconut, raisins, almonds and pistachios. Stir them into the rice. Cover the pan and cook for another 10 minutes, or until the rice is soft. Add a small amount of water if the rice is too firm. Remove the pan from the heat and let it stand covered for 15 minutes more before serving.

Serve warm with other dishes.

Serves 6

Variations: An interesting variation is prepared as follows: White rice is cooked in the conventional manner; when the rice is nearly finished, a drop each of 4 different vegetable colors is added in 4 different places around the edge of the pan. Then the cooking is completed. The color seeps down. When the rice is fluffed up and served, the 4 colors are visible but have not mixed together in the pan.

Munji
Kohlrabi Stir-Fry

2 tablespoons corn or peanut oil
3 garlic cloves, chopped fine
1 pound kohlrabi, peeled and
　sliced thin
1/2 teaspoon dried hot red chili
　flakes

1/2 teaspoon ground turmeric
1 teaspoon salt, or to taste
1 cup water

1. Heat the oil in a skillet and stir-fry the garlic for 1 minute. Add the kohlrabi and stir-fry for 2 minutes. Add the chili flakes, turmeric and salt, and continue to stir-fry.

2. Add the water, cover the pan, and cook until the kohlrabi is soft, about 15 minutes. Uncover the skillet and cook over moderately low heat until nearly all the liquid has evaporated.

Serve warm with other Kashmiri dishes.

Serves 6

Vangun Aur Masala
Eggplant Sauté

2 tablespoons corn or peanut oil
1/2 cup thin-sliced onion
1 teaspoon minced fresh
　gingerroot
2 garlic cloves, chopped fine
2 scallions, white part only, sliced
　thin
1/2 cup chopped tomato, fresh or
　canned
1/4 teaspoon dried hot red chili
　flakes

1/4 teaspoon freshly ground black
　pepper
1/2 teaspoon ground turmeric
1/4 teaspoon ground cinnamon
1 teaspoon salt, or to taste
3/4 cup water
1 pound small eggplants, 3,
　quartered lengthwise

1. Heat the oil and stir-fry the onion, gingerroot, garlic and scallions over moderate heat until golden. Add the tomato, chili flakes, black pepper, turmeric, cinnamon and salt. Stir-fry briskly for 2 minutes. Add 1 tablespoon water and stir-fry for another minute.

2. Add the eggplants and the balance of the water, stir for a moment, cover the pan, and cook over moderately low heat for 15 minutes.

Serve warm with rice.

Serves 4

Tomatar Vangun
Aromatic Eggplant and Tomatoes

This eggplant recipe is almost a simplified version of the preceding one. The difference is in the use of more tomato and less of the pungent flavorings—no garlic, ginger or chili. Both are delicious but may appeal to different tastes.

2 tablespoons corn or peanut oil
1/2 cup thin-sliced onion
2 cups chopped tomatoes, fresh or canned
1 teaspoon salt, or to taste
1/4 teaspoon freshly ground black pepper
1/2 teaspoon ground cinnamon
1/2 teaspoon ground turmeric
1 pound small eggplants, 3, quartered lengthwise
1/2 cup water

1. Heat the oil in a pan and lightly brown the onion over moderate heat. Add the tomatoes and stir-fry for 3 minutes to prepare the sauce.

2. Add the salt, black pepper, cinnamon and turmeric, and continue to stir-fry for 3 minutes. Add the eggplants and water and mix.

3. Cover the pan and cook the mixture for 15 minutes so that the eggplants are tender but still firm and the sauce thickened.

Serve warm with rice or chapatis.

Serves 6

Chaman Aloo
Cheese and Potatoes

3 tablespoons corn or peanut oil
1/2 pound Panir Cheese (see
   Index), cut into 2-inch squares
   1/4 inch thick
1/2 cup chopped onion
1/2 cup chopped tomato, fresh or
   canned
1/4 teaspoon dried hot red chili
   flakes

1 teaspoon salt, or to taste
1/4 teaspoon freshly ground black
   pepper
1 pound small potatoes, 6, peeled
   and quartered
1 cup water

1. Heat the oil in a skillet and brown the cheese squares on both sides over moderate heat for 2 minutes. Remove and set aside.

2. Add the onion to the same oil and lightly brown it. Add the tomato and stir-fry over moderate heat for 3 to 4 minutes to make a purée. Add the chili flakes, salt and black pepper and stir for a moment.

3. Add the potatoes and stir-fry for 2 minutes. Add the water and bring to a boil. Add the browned cheese, cover the pan, and cook until the potatoes are soft and the liquid has reduced somewhat, about 15 minutes.

Serve warm.

Serves 6

Nadru Ka Yeknee
Lotus Root in Yogurt Sauce

LOTUS

1 pound fresh lotus root, scraped and cut into 1/2-inch-thick diagonal slices
1/2 teaspoon ground cardamom
1/2 teaspoon freshly ground black pepper
1/2 teaspoon ground fennel seed
1/2 teaspoon ground cinnamon
1 whole clove
1/2 teaspoon minced fresh gingerroot
2 whole cardamom pods, cracked
1 teaspoon salt, or to taste
1 1/2 cups water

SAUCE

2 tablespoons corn or peanut oil
1/2 cup thin-sliced onion
1 whole clove
1 cup plain yogurt
1 cup reserved liquid
1 cardamom pod, cracked
1/2 teaspoon cuminseeds

1. Put lotus root and its spices and salt with the water in a pan, bring to a boil, and cook over moderate heat for 30 minutes, or until the lotus is tender. Remove the lotus and reserve the liquid.

2. Heat the oil for the sauce in a pan and lightly brown the onion and the clove over moderate heat. Remove the onion and set aside.

3. Off the heat add the yogurt to the oil and stir it in briskly. Add the browned onion, the reserved liquid, the cardamom and cuminseed. Bring to a boil over moderate heat and stir continuously for 5 minutes.

4. Add the lotus root and continue to cook and stir for 5 minutes more. The slightly tart, spicy sauce will thicken.

Serve warm with rice and other dishes.

Serves 6

Bundgobi Tulmut
Cabbage Stir-Fry

Cabbage, cauliflower, turnip, kohlrabi and white radishes are the popular winter vegetables in Kashmir. They are grown in profusion, are cheap, and all are easily prepared by this stir-fry method.

2 tablespoons corn or peanut oil
1 garlic clove, chopped
1 teaspoon minced fresh gingerroot
2 tablespoons minced onion
1 pound cabbage, shredded (5 cups)

1/2 teaspoon ground cardamom
1/4 teaspoon freshly ground black pepper
1 whole clove
1 teaspoon salt, or to taste
1 tablespoon water

1. Heat the oil in a saucepan or large skillet and fry the garlic and gingerroot over moderate heat for 1 minute. Add the onion and stir-fry for 2 minutes. Add the cabbage and continue to stir-fry for 2 minutes.

2. Add the cardamom, black pepper, clove, salt and water. Stir-fry for 1 minute. Cover the pan and cook for 5 minutes. Uncover the pan and stir-fry until the cabbage is completely wilted and dry. There is no sauce.

Serve warm with other dishes.

Serves 6

Zumroo Toor
Egg Curry

3 tablespoons corn or peanut oil
4 hard-cooked eggs, peeled
1 teaspoon minced fresh gingerroot
1 cup fine-chopped onions
3 scallions, white part only, sliced thin
1/2 cup chopped tomato, fresh or canned

1/4 teaspoon ground cinnamon
1/4 teaspoon ground fennel seed
1/4 teaspoon freshly ground black pepper
1/2 teaspoon ground turmeric
1/2 teaspoon salt
1 cup water

1. Heat the oil in a wok or skillet and brown the eggs on all sides over moderate heat for about 3 minutes. Remove the eggs and set aside.

2. Add the gingerroot, onion and scallions to the oil and stir-fry until the onions are light brown. Add the tomato and stir-fry for 2 minutes to make a sauce.

3. Add the cinnamon, fennel, black pepper, turmeric and salt. Stir-fry the mixture for 1 minute and add the water. Bring to a boil, stirring rapidly for a minute, and add the eggs. Cook the curry over moderately low heat for 15 minutes to thicken the sauce.

Serve with rice as a side dish.

Serves 4

Gawd
Fish Balls

Kashmir is not near the ocean but freshwater fish, which are plentiful, are found in the lakes and rivers. Trout are raised in government fish farms. Carp and other lake fish, which I was unable to identify, are sold in the bazaars by women who bring them in from the lakes. These fish balls were prepared with freshwater fish, but saltwater fish may be substituted.

1 pound fish fillets, ground fine
1/2 teaspoon salt
1/2 teaspoon ground fennel seed
1/2 teaspoon dried hot red chili
 flakes

1/2 teaspoon ground cuminseed
1/2 teaspoon ground gingerroot
1 tablespoon corn or peanut oil

1. Mix everything together and shape fish balls 1 inch in diameter.

2. Bring a saucepan of water to a boil. Carefully put the balls in the water, one by one, and cook over moderate heat for 8 minutes. Drain well.

Serve warm as an appetizer.

Makes 8 fish balls

Batak Cuen

Braised Duck with Cardamom

Although the lake region in the Vale of Kashmir abounds with swimming ducks and the countryside always seems to have ducks in the farmyards, Kashmiris do not really like them as food. They are raised for eggs and an occasional meal. This is the only recipe for duck that I found, but it is a good one.

2 tablespoons corn or peanut oil
2 cups thin-sliced onions
1 inch of fresh gingerroot, chopped fine
4 garlic cloves, chopped fine
1 duck, including giblets, 4½ pounds, cut into 10 pieces, loose skin and fat discarded
½ teaspoon dried hot red chili flakes
½ teaspoon ground turmeric
½ teaspoon ground cinnamon
6 cardamom pods, cracked
½ teaspoon freshly ground black pepper
1 teaspoon salt, or to taste
1½ cups water

1. Heat the oil in a large pan and fry the onions, gingerroot and garlic over moderate heat until golden. Add the duck pieces and stir-fry until they have been thoroughly browned, about 10 minutes.

2. Add the chili flakes, turmeric, cinnamon, cardamom, black pepper and salt. Stir-fry for another 2 minutes. Add the water, bring to a boil, cover the pan, and cook until the duck is tender, about 45 minutes. The sauce should be reduced to a thick mélange.

Serve warm with rice. Since American ducks are very fat, pour off as much accumulated fat as possible before serving.

Serves 6

Talmut Kooker
Fried Chicken with Sauce

2 tablespoons corn or peanut oil
1 cup fine-chopped onions
2 garlic cloves, chopped fine
1/2 teaspoon minced fresh
  gingerroot
1/4 teaspoon freshly ground black
  pepper
1/4 teaspoon ground cinnamon

1/2 teaspoon salt
1/2 teaspoon ground turmeric
1 cup water
1 chicken, 3 pounds, cut into 8
  serving pieces, including the
  giblets, or 2 Cornish hens, 1 1/2
  pounds each, halved

1. Heat the oil in a pan and brown the onions and garlic over moderate heat for about 3 minutes, or until golden. Add the gingerroot, black pepper, cinnamon, salt and turmeric. Stir-fry for 2 minutes, adding 1 tablespoon water.

2. Add the chicken and stir-fry for 5 minutes to brown the pieces. Add remaining water, cover the pan, and cook for 30 minutes, or until all the liquid has evaporated and the chicken is tender. Should the liquid evaporate too quickly, add another 1/4 cup water.

Serve warm with rice, chutney and vegetable dishes.

Serves 4

Kooker Pilau
Chicken and Rice

3 tablespoons corn or peanut oil
1 chicken, 3 pounds, cut into 8
   serving pieces, including the
   giblets, or 2 Cornish hens,
   quartered
1 cup fine-sliced onions
1 cinnamon stick, 3 inches, broken
   into halves

4 cardamom pods, cracked
1 teaspoon cuminseeds
2 whole cloves
1 teaspoon salt
4 cups water
2 cups raw rice, preferably
   Basmati, well rinsed

1. Heat the oil in a pan and brown the chicken pieces over moderate heat for 5 minutes. Remove chicken and set aside.

2. In the same oil stir-fry the onions until they are light brown. Add the cinnamon, cardamom, cuminseeds, cloves, salt and 1 cup water. Stir-fry for 2 minutes to form a sauce.

3. Return the chicken and add the rice. Stir well and add the balance of the water, 3 cups. Bring to a boil, cover the pan, and turn the heat to low for 30 minutes. Or you may bake the mixture in a 325°F. oven for 30 minutes. Should the rice appear too dry, add 1 or 2 tablespoons water.

Serve warm with chutney and vegetable dishes.

Serves 6

Kooker Shorba
Kashmir Chicken Curry

3 tablespoons corn or peanut oil
2 cups fine-sliced onions
3 garlic cloves, chopped fine
2 teaspoons minced fresh
   gingerroot
1 to 2 teaspoons dried hot red
   chili flakes, dissolved in 1
   tablespoon water
1½ cups water
1 teaspoon ground turmeric

2 whole cloves
1 teaspoon salt
1 chicken, 3½ pounds, cut into
   10 serving pieces, including the
   giblets
¼ teaspoon freshly ground black
   pepper
½ teaspoon ground cinnamon
2 cardamom pods, cracked
2 tablespoons Scallion Paste (see
   Index)

1. Heat the oil in a pan and fry the onions over moderate heat until golden, about 3 minutes. Add the garlic and gingerroot and stir-fry for 1 minute. Add the chili flakes and ¼ cup water and stir rapidly to develop a smooth sauce.

2. Add the turmeric, cloves, salt and chicken pieces. Continue to stir to brown the chicken. Add another ¼ cup water.

3. Add the black pepper, cinnamon and cardamom and continue to stir for 5 minutes. Add the balance of the water, 1 cup, and the scallion paste. Cover the pan and cook the curry over moderately low heat for 35 minutes, or until the chicken is tender and the sauce has thickened.

Serve warm with rice and other Kashmiri dishes.

Serves 6

Murga Aur Kanguchi
Chicken and Mushrooms

Mushrooms are commonly found in Kashmir. There is the famous *gucci*, a black wild mushroom (morel) that is sold dried and is expensive enough to be prohibitive for Kashmiris.

There are also fresh mushrooms in the bazaars that are the same as our domesticated supermarket mushrooms but with a more intense flavor. A large white mushroom is also available dried.

2 tablespoons corn or peanut oil
1 cup thin-sliced onions
2 garlic cloves, sliced thin
1 teaspoon minced fresh gingerroot
1/4 teaspoon dried hot red chili flakes
1 teaspoon ground turmeric
1 1/2 cups water
1 chicken, 3 pounds, cut into 8 pieces, loose skin and fat discarded

2 whole cloves
1/4 teaspoon ground cinnamon
1/4 teaspoon freshly ground black pepper
1 teaspoon salt
4 cardamom pods, cracked
1/2 pound small whole fresh mushrooms, well rinsed
1 small ripe tomato, quartered

1. Heat the oil in a pan and fry the onions, garlic and gingerroot over moderate heat until golden. Add the chili flakes and turmeric, stir-fry for 1 minute, and add 1 tablespoon water. Stir-fry rapidly and add the chicken. Brown for 5 minutes.

2. Add 1/4 cup water, the cloves, cinnamon, black pepper, salt and cardamom, and stir well. Add the mushrooms and tomato, stir-fry for a minute, then add the balance of the water.

3. Cover the pan and cook for 30 minutes to reduce the liquid and produce a thick sauce. The chicken should be tender.

Serve warm with plain white rice and other dishes.

Serves 6

Chook Charan
Wedding Liver

This liver with a sweet-and-sour flavor is often served at Hindu weddings. The liver which is twice cooked—boiled and fried—has a chewy texture that is unexpectedly attractive.

1 pound lamb liver	1/2 teaspoon ground turmeric
3 tablespoons corn or peanut oil	1 teaspoon ground fennel seed
1 teaspoon sugar	1/4 teaspoon ground cardamom
1/2 teaspoon dried hot red chili flakes	1/2 teaspoon salt
1 tablespoon tamarind paste, dissolved in 2/3 cup water	1/2 cup water

1. Cook the lamb liver in one piece in boiling water for 3 minutes on each side. Cool and cut into 1/2-inch cubes.

2. Heat the oil in a saucepan or skillet and over moderate heat brown the liver for 2 minutes. Add the sugar and chili flakes, stir for a moment, then add the tamarind liquid strained through a metal sieve. Add the turmeric, fennel, cardamom and salt.

3. Add 1/2 cup water and simmer the liver, uncovered, over moderately low heat for 15 minutes to reduce the sauce to a thick consistency.

Serve warm as a side dish.

Serves 6

Variation: Chicken livers may be used instead of the lamb. Cook 1 pound of the livers in boiling water for 3 minutes. Remove, drain well, and cut into 1-inch lobes. Brown pieces lightly in oil and continue as for the lamb liver. Chicken livers cooked this way make an attractive appetizer with drinks.

Kirnee

Lamb Kidney Stir-Fry

2 lamb kidneys, quartered   salt and pepper
1 tablespoon corn or peanut oil

1. Trim the kidneys of excess membrane and fat.

2. Heat the oil in a skillet and over moderate heat brown the kidneys all over for 3 minutes. Sprinkle with salt and pepper.

Serve immediately as an appetizer with drinks. Allow 1 kidney per person.

Kaed

Lamb Brains in Onion Gravy

2 tablespoons corn or peanut oil   1 teaspoon salt
1 cup plus 1 tablespoon fine-   1/4 teaspoon freshly ground black
  chopped onions   pepper
2 lambs brains, rinsed in cold   1/4 teaspoon ground turmeric
  water, loose membranes removed   1/4 teaspoon dried hot red chili
1/2 cup chopped tomato, fresh or   flakes
  canned

1. Heat the oil in a pan and fry 1 tablespoon onion over moderate heat until golden, about 2 minutes. Add the brains and fry on both sides for 5 minutes.

2. Combine together in a bowl 1 cup onions, the tomato, salt, black pepper, turmeric and chili flakes. Pour this over the brains and stir around to distribute in the pan. Cover the pan and cook over moderately low heat for 15 minutes, stirring now and then.

Serve warm as a side dish with rice and chutney.

Serves 4

Arbie Churma
Taro or Potato Chips in Sauce

oil for deep-frying
1 pound taro or potatoes, cut as
  for French fries
1 cup thin-sliced onions
3 garlic cloves, chopped fine
1/2 teaspoon ground turmeric
1/2 teaspoon salt
1/4 teaspoon freshly ground black
  pepper

1/4 teaspoon dried hot red chili
  flakes
1/4 teaspoon ground cardamom
1/4 teaspoon ground cinnamon
1 cup chopped tomatoes, fresh or
  canned

1. Heat the oil in a wok or skillet and crisp-fry the taro or potatoes (*arbie*) over moderate heat. Remove them and set aside.

2. Fry the onions in the same oil until light brown and crisp. Remove them and set aside.

3. Remove all but 1 tablespoon oil and over moderate heat fry the garlic, turmeric, salt, black pepper, chili flakes, cardamom and cinnamon for 1 minute. Add the tomatoes and stir-fry rapidly for 5 minutes. Add the crisp-fried onions and stir-fry for another minute.

4. Add the potato or taro chips to the sauce; stir them around for 2 minutes.

Serve immediately, warm, with other dishes.

Serves 6

Note: This is another of the Kashmiri dishes that is both inventive and aromatic, and a special favorite of vegetarians.

Kashmiri Bindi
Okra from Kashmir

1 teaspoon ground turmeric
1/2 teaspoon salt
1/4 teaspoon freshly ground black pepper

1 tablespoon water
1/2 pound fresh okra
3 tablespoons corn or peanut oil

1. Prepare a paste by mixing together the turmeric, salt, black pepper and water.

2. Rinse and dry the okra. Cut off the stem end. Make a 2-inch incision along the side of each okra. Stuff the okra with a few drops of the turmeric paste and rub some on the outside. Let stand for 10 minutes.

3. Heat the oil in a wok or skillet and over moderate heat stir-fry the okra for about 4 minutes until they change color.

Serve warm with rice and other Kashmiri dishes.

Serves 4

Kanguchi Aur Tomatar
Mushrooms and Tomatoes

1 tablespoon corn or peanut oil
1/2 cup chopped onion
2 garlic cloves, chopped fine
1/2 cup chopped tomato, fresh or canned
2/3 cup water
1/4 teaspoon freshly ground black pepper

1/4 teaspoon ground cardamom
1/4 teaspoon ground turmeric
1/2 teaspoon salt
1/2 teaspoon ground fresh gingerroot
3 whole cardamom pods, cracked
1/2 pound small fresh mushrooms, rinsed well

1. Heat the oil in a pan and over moderate heat fry the onion and garlic until golden, about 3 minutes. Add the tomato and stir-fry rapidly for 3 minutes. Add 1/2 cup of the water, the black pepper, ground cardamom, the turmeric, salt, gingerroot and cardamom pods. Cook for 3 minutes.

2. Add the whole mushrooms and the balance of the water. Continue to cook over moderate heat for 10 minutes to reduce the sauce so that it thickens.

Serve warm with rice as an accompaniment to other Kashmiri dishes.

Serves 4

Palak

Spinach Purée

The *palak* of Kashmir is a long leaf of pale green color. I have found the same green in Burma. Since it is not available, to my knowledge, in the United States, supermarket spinach or chard is a reasonable enough substitute and the preparation is authentic.

*1 pound spinach or Swiss chard,
   leaves only
1 tablespoon corn or peanut oil
1/2 teaspoon salt*

*1/4 teaspoon ground turmeric
1/4 teaspoon freshly ground black
   pepper*

1. Slice the leaves into thin strips. Rinse well. Put leaves in a pan with a few tablespoons of water. Cover the pan and cook over moderately low heat for 5 minutes to wilt leaves. Remove them and lightly press out the excess liquid.

2. Heat the oil in a pan, add the greens, salt, turmeric and black pepper, and stir-fry rapidly for 3 to 4 minutes. This will break down the leaves into more or less of a purée.

Serve warm with other dishes.

Serves 4

Nadru Chips
Lotus Root Chips

This is an appetizer unique in Indian cooking. Although the word "chips" is English, this is the word used by the Kashmiris. There is no word for it in their language, but in other regions it would be called a *pakora*.

Fresh lotus roots are usually available in New York's Chinatown and elsewhere. Canned lotus is imported, but I do not recommend it.

1 cup lotus root or more	¼ teaspoon dried hot red chili
½ cup besan (chick-pea flour)	flakes
½ teaspoon salt	3 tablespoons water or more
	oil for deep-frying

1. Cut the lotus into 3-inch-long sticks, ¼ to ½ inch wide. Rinse well to remove any sand that may be clinging.

2. Mix the *besan*, salt, chili flakes and water into a thick paste. Mix the lotus roots in the batter.

3. Heat the oil in a wok or skillet. Take the lotus roots, one by one, and shake off the excess batter. Fry them in oil over moderate heat until crisp and brown, about 2 minutes. Drain on paper towels.

Serve warm.

Serves 4 to 6

Aluva Koofta
Potato Fritters in Sauce

3 small potatoes, ½ pound, cooked whole in their skins
2 garlic cloves, browned in oil and chopped fine
1 tablespoon besan (chick-pea flour)
3 tablespoons corn or peanut oil
¼ cup minced onion

½ cup chopped tomato, fresh or canned
½ teaspoon salt
½ teaspoon ground fennel seeds
¼ teaspoon dried hot red chili flakes
1 cup water

1. Peel the potatoes and mash them with the garlic. Add the *besan* and knead the mixture as though it were dough. Roll into cylinders 3 inches long and ½ inch thick.

2. Heat the oil in a skillet and brown the *koofta*. Remove them and set aside.

3. In the same oil, brown the onion over moderate heat. Add the tomato, salt, fennel and chili flakes, and stir-fry rapidly for 2 minutes to prepare the sauce. Add the water and cook, uncovered, for 10 minutes, stirring frequently.

4. Add the *koofta* in a single layer. Simmer the mixture for 3 minutes, shaking the pan once or twice rather than stirring.

Serve warm with other vegetarian dishes and rice.

Serves 4

Note: The fritters (*koofta*) may be served as appetizers with drinks by simply browning them in the oil and draining briefly on paper towels so that they are dry and crisp.

Daum Aloo

Spiced Potatoes in a Sauce

1½ pounds potatoes, 8 small-size
¼ cup corn or peanut oil
1 cup thin-sliced onions
2 teaspoons minced fresh
  gingerroot
4 garlic cloves, chopped fine
½ teaspoon dried hot red chili
  flakes
½ teaspoon ground turmeric
1 cup water

2 tablespoons tamarind paste,
  soaked in 1 cup water for 30
  minutes, strained through a
  metal sieve
½ teaspoon ground cinnamon
¼ teaspoon freshly ground black
  pepper
½ teaspoon ground fennel seed
½ teaspoon ground cardamom
2 tablespoons Scallion Paste (see
  Index)

1. Cook the whole potatoes in water over moderate heat until they are nearly done but still firm. Cool and peel. With a wooden skewer poke 6 holes in each potato. Set aside.

2. Heat the oil in a wok or skillet and crisp-fry the onions over moderate heat for about 5 minutes. Remove the onions and set aside. In the same oil, brown the potatoes for about 3 minutes. Remove them and set aside.

3. Heat 1 tablespoon of the used oil in a pan and fry the gingerroot and garlic for 1 minute. Add the chili flakes and turmeric and stir-fry the mixture with 2 tablespoons of the 1 cup water. Add the crisp onions and continue to stir.

4. Add the potatoes, the tamarind liquid and the balance of the water. Add the cinnamon, black pepper, fennel, cardamom and scallion paste. Cook the mixture over moderately low heat for 15 minutes, or until the sauce thickens and the liquid has reduced by half.

Serve warm with other dishes.

Serves 6

All Yaknee
Gourd in Yogurt Sauce

The *all* is a green gourd found in Chinese markets. It looks like a very large cucumber with a smooth skin, which may appear slightly hairy. This is a Hindu recipe for the dedicated vegetarian.

Zucchini make an excellent substitute for the gourd and are more easily available. The texture is softer than the gourd so care must be taken not to overcook it since the firmness of the texture is part of the appeal of this fine vegetarian dish.

1 pound green gourd or zucchini	1/4 teaspoon freshly ground black
oil for frying	pepper
1 cup plain yogurt	1/4 teaspoon minced fresh
1 teaspoon ground fennel seed	gingerroot
1/2 teaspoon ground cuminseed	1/2 teaspoon salt

1. Scrape the skin off the gourd lightly; cut it open and remove the seeds. Cut the gourd into 2-inch pieces.

2. Heat the oil in a wok or skillet and lightly fry the gourd over moderate heat until wilted, about 3 minutes. Remove and set aside.

3. Put the rest of the ingredients in a saucepan and stir constantly over moderately low heat for 5 minutes. Add the fried gourd and continue to stir the mixture for 5 minutes more. The thick, slightly acid sauce will cover the gourd.

Serve warm with rice and other dishes.

Serves 4

All Ka Kofta
Gourd Fritters

½ pound sliced gourd or zucchini
¼ teaspoon salt
1 tablespoon besan (chick-pea flour)

¼ teaspoon ground fennel seed
¼ teaspoon ground cuminseed
oil for deep-frying

1. Chop the gourd in a processor to a coarse consistency but do not overprocess. Squeeze in a towel to remove water. Mix the pulp with salt, besan, fennel, cuminseed and 1 teaspoon oil. Shape into round cylinders 2 inches long and ½ inch in diameter.

2. Heat the oil in a wok or skillet. Brown the fritters on all sides over moderate heat for about 3 minutes. Drain on paper towels.

Serve warm as an appetizer.

Makes 6 fritters

Variation: Zucchini are a good substitute for the gourd, but you may find it necessary to double the quantity of besan if the vegetables are too moist.

All Namkin Toor
Squash and Yogurt Purée

This is a fine vegetarian preparation, which displays the inventiveness of the Kashmiri kitchen.

1 pound pumpkin or butternut squash, peeled and cubed
1 cup plain yogurt

1 teaspoon salt
2 teaspoons toasted cuminseeds, crushed but not powdered

1. Cook the squash in water until soft. Drain well.

2. Purée the squash, yogurt, salt and cuminseed together in a processor.

Serve chilled or at room temperature.

Serves 4

Subzi Rus
Mixed Vegetable Soup

In my opinion, this soup is a winner, one of the best purely vegetarian soups I have encountered in Asia.

4 small white turnips, 1/2 pound, peeled and quartered

3 carrots, 1/4 pound, sliced diagonally

4 small potatoes, 1/2 pound, peeled and quartered

2 medium-size onions, 1/4 pound, quartered

1/4 pound cauliflower, cut into 1-inch florets

1 teaspoon minced fresh gingerroot

2 cardamon pods, cracked

1/4 teaspoon freshly ground black pepper

1 teaspoon salt

3 cups water

1/2 cup chopped tomato, fresh or canned

1 tablespoon corn or peanut oil

1 teaspoon cuminseeds

1. Put all the ingredients except the tomato, oil and cuminseeds into a pan and bring to a boil. Cook over moderate heat for 20 minutes, until the vegetables are soft.

2. Add the tomato and simmer over low heat for 10 minutes.

3. Just before serving, heat the oil in a skillet and drop in the cuminseeds. Remove from the heat immediately and add seeds and oil to the soup. Mix well.

Serve hot.

Serves 4

Kashmiri Halwah
Semolina Sweet Dish

Semolina or *soojee* is a popular Indian sweet, sometimes prepared with *ghee*. The Kashmiri version has a bit more going for it with the coconut and poppy seeds. It is a rich dessert with dimension.

6 tablespoons butter or margarine
1½ cups semolina (soojee)
3 cups water
¾ cup sugar
6 cardamom pods, cracked

2 tablespoons raisins
¼ cup 2-inch-long thin slices of coconut
2 tablespoons poppy seeds, white or black (optional)

1. Melt the butter in a wok or skillet. Add the semolina and, stirring continuously, toast it over moderately low heat for about 4 minutes to a light tan color.

2. Mix together the water, sugar, cardamom and raisins, and bring to a boil. Add half of the coconut to the syrup and pour it all over the toasting semolina. Continue to stir rapidly for 3 minutes as the grain thickens. The consistency at this stage is like a cooked Cream of Wheat cereal (which it is), toasted and sweetened.

Serve warm sprinkled with the poppy seed, if used, and the other half of the coconut strips.

Serves 6

Mudur Chere
Apricot Sweet

The apricots of Kashmir are grown in the highlands of Ladakh, an adjacent Himalayan mountain region. The apricots are dried whole with their seed and one purchases them in the bazaars of Kashmir. They look like round, deep orange, hard, wrinked balls about ¾ inch in diameter. They are of extraordinary sweetness and flavor.

1/2 pound dried apricots
1 1/2 cups water
3 tablespoons sugar, or to taste
12 blanched almonds, halved
  lengthwise

2 slices of fresh gingerroot (1
  teaspoon)
4 cardamom pods, cracked
1 cinnamon stick, 2 inches, broken
  into halves

1. Soak the apricots in the water for 5 hours or more.

2. To the apricots and water add the sugar, almonds, gingerroot, cardamom and cinnamon. Bring to a boil and cook over moderately low heat for 15 to 20 minutes, or until half of the liquid has evaporated. The apricots will be soft and surrounded by a thick syrup.

Serve chilled.

Serves 6

Chaman Ka Shipt
Sweet Cheese

Panir is an adaptable home-style cheese that responds to any seasoning. This dessert is simple and delicious. The amount of sugar may be increased or decreased according to personal preference. The preference of most Hindus is the sweeter the better.

2 tablespoons corn or peanut oil
1 cup Panir, Cheese (see Index),
  cut into 1/4-inch cubes

1 cup water
1 teaspoon ground turmeric
1/4 cup sugar

1. Heat the oil in a saucepan or skillet and brown the cheese cubes lightly over moderate heat.

2. Bring the water and turmeric to a boil. Add the cheese and oil and cook over moderate heat for 2 minutes.

3. Add the sugar and continue to cook for 10 minutes, when the liquid will evaporate somewhat and a sticky syrup remain.

Serve warm.

Serves 4

Chaman Ka Kaliya
Cheese in Fennel Sauce

2 tablespoons corn or peanut oil
1/2 pound Panir, Cheese (see
  Index), cut into 1/2-inch cubes
1 cup water
1/4 teaspoon ground turmeric

1/2 teaspoon salt
1 teaspoon ground fennel seed
1/2 teaspoon ground fresh
  gingerroot

1. Heat the oil in a wok or skillet and over moderate heat brown the cheese cubes for 3 minutes.

2. Add the water and bring to a boil. Add the turmeric, salt, fennel and gingerroot. Simmer over moderately low heat for 10 minutes to reduce the liquid somewhat and thicken the sauce.

Serve warm as a side dish.

Serves 4

Shahi Chaman
Royal Cheese

This is a Hindu recipe that goes well with rice and other nonmeat dishes. It is called Royal Cheese by the Kashmiris because they consider that, with all its aromatic spices, it is fit for royalty.

3 tablespoons corn or peanut oil
12 squares of Panir, Cheese (see
  Index), 2 inches square and 1/4
  inch thick
1/2 cup chopped ripe tomato
1/2 cup water
1/2 teaspoon salt
1/2 teaspoon sugar

1/2 teaspoon dried hot red chili
  flakes
1/2 teaspoon ground fennel seed
1/2 teaspoon ground fresh
  gingerroot
1/2 teaspoon ground cuminseed
1/2 teaspoon ground cardamom

1. Heat the oil in a wok or skillet and lightly brown the cheese squares over moderate heat. Remove the cheese and set aside. Remove all but 1 tablespoon oil.

2. Reheat the tablespoon of oil, add the tomato, and stir-fry over moderate heat for 3 minutes. Add the water, salt, sugar and spices. Stir well to produce a relatively smooth sauce. Simmer for 5 minutes.

3. Return the cheese squares and continue to simmer over moderately low heat for 10 minutes more. The sauce is spicy and should be thick.

Serve warm.

Serves 4

Mooj
White Radish Chutney

In Kashmiri homes the chutney would be pounded in a round stone mortar with a solid wooden pestle, instead of being put through a processor. The semihot chili used here is first green and then turns red as it matures. It is also known as "elephant's trunk" because of its curved shape.

1 cup sliced peeled white radish
2 inches of fresh semihot green
  chili, sliced
1/2 teaspoon salt

1/2 cup shelled walnut meats
1 teaspoon white or cider vinegar
  (optional)

1. Process the radish and chili to a coarse purée.

2. Add the salt and walnuts and continue to process to a smooth consistency. Add the vinegar, if used, and incorporate it into the chutney.

Serve with any kind of Kashmiri food.

Makes 1 cup

Mooj
Radish Salad

Restaurants automatically put a platter of *mooj* before diners. This is done in the home too for a textural contrast to the other foods that are served.

1 cup sliced peeled white radishes
1 small tomato, sliced thin
1 small onion, sliced thin

salt and freshly ground black
pepper
lemon quarters

Put the radish slices on the bottom of a serving platter. Top them with the tomato and place the onion slices over that. Sprinkle with salt and pepper to taste.

Serve with Kashmiri foods, garnished with lemon quarters.

Serves 4

Chukwangan
Eggplant Pickle in Tamarind

4 long Japanese eggplants, about
  1¼ pounds
4 cups water
oil for pan-frying
1 cup fine-sliced onion
1 teaspoon minced fresh
  gingerroot
¼ teaspoon freshly ground black
  pepper
1 teaspoon salt

¼ teaspoon ground cardamom
½ teaspoon dried hot red chili
  flakes
1 whole clove
4 cardamom pods
2 tablespoons tamarind paste,
  soaked in ½ cup hot water for
  30 minutes, strained through a
  metal sieve
¾ cup water

1. Cut the eggplants down the center from the bottom to within 1 inch of the stem. Bring 4 cups water to a boil and simmer the eggplants over moderate heat for 3 minutes. Drain and dry them on paper towels. Set aside.

2. Heat oil in a skillet and brown the eggplants on all sides over moderate heat for 3 to 4 minutes. The skin will become crisp. Remove eggplants from the oil and set aside.

3. In the same oil brown the onion and gingerroot over moderate heat for 3 minutes. Add the black pepper, salt, ground cardamom, chili flakes, clove and cardamom pods. Stir-fry for 2 minutes.

4. Add the tamarind liquid and the water and stir firmly and rapidly to reduce the sauce to a purée. Return the eggplants, cover the skillet, and cook over moderately low heat for 10 minutes to reduce the sauce, which will be thick and dark.

Serve at room temperature as a spicy condiment or side dish.

Serves 6 to 8

Pisahua Pran
Scallion Paste

The Kashmiri *pran* is really a 2-inch-long onion set that has just sprouted and then been allowed to dry. It is sold in the bazaar, dried, and is used as far as I know only in the form of a cooking ingredient, a fried paste which is used to flavor many sauces. The white part of a scallion is the closest one can come to this onion but it serves the purpose well. The paste may be stored in the refrigerator for 1 week.

¹/₄ cup corn or peanut oil   *¹/₂ cup water*
2 cups thin-sliced scallions, white
    part only

1. Heat the oil in a wok or skillet and lightly brown the scallions over moderate heat for about 4 minutes. Remove scallions from the oil.

2. Crush the scallions and water to a smooth paste in a processor.

The
Tibetan
Kitchen
of
Darjeeling

On the northernmost border of India, a few rugged miles from the great plateau that is Tibet, lies the beautiful and mysterious hill station of Darjeeling. The foothills of the Himalayas completely surround the town, and its central market is a congregating place for mountain people from Nepal, Bhutan, Sikkim and Tibet, who come to trade their wares. In the course of their trading, the Tibetans had, over the centuries, established a small community there. When I lived in India I became familiar with the dietary habits and folklore of the Tibetans from spending so much time with them. It was then that I first became intrigued with their cuisine.

When, in 1959, the Dalai Lama fled his country with thousands of his countrymen and settled in Darjeeling, my interest was intensified and took focus. Since that time, I have cooked with Tibetans in New York City as well as with the former chef of the Dalai Lama in India. We cooked the foods of several Tibetan regions, using local ingredients and reproducing the authentic flavors of the dishes. In an area so close to Tibet, their traditional foods were available and there was little need for substitution.

Cuisines logically develop on what is easily and immediately available within the precincts of a region, and therefore it is natural that the cuisine of Tibet combines the seasonings and techniques of the cooking of both China and India and the fruits, vegetables, meat and grains that could be grown at high altitudes. The food is that of both a mountain people who are meat eaters because that is what will sustain them at rigorous altitudes, and of the strict vegetarians—members of the great Buddhist society in which meat is forbidden. The broad, open plateaus and the valleys support large herds of sheep and yaks to supply meat, wool and milk products. Barley, a hardy grain, is grown extensively and is eaten in the form of *tsamba*, the toasted mash, and in *chang*, the native beer. Both tea and beer are considered to be food and are consumed in quantity. The traders, moving from India to China and back through Tibet, also brought in many foods and spices grown elsewhere, but sugar cane, being a tropical plant, was not among them. Therefore a taste for sweets never developed and there are no desserts.

Stir-frying, the most basic and easiest method of combining meat, vegetables and sauces, is a principal technique of Tibetan cooking.

241

Steaming the varieties of plain and stuffed breads (mo mo) is next in importance. None of the cooking techniques is so formidable that it is intimidating in the American kitchen, nor are the ingredients used in this cooking too hard to find. Adventurous cooks, especially if they have a knowledge of Indian or Chinese cooking, will have no problem in assembling a Tibetan dinner.

Tea

Tea comes from the leaves of a tree or shrub (camellia sinensis) that is a native of Assam, India. The plant grows wild from India to China. It is known to have been cultivated in Szechuan Province during the Earlier Han Dynasty (202 B.C.–A.D. 9). Tea did not come into general use in China before the sixth or seventh century. It was introduced into Japan about 1000 A.D. It was first used in Tibet before the middle of the eighth century. These are the cold historical facts regarding the most prevalent Tibetan beverage and one that is an absolute necessity of life.

The tea for the Tibetan market is grown in the district of Yachow (Yaan) in western Szechuan and is (or was) prepared by using the leaves and twigs of the tea plant, which are sun-dried, fermented, steamed and pressed into molds.

To prepare tea in the unique Tibetan fashion, a chunk of the tea brick is broken off and boiled in water with salt. It is then churned in a butter churn where yak butter is added according to personal preference and economic status. Sometimes, tsamba (toasted barley flour) is added to enhance the flavor. The result is indescribable.

In one account of this national addiction, it was indicated that nomadic Tibetans could drink 50 to 80 cups of tea during the day in their high, cold, rugged land. So one has a vision of the entire Tibetan plateau awash in tea, rivers of it being brewed, buttered, churned and drunk in a continuous ritual, eternal and unending. Millions of Tibetans floating in a sea of tea.

Although not everyone's cup of tea, for the Tibetans, whose principal diet may consist of this mixture, it is the staff of life, stimulating and nourishing. It contains both tannin and caffeine.

Gya Tuk

Chinese Noodle Soup, Tibetan Style

The Gya Tuk is a family-style soup, a hearty meal, for cool days. It is traditionally served with pickled radish and vegetable dishes.

1/2 pound fresh Chinese egg noodles
3 cups water
2 teaspoons corn or peanut oil
1/4 cup chopped onion
1/2 pound ground beef
1/4 teaspoon salt
1/4 teaspoon five-spice mix (optional)
1 tablespoon soy sauce
2 teaspoons minced fresh gingerroot

4 garlic cloves, chopped fine
2 teaspoons butter
2 eggs, beaten
5 cups chicken broth with 1 teaspoon soy sauce
4 scallions, sliced thin
1 soybean cake (tofu), cut into 1/4-inch cubes
Chinese-style dark vinegar

1. Boil the noodles in the water for 3 minutes so that they are cooked but still *al dente*. Drain under cold water. Set aside.

2. Heat the oil in a skillet and fry the onion over moderately low heat for 2 minutes. Add the beef, salt and five-spice mix, and stir-fry for 3 minutes. Add the soy sauce, gingerroot and garlic, and stir-fry for 3 minutes more. Set aside.

3. Heat the butter in a skillet. Over moderate heat add the eggs and make a standard flat omelet. Cool omelet and cut into 1/4-inch cubes.

4. Bring the chicken broth and soy sauce to a boil in a saucepan over moderate heat. Add the noodles for 1 minute to heat through. Remove the noodles and divide them equally into 5 or 6 soup bowls. Add 1 tablespoon of the egg, some scallion, fried beef mixture and bean cake to the top of the noodles. Then add very hot broth to each dish.

Serve hot with a Chinese-style vinegar to sprinkle over the soup, as much as wanted.

Serves 5 or 6

Then-Thu
Stretched Dough Soup

Here is another imaginative and hearty Tibetan soup. It is substantial and comforting on cold days and freezing evenings.

DOUGH

1 cup white flour
1 cup whole-wheat flour

3/4 cup cold water

SOUP

1 pound white Chinese radish, peeled
1 tablespoon corn or peanut oil
1 medium-size onion, sliced (1/2 cup)
1 pound round or sirloin steak, cut into 1/2-inch cubes

4 cups water
4 cups beef broth
1 teaspoon caraway seeds
1 teaspoon salt, or to taste
1/2 cup cottage cheese
1 cup shredded Chinese cabbage, green part only

1. Mix both flours and the water into a dough. Knead it for 5 minutes until smooth and firm. Let the dough rest for 10 minutes before using, or make it several hours in advance, wrap it in wax paper, and refrigerate until ready to use.

2. Quarter the radish lengthwise and cut each quarter across into thin slices.

3. Heat the oil in a large pan and fry the onion slices over moderate heat for 1 minute. Add the beef cubes and stir-fry for 5 minutes as the color changes. Add the water, broth, caraway seeds, salt and radish slices. Bring to a boil, cover the pan, and cook for 20 minutes

4. In the meantime, as the soup cooks, cut the dough into 2-inch chunks. Lightly oil your fingers and palms and with your hands roll the dough into 6-inch-long cigar shapes.

5. Flatten out the dough cigars with a rolling pin into flat, long, thin strips, the thinner the better, about 24 inches long and 1 inch wide. Pull and stretch the strips to make them as thin as possible.

6. Pull off 1-inch pieces of the dough strips and drop into the boiling soup. Continue until all the dough is used, stirring occasionally.

7. When all the dumplings are in the soup, add the cottage cheese and cabbage. Stir well. Cook for 15 minutes to blend the flavors. The total cooking time for the soup is about 45 minutes from the first step in the preparation.

Serve hot.

Serves 8

Variation: One cup spinach leaves can be substituted for the cabbage.

All white flour can be used, but it will alter the color of the soup somewhat and the mixture of flours does give additional body to the soup.

Faktu
Beef and Radish Soup

1 tablespoon corn or peanut oil
1 pound rump or sirloin steak, cut into ¹/4-inch dice
1 tablespoon minced fresh gingerroot
3 cups water
1 teaspoon salt, or to taste

¹/4 teaspoon freshly ground black pepper
2 cups small or medium-size pasta shells
2 cups ¹/4-inch-thick diagonal slices of white radish
1 teaspoon cornstarch dissolved in 1 tablespoon water

1. Heat the oil in a saucepan and stir-fry the beef and gingerroot over moderate heat for 3 minutes. Add the water, salt and black pepper. Bring to a boil.

2. Add the pasta shells and radish slices. Simmer over moderately low heat for 15 minutes, or until the shells are soft but still *al dente*.

3. Add the cornstarch mixture and simmer for 3 minutes more.

Serve warm in soup bowls with a hot chili chutney on the side.

Serves 6

Chu Rul

Fermented Cheese Soup

This is a delicious and highly nutritious soup. It is eaten with *tsampa* or *pali*, a Tibetan flat bread.

There are three types of milk available in Tibet from which cheeses and other milk products are made. The first is from the *dri*, the female of the species (the yak is the male). The conventional milk cow produces milk for cheese, and lastly the *zomo*, which is the crossbreed of the yak and the cow. The *zomo* give a fine quality milk, which is much prized.

Tibetan blue cheese, called fermented cheese, is derived from buttermilk after the butter has been churned. The curd is poured into porcelain jugs and allowed to ripen a length of time to develop the blue veins. This process results in a blue cheese similar to the various European varieties. In Darjeeling cow's milk and cream are readily available and so the cheese used there is much like ours.

¼ cup chopped onion	2 ounces blue cheese, mashed (¼
1 teaspoon butter	cup)
½ pound round or sirloin steak,	3 ounces cream cheese, mashed
cut into ½-inch cubes	2 garlic cloves, chopped fine
4 cups water	1 cup cottage cheese
½ teaspoon salt, or to taste	2 scallions, sliced thin

1. Fry the onion in butter in a saucepan over moderate heat for 1 minute. Add the beef and stir-fry for 5 minutes.

2. Add the water, salt, blue cheese and cream cheese and bring to a boil. Add the garlic and 2 minutes later the cottage cheese. Stir slowly to blend the various flavors.

3. Cook for 5 minutes. Add the scallions and serve hot.

Serves 6 to 8

Note: Do not overcook the soup since, according to the Tibetans, the flavor of the cheese will disappear.

Variation: For the dedicated vegetarian, omit the steak from the ingredients but follow the same steps.

Gim Mo Mo
Steamed Rolls

The Tibetans mix a cup of flour with water to form a sticky dough for these rolls. The dough is placed in a covered dish and allowed to ferment in a warm spot for 3 days. The fermented dough ball is then mixed with a type of baking soda that I have been unable to track down. It is this style of leavening that is used to produce the traditional Gim Mo Mo, but we must make do with yeast.

1½ teaspoons active dry yeast   *2 cups plus 6 tablespoons flour*
1 cup warm water (about 110°F.)   *1 tablespoon corn or peanut oil*

1. Dissolve the yeast in the warm water. Mix this with 2 cups flour. The mixture is a thin, light sticky dough. Let it rise in a well-covered bowl in a warm spot for 45 minutes, until doubled in bulk.

2. Add 5 or 6 tablespoons flour and knead the dough until it is easy to handle. It will be a soft, spongy dough ball.

3. On a floured board, roll out the dough into a large oval pancake about 20 inches in diameter and ¼ inch thick. Dust with flour if needed. Rub the surface of the pancake with oil and roll it up into a long sausage. Press the sausage down into a ½-inch-thick flattened shape.

4. Cut the dough sausage into 3-inch pieces. Slash 3 times almost all the way through each piece equidistant but not to the outer edge of the dough. Lift up the piece and open the 3 vents. Then take the 2 outer strips, bend them down, then up through the *center* vent opening.

5. Using a Chinese-style steamer, oil the bottom of the steamer trays. Place the twisted rolls into the trays 1 inch apart. Steam them over moderate heat for 30 minutes.

Serve warm.

Makes about 15 rolls

Note: The rolls can be reheated the following day in a 200°F. oven for 5 minutes or can be toasted lightly in an electric oven toaster. They can be refrigerated for 3 days after steaming and cooling.

Logo Mo Mo
Steamed Bread in the Shape of a Soup Bowl

1½ cups flour
½ teaspoon baking soda
1 teaspoon baking powder

1½ cups water, approximately
1 tablespoon corn or peanut oil

1. Mix first 3 ingredients together with about ¾ cup of water and knead the mixture into a firm smooth dough. Dust with flour when necessary if too sticky to handle easily. Shape into a round ball.

2. Shape into a bowl (logo) by pushing a depression into the dough ball about 5 inches in diameter and 4 inches deep, like a large mushroom cap.

3. Heat the oil in a saucepan over moderate heat. Place the logo (the dough bowl) edge side down into the oil and fry for 1 minute. Add the rest of the water, cover the pan, and steam cook for 10 to 12 minutes.

4. Pour off the water that remains and dry out the logo in the covered pan for 2 minutes. The logo will expand into a rather thick, steamed bread shaped like a soup bowl.

Serve the logo warm with any soup or meat dishes.

Makes 1 logo

Shapali
Fried Stuffed Dumpling

FILLING

¼ cup fine-chopped onion
2 garlic cloves, chopped fine
1 inch of fresh gingerroot, chopped fine
1 cup chopped fresh spinach or Chinese cabbage

¼ pound ground beef
½ teaspoon salt
1 tablespoon dark soy sauce
¼ teaspoon five-spice mix
1 tablespoon cold water

PASTRY

2 cups flour   ³/₄ cup cold water, approximately

¹/₂ cup corn or peanut oil for
  cooking, approximately

1. Mix all the filling ingredients together and set aside.

2. Mix the flour and water into a moist soft dough. Add 1 or 2 more tablespoons flour if the dough is too sticky to handle. Knead for 10 minutes. Set aside and allow the dough to rest for about 1 hour.

3. Cut the dough into 2-inch pieces and roll them into balls with lightly floured hands. Set the balls aside on a floured board. They will be soft and spongy.

4. Roll out each dough ball into a round pancake 3 to 4 inches in diameter. Pull out the edges to stretch the pancake to the desired size. Fill it with 1 heaping tablespoon of the beef mixture. Close the pancake by folding up the edges and by pinching and pulling the dumpling (which you revolve as you close it up) into a round sealed ball.

5. Heat 1 tablespoon oil in a skillet over medium heat. Flatten the filled dumpling with a rolling pin until it is a bit more than ¹/₄ inch thick and about 4 inches in diameter. Fry for 2 minutes on each side until lightly browned. Drain briefly on paper towels. Continue until all the dumplings are fried, adding a teaspoon or so of oil when necessary.

Serve warm. *Shapali* can be eaten hot, at room temperature or cold. They are traditionally eaten on picnics or with other dishes in the home.

Makes 12

Variation: Tibetan wheat flour is white but not the highly bleached supermarket variety found in the United States. One could make the pastry by using one quarter whole-wheat flour and three quarters white flour, a more natural mixture.

The Tibetan upper classes used the white flour and the peasant classes traditionally used the whole-wheat flour since it was cheaper; the same condition prevailed in Darjeeling. Today, we have almost reversed the practice since the whole-wheat dumpling has an interesting texture and cost doesn't enter into the calculation at all.

Mo Mo
Steamed Meat Dumplings

DOUGH

2 cups flour   3/4 cup water, approximately

FILLING

1 pound ground beef   3 garlic cloves, chopped fine
1 medium-size onion, chopped fine 1 teaspoon salt
   (1/2 cup)   2 teaspoons soy sauce
1/4 teaspoon freshly ground black 1 tablespoon cold water
   pepper
1 inch of fresh gingerroot, chopped
   fine

1. Mix the flour and water into a smooth but soft dough. Use as much water as necessary and dust with flour if dough is too sticky. Knead for 5 minutes. Set aside.

2. Mix all the filling ingredients together. Set aside.

3. Prepare a long sausage 1 inch in diameter with the dough. Cut or tear off 1-inch pieces of dough and roll them into balls. Roll out the balls on a well-floured board to discs 4 inches in diameter.

4. Place 1 heaping tablespoon of the filling in the center of each dough disc. Pinch together the two sides, then do this pinching/folding motion to the entire dumpling to make a round ball closed together at the top.

5. Rub the steamer racks in a Chinese-style steamer with oil. Place the dumplings on the rack over hot water. Steam over moderate heat for 20 minutes.

Serve warm with soy sauce as a dip.

Makes 14 dumplings

Variation: Some cooks prepare the *mo mo* dough with 1 teaspoon baking powder, which gives the dough a more spongy texture. You may wish to do this.

Stuffing Variations:

CHEESE AND VEGETABLES

1 small carrot, sliced	1¹/₄ cups farmer's cheese
¹/₂ cup sliced green beans	¹/₂ teaspoon salt
¹/₄ cup green peas, fresh or frozen	¹/₂ teaspoon pepper
¹/₂ cup shredded cabbage	

1. Blanch the carrot, green beans, peas and cabbage separately in boiling water for 2 minutes. Drain well.

2. Chop the carrot, green beans and cabbage to fine pieces. Green peas remain whole.

3. Mix the chopped vegetables, cheese, salt and pepper together. Use this stuffing to prepare the *mo mo*.

LAMB STUFFING

1 pound ground lamb	¹/₂ teaspoon salt
1 small onion, chopped fine (¹/₄ cup)	1 teaspoon soy sauce
¹/₂ inch of fresh gingerroot, chopped fine	

Mix everything together and use as a stuffing. Note that this is a simpler meat stuffing than that of the beef. However, the same flavorings may be used with the lamb as for the beef.

CHICKEN AND PORK

Ground chicken or pork are also used as *mo mo* stuffings. You may season these meats simply, like the lamb, or give them the stronger flavors used with the beef.

Tea Mo Mo
Plain Steamed Dumplings

2 cups flour
about ³/₄ cup water

1 teaspoon baking powder
2 tablespoons corn or peanut oil

1. Mix flour, water and baking powder together to make a moist but not sticky dough. Dust with flour and knead on a floured board for 5 minutes. Let the dough rest, covered, for 30 minutes.

2. Cut off an egg-sized piece of dough and roll it out to a strip 6 inches long and 1 inch wide. Rub oil over the surface of the strip, then fold it over in half. Roll up the half. Continue to shape the rest of the dough.

3. Cut an incision ¹/₄ inch deep and 1 inch long with a sharp knife into the top of each rolled dumpling.

4. Put all the dumplings on the oiled rack of a Chinese-style steamer. Steam over hot water over moderate heat for 15 minutes.

Serve warm with any Tibetan food.

Makes 6 dumplings

Variation: The tea *mo mo* may be prepared with half whole-wheat and half white flour.

Tsel Mo Mo
Boiled Cabbage Dumplings

2 cups flour
³/₄ cup cold water, approximately
2 Chinese soybean cakes (tofu)
2 tablespoons corn or peanut oil
2 cups chopped Chinese or round head cabbage
¹/₂ teaspoon salt
¹/₄ teaspoon freshly ground black pepper
2 garlic cloves, chopped fine

¹/₂ inch of fresh gingerroot, chopped fine
1 medium-size onion, chopped fine (¹/₂ cup)
1 scallion, green part only, sliced thin
2 teaspoons soy sauce
1 tablespoon sesame butter (tahini)

1. Mix the flour and cold water into a soft, smooth dough. Knead for 5 minutes, until smooth, adding 1 to 2 tablespoons more flour if the mixture is sticky. Set aside and let the dough rest, covered, for 1 hour.

2. Cut the soybean cakes into 1/4-inch-thick slices. Heat the oil in a skillet and fry the slices over moderate heat until light brown. Remove and cool. Coarsely chop the slices.

3. Mix together the cabbage, salt, black pepper, garlic, gingerroot, onion, scallion, soy sauce, sesame butter and chopped bean cake.

4. On a floured board cut the dough into 2 equal strips. Roll out each strip between your palms into rounded lengths about 14 inches long. Cut each strip into 3/4-inch-thick slices, dust with flour, and press into flat discs 2 inches in diameter.

5. Prepare the dough wrapper by rolling out each pressed disc into a thin disc 3 inches in diameter.

6. Place 1 heaping teaspoon of vegetable stuffing in the center of the wrapper that rests in your palm. Pinch together one end of the wrapper, push the stuffing firmly inside, then continue to pinch the dough together at the top of the dumpling. Revolve the *mo mo* in your hand as you pinch and turn. Make certain that the *mo mo* is well sealed so that it does not open during cooking. Prepare all the *mo mo* and set aside.

7. In a large pan bring water to a rolling boil over moderate heat. Add about 8 *mo mo* at a time and cook, uncovered, for 7 minutes. Remove them with a slotted spoon and serve immediately.

Serve hot with soy sauce as a dip.

Makes about 20 dumplings

Note: The *mo mo* may be cooked, cooled and refrigerated for about 4 days. Reheat briefly in a steamer when wanted.

The *mo mo* may also be frozen in the *uncooked* state for long periods of time. They should be dusted with flour prior to freezing in aluminum-foil packages. They should be thawed out for 1 hour before cooking.

Bopik
Stuffed Beef and Vegetable Pancake

PANCAKE

2 cups flour
3/4 cup cold water, approximately

2 tablespoons melted butter or margarine

FILLING

3 tablespoons corn or peanut oil
3 scallions, sliced diagonally into 1-inch-long pieces
1/4 pound flank or sirloin steak, sliced thin
1/2 teaspoon salt
1/4 teaspoon pepper

1 medium-size carrot, cut into julienne (1/2 cup)
2 cups thin-sliced celery
4 ounces bean thread noodles (phing) (see Note)
1 tablespoon soy sauce
3 tablespoons water

1. Mix the flour and enough water to make a firm dry dough. Knead on a floured board for 5 minutes.

2. Roll out the dough into a 24-inch-long sausage, 1 inch in diameter. Cut into 1/2-inch-wide slices. Dust the cut ends with flour and press them out into 2 1/2-inch discs. Butter one side of each disc and press two of them together on the buttered sides. This will make 12 sandwiches.

3. Roll out each sandwich into a 6-inch-round pancake. Prepare all the sandwiches this way.

4. Place a dry skillet over moderate heat. Fry the sandwich for 1/2 minute on each side. Set aside for a moment and pull the two halves apart into 2 thin pancakes. Put them in a covered dish lined with a paper towel. Fry and separate all the sandwiches this way.

5. Heat the 3 tablespoons oil in a wok or skillet and stir-fry the scallions and steak for 1 minute. Add the salt, pepper, carrot, celery and bean threads and stir-fry for 2 minutes. Lastly, add the soy sauce and water and stir-fry for 2 minutes more. Set aside.

TO SERVE

Take 1 thin pancake and place on it as much of the mixture as you wish, then roll it up like a sausage.

Serve as an appetizer or for lunch or dinner with other dishes.

Serves 6

Note: The bean thread noodles must be soaked in hot water for 10 minutes, drained well, and cut into halves with scissors before using.

Prepared Shanghai-style round pancakes may be purchased in Chinatown food markets. They are found on refrigerated shelves. They are useful but the homemade variety is preferable.

Pal Tsal Ngopa
Fried Beef with Chinese Cabbage

Pal tsal is freely translated as Chinese cabbage. Like many Tibetan dishes, this particular one is assembled as a stir-fry. The original recipe uses mustard oil, another popular ingredient in Tibet.

Asian food shops feature many types of soy sauce including a dark sauce and one known as mushroom soy sauce. Tibetan friends in New York use both of these.

2 tablespoons corn or peanut oil
1 small onion, sliced (¼ cup)
½ pound round or sirloin steak, cut into ½-inch cubes
3 or 4 garlic cloves, chopped fine
2 tablespoons dark or mushroom soy sauce

¼ teaspoon five-spice mix
½ teaspoon salt
1 pound Chinese cabbage, cut into 2-inch-wide slices
1 inch of fresh gingerroot, chopped fine

1. Heat the oil in a wok or large skillet and stir-fry the onion over high heat for 2 minutes. Add the beef, stir-fry for 1 minute, then add the garlic, soy sauce, five-spice mix and salt. Stir well.

2. Add the cabbage and gingerroot, cover the wok, and fry for 5 minutes to reduce the bulk of the cabbage. Uncover; stir well.

Serve hot.

Serves 4

Bhak Tsa Maku

Buttered Sweet Shells with Cheese

2 cups flour
4³/4 cups water, approximately
3 tablespoons sugar
8 tablespoons butter or margarine

1 tablespoon Tsamba Ma Sen,
  following recipe (optional)
¹/2 cup cottage or farmer's cheese

1. Mix the flour with enough water, about ³/4 cup, to make a firm dough. Knead until smooth and dust with flour if dough is too sticky.

2. Roll out the dough into long cigars ¹/2 inch in diameter. Tear off ¹/2 inch of dough, press it in your palm with a thumb and roll it slightly away from you to get the curved shape of a shell. Shape shells from all the dough.

3. Bring the 4 cups water to a boil, drop in the shells, cover the pan, and cook over moderate heat for 5 minutes, until *al dente*. Drain well.

4. Return the shells to the pan, add the sugar, butter, *tsamba* if used, and cottage cheese. Mix well over low heat for 2 minutes.

Serve warm with coffee, tea or as a snack at any time.

Serves 6

Note: This is not a daily food but one that is usually served at special events. It is a festive dish.

Tsamba Ma Sen

Toasted Barley Meal with Butter

Barley is the staple cereal of Tibetans and *tsamba* is a staple dish. Originally carried by the nomads wandering the heights of the Tibetan plateau, the receipe for this dish is more of historical than practical import.

2 cups barley
¹/2 cup hot water, approximately

1 tablespoon butter

1. Toast the barley in a dry skillet over moderately low heat for 5 minutes, or until it turns a light brown color. Grind it to a flour in a processor.

2. Mix the flour and water together into a moist but crumbly mixture. Take a soup bowl and press the *tsamba* quite firmly into the dish. Invert the bowl over a serving plate. Dot with the butter and serve with a spoon.

Tsamp Tuk
Creamed Barley

The *tsamp tuk* is a ceremonial dish, but it can be eaten daily by lamas or other Tibetans who do not eat meat or eggs.

1 cup raw barley, well rinsed under cold water
5 cups water
¹/₄ cup dairy sour cream
¹/₂ cup plain yogurt

2 tablespoons grated Parmesan-type cheese
¹/₄ cup sugar
2 tablespoons raisins, soaked in hot water for 10 minutes, drained

1. Cook the barley in water in a covered pan over moderately low heat for 20 minutes. Stir now and then. After that, turn off the heat and leave the pan covered to steam the barley for 10 minutes more. The water will have been completely absorbed.

2. Add the sour cream, yogurt, cheese, sugar and raisins. Stir well and simmer over low heat for 3 minutes.

Serve warm or at room temperature.

Serves 6 to 8

Shabri

Lamb Balls in Sauce

The *shabri* is an attractive and tasty party dish, which can be made in quantity for large groups. It has the traditional Tibetan seasonings of ginger and garlic.

MINIATURE MEATBALLS

2 pounds lamb, ground
1 egg, beaten
1 teaspoon salt
1/2 teaspoon freshly ground black pepper

1 tablespoon cornstarch or rice flour
3 tablespoons cold water

1/4 cup corn or peanut oil

SAUCE

1/2 cup shredded cabbage
1/2 cup thin-sliced carrot
1 tablespoon corn or peanut oil
1 teaspoon minced fresh gingerroot
1 garlic clove, chopped fine

1 tablespoon minced onion
1 tablespoon soy sauce
1/4 teaspooon freshly ground black pepper
2 cups chicken or beef broth

1. Mix the lamb, egg, salt and black pepper together.

2. Dissolve the cornstarch in the water. Dip your fingers into the cornstarch solution, take 1 heaping teaspoon of the lamb mixture, and roll it into a ball about 3/4 inch in diameter. The cornstarch will hold it together. Shape all the meatballs.

3. Heat the oil in a skillet and brown the meatballs over moderate heat for 2 minutes. Drain well and set aside.

4. Blanch the cabbage and carrot separately in boiling water for 2 minutes. Drain well.

5. Heat the oil in a skillet and stir-fry the gingerroot, garlic and onion over moderate heat for 2 minutes. Add the blanched vegetables and stir-fry for 2 minutes more.

6. Add the meatballs, soy sauce, black pepper and broth. Bring to a boil and cook over moderately low heat for 5 minutes.

Serve warm with rice, noodles (*phing*) or Tea Mo Mo (see Index).

Serves 6

Phing
Bean Threads with Beef

Phing is not really a soup but could perhaps be considered a stew. The *phing* (bean threads) come in several thicknesses. The one used here is like a medium-thin spaghetti and is called Long Rice or Saifun. It is made of mung bean and potato flour and is purchased dry in packages.

1/4 pound bean threads
1 tablespoon corn or peanut oil
1 tablespoon minced onion
1/2 pound flank or sirloin steak,
  cut into thin 2-inch slices
1 garlic clove, chopped fine
1 teaspoon minced fresh
  gingerroot
1 cup beef broth
2 tablespoons soy sauce
1/4 teaspoon salt
1/8 teaspoon five-spice mix

1. Soak the bean threads (*phing*) in hot water for 15 minutes. The threads will swell slightly and become translucent. Drain, and cut into 3-inch pieces with scissors.

2. Heat the oil in a skillet and stir-fry the onion over moderate heat for 1 minute. Add the steak and stir-fry for 1 minute. Add the garlic and gingerroot and continue to stir-fry for 1 minute.

3. Add the broth, soy sauce, salt, five-spice mix and bean threads, and cook for 3 minutes.

Serve warm with the traditional accompaniment, rice.

Serves 4

Dang-Tsal
Beef and Vegetable Fry

This dish is prepared in two shifts, always cooked separately but served together. *Dang-tsal* means "cold vegetables" but the reason for this is a puzzle to me.

1 pound cauliflower, cut into 2-inch florets

1¹/₂ cups green peas, fresh or frozen

2 tablespoons corn or peanut oil

1 medium-size onion, sliced (¹/₂ cup)

2 garlic cloves, chopped fine

1 inch of fresh gingerroot, chopped fine

¹/₂ pound flank or sirloin steak, cut into julienne

1 teaspooon salt, or to taste

¹/₄ teaspoon freshly ground black pepper

2 tablespoons light soy sauce

¹/₂ cup beef broth

1. Blanch the cauliflower and peas separately in boiling water for 2 minutes. Drain well. If frozen peas are used, this step is not necessary.

2. Use half of all the rest of the ingredients for each vegetable. Heat the oil in a wok or skillet and stir-fry half of the onion, garlic and gingerroot over moderate heat for 1 minute. Add half of the beef and stir-fry until the color changes, about 2 minutes. Add half of the salt, black pepper and soy sauce and stir-fry for 1 minute.

3. Add the cauliflower and continue to stir-fry for 2 minutes. Add half of the broth and continue to fry for 2 minutes more.

4. Do the same for the green peas, using the remaining half of all the ingredients.

Serve warm with a separate dish for each vegetable.

Serves 6

Variation: One-half pound boneless raw chicken, both light and dark meat, can be substituted for the beef steak.

Chenpa
Beef Kidney Sauté

The vegetables provide additional texture to this beef kidney dish. Other vegetables sometimes used are green beans, summer squash, or even white turnip—always in combinations of three vegetables.

2 small beef kidneys
1 small carrot, sliced
1/2 chayote, peeled and sliced
1/2 cup 1-inch cauliflowerets
2 tablespoons corn or peanut oil
1 small onion, chopped (1/4 cup)
3 garlic cloves, chopped fine
1 inch of fresh gingerroot, chopped fine

1/2 teaspoon salt, or to taste
1/4 teaspoon freshly ground black pepper
1 tablespoon soy sauce
3/4 cup beef or chicken broth
2 teaspoons cornstarch dissolved in 1 tablespoon water

1. Halve the kidneys and trim out the inner ligaments and vessels. Cut the kidneys into 2-inch cubes and score them crisscross on the outer part. Rinse in cold water. Set aside.

2. Blanch the carrot, chayote and cauliflowerets in boiling water for 5 minutes. Drain well.

3. Heat the oil in a wok or skillet and stir-fry the onion, garlic and gingerroot over moderate heat for 2 minutes. Add the kidneys and stir-fry for 2 minutes. Add the salt, black pepper, soy sauce and vegetables, and stir-fry for 1 minute.

4. Add the broth and the cornstarch mixture and continue to stir for 3 minutes more to cook all the ingredients.

Serve warm with rice, any kind of *mo mo* and chutney.

Serves 4

Shaptak
Beef and Chili

Tibetans love garlic, chili and ginger, their most important flavorings. Both chili and ginger are grown in India, Nepal and Bhutan.

Sha means "meat"; *ptak* means "fried." Yak was the fried meat in the original recipe.

1 tablespoon corn or peanut oil
1 small onion, chopped fine (¹/₄ cup)
1 pound round or flank steak, cut into thin slices 2 inches long
¹/₂ teaspoon salt
4 garlic cloves, chopped fine

1 inch of fresh gingerroot, chopped fine
¹/₂ teaspoon five-spice mix
2 fresh green semihot chilies, seeds removed, sliced into coarse pieces
2 tablespoons soy sauce
2 tablespoons hot water

1. Heat the oil in a wok or skillet and stir-fry the onion over high heat for 1 minute. Add the beef and stir-fry rapidly for 2 minutes. Add the salt, garlic, gingerroot and five-spice mix, and continue to stir-fry.

2. Add the chilies, soy sauce and water. Stir-fry for another minute to distribute the flavors.

Serve warm with rice, *mo mo* and hot sauce.

Serves 6

Chelay
Tender Tongue Fry

1 fresh beef or veal tongue, 2 to 3 pounds
6 cups water
1 tablespoon corn or peanut oil
1 garlic clove, chopped
1 teaspoon minced fresh gingerroot

1 small onion, chopped (¹/₄ cup)
¹/₂ teaspoon salt
¹/₄ teaspoon black pepper
¹/₂ teaspoon dried hot red chili flakes
1 tablespoon soy sauce

1. Cover the tongue with water in a pan and cook over moderate heat, covered, until the tongue is tender, 1½ hours or more. Peel the tongue and cut it into ¼-inch thick slices.

2. Heat the oil in a skillet and stir-fry the garlic, gingerroot and onion over moderate heat for 2 minutes.

3. Add the tongue slices, salt, black pepper, chili flakes and soy sauce. Stir-fry for 3 minutes to coat the tongue with the flavorings. This is a dry fry without sauce.

Serve warm with other dishes.

Serves 4

Fak Sha Shapta
Pork Stir-Fry

The influence of China is paramount in this stir-fry. Only serving it with the *mo mo* makes it Tibetan.

2 tablespoons corn or peanut oil
¼ cup thin-sliced onion
1 garlic clove, chopped
1 teaspoon minced fresh gingerroot
½ pound boneless pork, cut into slices 2 inches long and 1 inch wide

1 tablespoon soy sauce
¼ teaspoon salt
¼ teaspoon freshly ground black pepper

1. Heat the oil in a wok or skillet and stir-fry the onion, garlic and gingerroot over high heat for 2 minutes. Add the pork slices and continue to stir-fry for 3 minutes more to cook the meat thoroughly.

2. Add the soy sauce, salt and black pepper and stir-fry for 2 minutes more.

Serve warm with, preferably, the Logo Mo Mo (see Index).

Serves 2

Gyako
Tibetan Hot Pot

Gyako is the Tibetan antidote to the intense cold of their high plateau. A production suitable for groups or family gatherings, most of the preparation can be done ahead and then assembled after the guests arrive. It is not apartment-house cooking unless you have an open balcony, but is more appropriate for warm autumn afternoons or evenings around the picnic table. The hot pot is a necessity for this recipe, and you will find that sitting around it, savoring the contents and being warmed vicariously by the charcoal in the chimney, becomes an exotic and romantic experience. Mongolian hot pots of various sizes always seem to be available for sale in Chinatowns, and some New York restaurants feature a variation of *gyako* on their menus during the cool months.

BEAN THREADS AND VEGETABLES
2 ounces thin bean thread noodles (phing)

3 cups water

2 cups coarse-shredded cabbage

1/2 cup thin-sliced carrot

MUSHROOMS AND TREE EARS
1/2 cup dried mushrooms

1/2 cup tree ears

2 cups hot water

FLAVORINGS
1 tablespoon soy sauce

1/4 teaspoon freshly ground black pepper

3 scallions, sliced diagonally, 1/4 inch wide

MEAT AND BROTH
1 pound boneless chuck, in one piece

1/2 pound boneless pork, in one piece

1 whole chicken breast, halved

1 small onion

6 cups water

PORK CUBES
1 egg, beaten

3 tablespoons flour

1/4 teaspoon salt

1 tablespoon water

1/2 pound boneless pork, cut into 1/2-inch cubes

1/4 cup corn or peanut oil

BEEF BALLS AND PATTIES

1 pound ground beef	*1 tablespoon cornstarch dissolved*
1 egg, beaten	*in 2 tablespoons water*
¹/₂ teaspoon salt	
¹/₄ teaspoon freshly ground black	
pepper	

TOFU

*2 Chinese soybean cakes, cut into
12 cubes each*

1. Soak the bean threads in 2 cups warm water for 15 minutes. Drain and set aside.

2. Bring 1 cup water to a boil and cook the cabbage and the carrot together for 2 minutes. Drain. Add the cabbage to the bean threads and set the carrot aside.

3. Soak the mushrooms and tree ears together in the hot water for 20 minutes. Rub them to remove any sand. Drain and squeeze dry to remove excess liquid. Break off the stems of the mushrooms and discard them. Slice the mushroom caps into ¹/₄-inch-wide strips; leave the tree ears in lobes. Add to the bean threads and cabbage.

4. Mix the soy sauce and black pepper into the bean thread mixture. Set the scallions aside for garnish.

5. Put the beef, pork and chicken with the onion and water into a large saucepan and bring to a boil over moderate heat. Cook, covered, for 30 minutes. Remove the chicken, and continue to cook the beef and pork for another 30 minutes or until tender. Cut the meat into neat slices and reserve the broth.

6. Prepare a smooth batter by mixing the egg, flour, salt and water for the pork cubes. Dip the pork cubes into the batter and brown them in the oil over moderate heat for 3 minutes. Set the pork cubes aside and reserve the oil.

7. Mix the beef, egg, salt and black pepper together and prepare the meatballs and patties. First dip your fingers into the cornstarch solution, and then take about a heaping teaspoon of the beef mixture and roll into a meatball 1 inch in diameter. Prepare all the meat in this way, then flatten half of the balls into patties ¹/₄ inch thick.

(recipe continues)

8. Reheat the oil used with the pork cubes and over moderate heat brown the meatballs and patties for 2 minutes. Drain well and set aside.

9. When ready to serve, mix half of the chicken, pork and beef slices in the bean thread mixture and place this mixture on the bottom of the hot pot bowl. Distribute the pork cubes over this mixture and on top of that scatter the beef balls and patties. The carrot slices are put on top of the patties and the balance of the chicken, pork and beef slices on the carrot slices. Put the tofu cubes on top.

10. Add 4 cups of the reserved hot meat broth slowly to the bowl and scatter the scallions over all.

11. Half-fill the inner chimney with hot charcoal embers and place the cover over the bowl, which slips over the chimney. Wait 10 minutes for the mixture to simmer. Remove the cover and invite each diner to help himself to a sampling of all the ingredients. As the soup is used up, the remaining broth should be added to the pot.

Serves 8

Jasha
Baked Honey Chicken

2 teaspoons chopped fresh
  gingerroot
2 garlic cloves, chopped
1/4 cup chopped onion
2 tablespoons honey

2 tablespoons soy sauce
1 chicken, 3 pounds, cut into 10
  pieces, including giblets, loose
  skin and fat discarded
3 scallions, green part only, sliced

1. Mix the gingerroot, garlic, onion, honey and soy sauce together and pour over chicken, including the giblets. Marinate for 1 hour.

2. Heat the oven to 450°F. Put the chicken into a heatproof glass baking dish and bake for 30 minutes, turning the pieces over once. Scatter the scallions over the chicken 5 minutes before it is ready to serve.

Serve warm with other dishes.

Serves 4

Note: You may broil rather than bake the chicken, if you prefer. The end result is similar, but to me the baking seems less hectic.

Chasha
Tibetan Chicken Curry

The country chickens of Darjeeling are small, about 2 pounds each, and have firm flesh. They never quite fall apart like our supermarket-chickens but retain their lean country texture. For this reason, 2 Cornish hens, weighing about 1½ pounds each and quartered, make a good substitute in this recipe. This is one of the very few Tibetan recipes that calls for turmeric.

3 tablespoons corn or peanut oil
2 medium-size onions, chopped
  (³/₄ cup)
2 teaspoons minced fresh
  gingerroot
3 garlic cloves, chopped fine
¼ teaspoon dried hot red chili
  flakes

1 chicken, 3 pounds, cut into 10
  serving pieces, loose skin and fat
  discarded
1 teaspoon salt, or to taste
¼ teaspoon freshly ground black
  pepper
1 teaspoon ground turmeric
1 cup water

1. Heat the oil in a saucepan or skillet, add the onions, and stir-fry for 1 minute. Add the gingerroot, garlic and chili flakes. Stir-fry for 2 minutes to brown lightly.

2. Add the chicken, salt, black pepper and turmeric and stir-fry for 5 minutes to brown the chicken.

3. Add the water, cover the pan, and cook over moderately low heat for 30 minutes, or until the chicken is tender and the sauce has reduced and thickened.

Serve warm with rice and Tea Mo Mo, Plain Steamed Dumplings (see Index).

Serves 4

Chasha Teeroo
Ground Chicken Curry

This is an example of India and China joining together to produce a curry. Indian flavorings and Chinese technique give this a character of its own.

¹/₂ cup 1-inch pieces of cauliflower
1 tablespoon corn or peanut oil
1 small onion, chopped (¹/₄ cup)
¹/₂ teaspoon minced fresh gingerroot
1 small garlic clove, chopped
¹/₂ teaspoon minced fresh hot green chili

1 cup ground raw chicken
¹/₄ teaspoon ground turmeric
¹/₂ teaspoon salt
¹/₄ cup green peas, fresh or frozen
¹/₂ cup beef or chicken broth
1 teaspoon cornstarch dissolved in 1 tablespoon water
1 scallion, sliced thin

1. Blanch the cauliflower in boiling water for 3 minutes. Drain well.

2. Heat the oil in a wok or skillet and fry the onion, gingerroot, garlic and chili over moderate heat for 2 minutes. Add the chicken, turmeric and salt and stir-fry for 2 minutes.

3. Add the cauliflower, peas and broth, bring to a boil, and add the cornstarch mixture. Stir-fry for 2 minutes more to combine the flavorings. Garnish with scallion.

Serve warm with any kind of *mo mo* (steamed dumplings).

Serves 6

Chadi Chimba Tang Tse
Chicken Liver Stir-Fry

The livers from the country chickens were tender, pink melting tidbits when prepared in this fashion. The thin slices allowed a quick stir-fry that retained the texture, a smooth one, that was characteristic of the mountain chickens raised in the chilly altitudes of Darjeeling.

1 tablespoon corn or peanut oil
1/4 cup thin-sliced onion
1 garlic clove, chopped
1/2 pound chicken livers, divided
   into lobes and halved

1/2 teaspoon salt
1/4 teaspoon freshly ground black
   pepper
2 teaspoons soy sauce
1 scallion, sliced thin

1. Heat the oil in a wok or skillet and stir-fry the onion and garlic over high heat for 1 minute.

2. Add the liver slices and stir-fry for 2 minutes, adding the salt, pepper and soy sauce. Stir in the scallion for 1 minute and serve immediately.

Serve warm with *mo mo* or rice and other dishes.

Serves 4

Gonga Mana
Spiced Eggs (An Omelet)

4 eggs, beaten
1/4 teaspoon salt
1/4 teaspoon freshly ground black
  pepper
1/2 teaspoon five-spice mix

2 tablespoons dairy sour cream
2 teaspoons grated Parmesan-type
  cheese
1 tablespoon corn or peanut oil
1 small ripe tomato, sliced thin

1. Mix the eggs, salt, black pepper, five-spice mix, sour cream and cheese together.

2. Heat the oil in a skillet over moderately low heat. Pour the egg mixture into the skillet and cover it with the sliced tomato. Fry slowly until the eggs are well set, then turn the omelet over. Brown lightly on the other side.

Serve warm with steamed rolls (*mo mo*) for lunch.

Serves 2

Gonga Tson
Scallion Eggs (An Omelet)

This is another Tibetan lunch preparation to be eaten with *mo mo*.

4 eggs, beaten
1/4 teaspoon salt
1/4 teaspoon freshly ground black
  pepper

3 scallions, sliced thin
2 teaspoons corn or peanut oil

1. Beat the eggs, salt, black pepper and scallions together.

2. Heat the oil in a skillet over moderately low heat. Pour in the egg mixture and fry the omelet slowly until the eggs are firmly set. Turn over and brown the other side lightly.

Serve warm with steamed rolls (*mo mo*).

Serves 2

Subjij
Vegetable Cutlet

These cutlets are so dense in texture that you will not notice the absence of meat when they are served. Perfect for a vegetarian meal.

¹/₂ cup 1-inch cauliflowerets
¹/₂ cup potato cubes
¹/₂ cup green peas, fresh or frozen
¹/₂ cup 1-inch pieces of green
  beans
¹/₂ cup thin-sliced carrot
 1 teaspoon salt

¹/₂ teaspoon freshly ground black
  pepper
2 eggs, beaten
2 tablespoons flour
1 tablespoon chopped parsley
¹/₂ cup toasted bread crumbs
¹/₂ cup corn or peanut oil

1. Cook the vegetables separately in water until tender but not overcooked. Drain well. Mash these together in a processor with the salt and pepper.

2. Mix the eggs, flour and parsley into a batter.

3. Shape about ¹/₂ cup of the vegetable mixture into a round ball. Flatten out the ball into an egg-shaped cutlet ¹/₂ inch thick.

4. Dip the cutlet into the batter and then into the bread crumbs.

5. Heat the oil in a skillet and brown the cutlets over moderate heat for 2 minutes on each side. Drain briefly on paper towels.

Serve warm.

Makes 6 cutlets

Ba Lee Shoga
Potato Fry with Pancake

This is a winter dish in which each diner helps himself to the pancakes and potatoes, taking as many as he wishes. A substantial food, it is vegetarian and yet satisfying for those living in cold climates. The potato fry is a recipe that can be served alone, as well as with the pancakes.

PANCAKE

1½ cups flour
½ cup plus 1 tablespoon cold
 water

3 tablespoons corn or peanut oil,
 approximately

POTATOES

1 tablespoon corn or peanut oil
2 garlic cloves, sliced thin
 lengthwise
½ cup thin-sliced onion
1 pound potatoes, peeled, sliced as
 for French fries
½ teaspoon salt

½ teaspoon freshly ground black
 pepper
2 tablespoons sesame butter
 (tahini)
1 tablespoon soy sauce
¼ cup water

1. Mix the flour and water into a dough and knead until smooth. Add a little more flour if the dough is too sticky to be manageable. Cover the dough and let it rest for 15 minutes.

2. On a well-floured board, roll out the dough to a circle about 16 inches in diameter. Spread 1 tablespoon oil over the dough circle and paint the entire surface. Roll the circle up like a jelly roll. Cut this into 3 equal pieces.

3. Twist each piece like a corkscrew and push both ends in toward the middle like an accordion. Press this ball with the heel of the hand into a round disc 4 inches in diameter. Roll out the disc into an 8-inch pancake about ⅛ inch thick. Prepare 3 pancakes.

4. Heat 2 teaspoons oil in a skillet and over moderate heat fry a pancake on both sides until light brown and crisp. Fry the other pancakes. Set aside and keep them warm.

5. To prepare the potatoes, heat the oil in a skillet and stir-fry the garlic and onion over moderate heat for 2 minutes. Add the potatoes and stir-

fry for 5 minutes. Add the salt, black pepper, sesame butter and soy sauce. Mix well, cover the skillet, and fry for 10 minutes.

6. Add the water, again cover the skillet, and continue to fry for 10 minutes more to evaporate the water and make the potatoes brown and dry.

7. Cut each pancake into thirds, which can be pulled open into a sort of pocket. Fill these with the potato mixture.

Serve warm.

Serves 4

Bazal Medok Armo
Sweet Cauliflower

The food cooked by the lamas is not complicated. There is an economy of flavorings—a little sweet, a little sour—that allows the natural flavor of the vegetable to come through.

1 pound cauliflower, cut into 1-inch pieces (about 3 cups)	*¹/₄ teaspoon salt*
2 cups boiling water	*3 tablespoons dairy sour cream*
	2 tablespoons honey

1. Drop the cauliflower into the boiling water, add the salt, cover, and cook for 2 minutes. Drain well.

2. Return the cauliflower to the pot, add the sour cream and honey, and simmer over low heat for 5 minutes.

Serve warm.

Serves 4

Bazal Medok
Cauliflower Fry

I was taught this dish by a lama, a complete vegetarian. The seasoning is not assertive but does provide contrast to the cauliflower.

2 tablespoons corn or peanut oil
1 medium-size onion, sliced (1/2 cup)
1 pound cauliflower, cut into 1-inch pieces (about 3 cups)
1/4 teaspoon salt

1/4 teaspoon freshly ground black pepper
1 teaspoon soy sauce
1 tablespoon sesame butter (tahini)
1/4 cup water

1. Heat the oil in a skillet and stir-fry the onion over moderate heat for 2 minutes. Add the cauliflower and stir-fry for 3 minutes.

2. Add all the other ingredients, cover, and cook for 10 minutes.

Serve hot with other dishes.

Serves 4

Variation: Four cups shredded cabbage may be used instead of the cauliflower; the cooking time is the same.

Tupa Menda
Buttered Fruit Rice

Tupa menda is a ceremonial dish served at weddings and on special occasions. It is dry butter-rich rice—not a food for daily consumption. Tibetan freshly churned butter, which I tasted in Darjeeling, has a faint dairy taste and is unsalted.

2 cups raw rice, rinsed and drained well
¼ pound butter (8 tablespoons)
3½ cups water
¼ teaspoon salt
¼ cup raisins
¼ cup dried apricots, cut into ¼-inch dice

1. Brown the rice in 7 tablespoons of the butter over moderate heat for 3 minutes. Add the water and salt and bring to a boil. Turn heat down to low, cover the pan, and cook for 5 minutes.

2. Add the raisins and apricots and stir once. Continue to cook, covered, for 5 minutes more. Remove from heat and let the rice stand for 20 minutes.

3. Give the rice a good mixing with a wooden spoon and add the other tablespoon of butter.

Serve at room temperature.

Serves 4 to 6

Daysi
Rice and Raisins

Daysi is a ceremonial dish offered on good and auspicious occasions. For our purposes, it should be considered a snack with tea or coffee or a straightforward dessert.

2 cups raw rice, rinsed and
  drained
3¼ cups water

4 tablespoons butter or margarine
1 cup raisins
2 to 3 tablespoons sugar

1. Put the rice and water in a saucepan and bring to a boil. Lower the heat immediately and cook covered for 7 minutes, or until the water has been absorbed by the rice.

2. Add the butter and raisins and stir well. Heat for 2 minutes more. Remove from the heat and keep the pan covered until ready to dine.

Serve warm or at room temperature, sprinkled with as much sugar as you like.

Serves 6

Shaman
Hot Chili Paste

Tibetans are fond of hot chili so this *shaman* will be authentic if made as hot as you wish by adding more chili or "hot oil," a red chili oil purchased in Asian groceries.

1 tablespoon sliced fresh hot green
  or red chili
1 teaspoon oil

¼ teaspoon salt
1 garlic clove, sliced
2 tablespoons chopped ripe tomato

Grind all the ingredients together in a mortar or processor into a fairly smooth paste.

Serve with meat or vegetarian dishes, especially with a white radish salad.

Seme Mandu
Hot Chili Chutney

¹/₄ cup ripe tomato slices
2 small garlic cloves, sliced
1 tablespoon fresh coriander

¹/₂ teaspoon salt
2 teaspoons sliced fresh hot red or
green chili

Process everything together into a smooth paste. Press it through a metal sieve to remove coarse pieces.

Serve at room temperature with any Tibetan food.

Sepen Mangthur
Hot Chili Sauce

Sepen mangthur is freely translated as "round red chili." It is used sparingly as a table condiment.

¹/₂ teaspoon caraway seeds
¹/₄ cup hot water
1 tablespoon dried hot red chili
flakes

1 tablespoon plain yogurt
¹/₈ teaspoon salt

1. Soak the caraway seeds in 2 tablespoons hot water for 5 minutes. Add the balance of the water, the chili flakes, yogurt and salt and mix well.

2. Let the sauce stand for 15 minutes before serving to blend the flavors. For a hotter, thicker sauce, reduce the amount of hot water by 1 or 2 tablespoons.

Serve at room temperature with any kind of Tibetan food.

Bibliography

Brooklyn Botanic Garden. *Oriental Herbs and Vegetables.* Brooklyn Botanic Garden Record, Vol. 39. Brooklyn: Brooklyn Botanic Garden, 1983.

Cornell University. *Hortus Third Dictionary of Plants.* New York: The Macmillan Company, 1976.

Elias, Flower, and Cooper, Judith Elias. *The Jews of Calcutta.* The Jewish Association of Calcutta, 1974.

Karkaria, Bachi J., "Meet Mr. Dhansakia." *Calcutta Statesman,* 1982.

Kunzang, Rechung Rinpoche Jampal. *Tibetan Medicine.* Berkeley, Calif.: University of California Press, 1976.

Limond, Dora. *The Anglo-Indian Cookery Book.* Calcutta: L. O. H. de Silva, ca. 1920.

Mehta, Jeroo. *101 Parsi Recipes.* Bombay: Jeroo Mehta Dolphin, 1983.

Musleah, Ezekiel N. *On the Banks of the Ganga—The Sojourn of Jews in Calcutta.* North Quincy, Mass.: Christopher Publishing House, 1975.

Nanavutty, Piloo. *The Parsis.* New Delhi: National Book Trust, 1977.

Newark Museum. *Catalogue of the Tibetan Collection.* Newark, N.J.: Newark Museum, 1971.

Olson, Eleanor. "Tibetan Tea." Unpublished dissertation, Newark Museum.

The Oxford Book of Food Plants. London: Oxford University Press, 1975.

Spear, Percival. *India: A Modern History.* Ann Arbor, Mich.: The University of Michigan Press, 1961, 1972.

Stein, R. A. *Tibetan Civilization.* Translated by J. E. Stapleton. Stanford, Calif.: Stanford University Press, 1972.

Tung, Rosemary Jones. *A Portrait of Lost Tibet.* New York: Holt, Rinehart and Winston, 1980.

Index

Made in the USA
Las Vegas, NV
27 January 2021